ACKNOWLEDGEMENTS

I dedicate this book to J.B.W. A year after my return he'd asked about my day. I told him my day had been singularly unproductive. He looked at me quizzically. "Didn't you tell me you are writing a book about how your travels changed you? I don't know anyone else who has written a book." You light up my life. For the past seven years you have believed that I would get these books published.

My heartfelt thanks to:

My Dad, whose nearly last words to me were, "Finish your book!" He walked through the Pearly Gates and saw them close behind him before he could read this, but I know he would be proud.

Mom, my brilliant children, all my siblings, their children and their children. They all think I am wonderful. Thanks for always believing in my superpowers.

A good friend, my neighbour D. Y. in B.C. When I returned from my trip, he told me that he read my blog until he reached his saturation point. At some point he crossed over from thinking, "I could do this too, I would like to be there with her," to thinking, "it's too much, she must have something unique in her DNA that allows her to achieve something this momentous, this incredible. Something I don't have."

My neighbour N. D. in B.C. who cheers for me, YAY!, with her hands in the air! She encourages me to not wait for a travel companion but to just go explore with only myself for company.

H., my dynamic, beautiful young friend from Bible College days, a true friend, prayer general and lifter of my spirits.

Crawford, my fellow Gospel Rider, who praised me for overcoming my fears, which is what usually keeps people in their rocking chairs. He welcomed me home, saying that I would always be one of the guys no matter how far away I travelled!

D., the cycling Scotsman, a friend who is very humble about his great accomplishment of cycling across Canada. His adventurous spirit catapulted me into a world of new possibilities. He helped edit my early drafts.

Doris, *mi mejor amiga,* (my best friend) who always tells me I am a moonbeam and encourages me to let my iridescent and youthful qualities shine through.

Lesley, my ever-pragmatic friend, who encouraged me on my journey by offering the 3L's as my travelling tips: Lipstick, Life Jacket and Life-giving EpiPen.

M.S., my lifelong friend whose giftings with the English language have inspired me to explore my own written voice.

Each and every beautiful American, Mexican, Chileano, Argentinian and every other nationality person whom my life intersected with during my travels.

My neighbour Francis, thanks for your prayers.

J.M., my hiking-adventure buddy in Alberta, thanks for your encouragement.

All my other friends and extended family members both in Alberta and B.C., who all enrich my life. You have each encouraged me along my writing path, and kept me focused.

My fellow riders in Gospel Riders. These are my band of brothers and sisters in Christ who encourage, hold me accountable, and love me.

Clarabelle, for the joy you infuse into my journey and for your years of encouragement. And for your whimsi-girl painting of me writing at my desk, entitled, "It's when God holds my pen, that's when I write."

My writing coaches who taught me how to shape my journal entries into the structure of a memoir and use a braided narrative, the 3 Cs, and define my algorithm: Betsy Warland, J. Thorn, Marion R.Smith.

Tyler, for your Burning Light Congregation: our Tuesday evening writing group at the museum, where you taught us all of us particles to love writing. And turn improbabilities into possibilities.

D.B., for poring over my many drafts with your legal secretary eyes and editing as no other could.

L.M. and Olive for carefully proofreading and finding the last of my mistakes.

ChatGPT, for your editing suggestions (some of which are absurd, some of which I incorporated) and for my brother for suggesting I try ChatGPT.

My Lord and Saviour Jesus Christ: *Psalms 28:7 Adonai* is my strength and my shield. My heart trusts in Him, and I was helped. Therefore my heart leaps for joy, and I will praise Him with my song. *Tree of Life version.*

Travelling Into the Patagonian Wind

A Solo Journey to Joy

RUTH D. STALLARD

WestBow Press books may be ordered through booksellers or by contacting:

WestBow Press
A Division of Thomas Nelson & Zondervan
1663 Liberty Drive
Bloomington, IN 47403
www.westbowpress.com
844-714-3454

ISBN: 979-8-3850-3062-0 (sc)
ISBN: 979-8-3850-3063-7 (hc)
ISBN: 979-8-3850-3061-3 (e)

Library of Congress Control Number: 2024916214

Print information available on the last page.

WestBow Press rev. date: 11/26/2024

PREFACE

Barely able to move, my muscles stiff, my stomach hollow with hunger, yet filled with a satisfying elation, I sank onto the hard tile floor and leaned against a flamenco-red couch in the communal space at *Refugio Paine Grande*, knowing I had to decide how to proceed. Should I use my last 15,000 *pesos* to pay for the twenty-minute catamaran ride across *Lago Pegoe* or save my money for an enormous supper by walking another two hours to the bus stop? Finally, I resigned myself to the thrifty approach—I would walk. As I watched my phone's battery charge, I sensed eyes observing me. I looked up to see a blonde woman, her head tilted, studying me from across the arm of the hostel couch.

"We just can't disconnect from civilization, can we?" she said with a knowing grin. "Hi, I'm Dagmar, from Denmark."

She patted the seat beside her, inviting me to join her, and we chatted like old friends. "After the high of the *Torres del Paine* trek, Fitz Roy in *Argentina* should be next for you, my friend," she said.

Ouch. I winced, and quickly changed the subject.

She invited me to hike to a nearby lookout over *Lago Pegoe*. We shared yogurt and crackers atop the most inviting of the rocks. The flat, azure surface of the lake below served as a mirror reflecting the verdant hills and the playful, scattered cumulus clouds.

Dagmar reached into her bag, and said, "Oh! I just remembered. I have an extra ticket for the ferry. Yes, a guy in my trek group bought a round-trip ticket but he decided to walk. Here, it's yours."

Overwhelmed by her unexpected generosity, I leaped off my rock, enveloped her in a spontaneous bear hug, and silently breathed a prayer of heartfelt thanks for the extraordinary gift from a perfect stranger.

The ferry cut across the lake's deep blue waters, and I felt the shoreline with its craggy peaks retreat behind me, knowing that the visual feast of the past days would soon reside only in memory. My heart tensed at the thought of leaving this wild, untamed beauty behind. "Captain, please turn back," I whispered, barely audible over the engine's gurgle. I wasn't ready to leave; the vastness of the *Torres del Paine* National Park had pushed me beyond the limits of my familiar world. For five days, I'd lived at the raw edge of my endurance, trekking through wild trails and sweeping peaks and into a truth I had long avoided, exploring landscapes within myself as much as those around me. Continuing to move forward meant breaking free from the roles I had always known—daughter, sister, friend, mother—to uncover who I might be beyond them. The farther the ferry carried me from the rugged landscape, the more I pondered—how curious that a Canadian would travel alone all the way to Chile to begin her searching and fearless moral inventory. The journey had only begun to transform me, helping me to find joy and a voice that had longed to be released. *And when I reach The Lodge? I wonder what awaits me there.*

CHAPTER 1

Leah: At the Crossroad of Duty and Desire

ON THE AFTERNOON OF JULY 4, 2014, I LEANED FORWARD FOR THE THIRD time and locked my bare legs under my canoe seat. The mesmerizing current threatened to knock me off balance and spin my craft out of control. I plunged my paddle deep into the frothy river, summoning every muscle in my being, yet still the surging current and the daunting wind in my face forced me, in reverse, toward the red danger-zone ropes at the base of the Stave Dam. I steered into a mass of tall, brown-topped cattails, and my canoe stopped. Either the midafternoon sun or over-exerting myself caused my cap to stick to my brow. The cataracts roaring down the spillway showered my spent muscles with a cool spray scented with the heart of the ocean.

My pulse slowed. *Now I can think.* I groaned. *When will I master the complexity of a tidal river?* My scientific mind made me wonder how a river could flow both uphill and downhill. To explain the phenomena, a native friend helped me visualize Moon and Tide as the two eternal dance partners of creation. Gravity sluiced Water over the Stave Dam, then drew her south through the narrow banks of the Stave River until she met the wide, muddy Fraser River, where they flowed, molecules entwined, downhill to the Pacific Ocean near Vancouver. But twice daily, Tide responded to Moon's invitation, and forced Ocean's Water up into the mouth of the Fraser River, and north into the Stave's channel until the dam's concrete towers halted the current. Tide lay unresponsive for many hours until she awakened and yielded once again to Moon's attraction, and Water was swept back toward the ocean. Moon has the power to make the river flow uphill, against gravity. This I understood.

My intention to check my tide tables had fallen out of my head somewhere between completing my first morning job and feeling the urgency to put-in while the sun still shone; therefore, I failed to calculate the correct time to return. If I had waited for the tide to turn, I could have effortlessly paddled downstream, both when leaving home and when returning. *My tide-timing is so off today! I've been on the water for two hours and I really, really need to get home before the sun tucks in behind the mountain for the night at four-thirty.* My canoe—my means of exercising and exploring the marshlands—bobbed gently, gunnels rhythmically scratching against the cattails. After a few breaths to restore my strength, I back paddled, then steered my canoe straight into the current, using rapid, forceful strokes to distance myself from the dam. The canoe—an immense, bright yellow salmon—inched ahead, one fin stroke at a time. Shortly, my modular came into view, and I saw the tulips in full bloom beneath my living room window.

A few minutes later, feeling as though every cell in my body had turned to mush; but pumped with adrenaline and ready to do it all again because of my success in overpowering the tide, I nosed the canoe into the west bank where the blackberry bushes guarded my dock. At that precise moment, my cell phone lit up with the call that would prove to rock my world. Mom's familiar bluebird picture filled the screen. *Mom just called yesterday; must be something important.* Holding my paddle across my knee, I balanced the phone on my shoulder, slowed my breathing, and said in a calm voice, "Hello, Mom."

"Hello, dear. Oh, good, you're at home. Dad's here, too, on the speaker phone."

"Hi, Dad. I'm actually canoeing right now. Remember, cell phones are portable." *I'm sure my kids believe I'm a technology Luddite as well.*

"Yes, of course." She laughed at our little joke. "So, we heard that Leah is out of the hospital now, and she doesn't want to go back to live with her temporary caregiver. We can't take her because we're in the middle of our move, and I doubt she would like our winters in Calgary. And since she'll need to finish high school, she'll need someone who can drive her every day."

Where is she going with this? I didn't have to wait long.

"What if you took Leah in? You could guide her back to a normal life. Few people are more patient and loving than you. You did mention last year that you were thinking of taking in foster children."

All this from the woman I had known and trusted for a long, long time, the woman with a caring mom's heart toward anyone living in difficult circumstances. I couldn't tell her what my heart desired to say, for fear of hurting her feelings: "I want to spend my semi-retirement years pursuing my interests: being a caretaker for Leah isn't on my agenda. I'm quite content working part-time, canoeing, and motorcycling here in this beautiful place." *I enjoy the freedom of my solo world. I think Mom is calling me because she knows I act quickly and that I seldom refuse any request. And she knows I'm a considerate daughter, so I need to say something nicer.*

"Shared Psychotic Disorder sounds serious to me. When I visited Leah in the hospital, she wouldn't make eye contact, and I couldn't understand her speech. She looked so lost. Oh, I'm at the shore now. I'm going to need both hands. Can I think it over and get back to you? It's been almost thirty years since I've had a teenager in my home."

"Of course, dear. Take your time. I love you. Bye for now."

"Bye. Love you too, Mom and Dad."

After tying my canoe, the *S. S. Stallard*, to a large spruce tree, I scrambled up the bank, ran through my front door, turned on my computer, switched back into work mode, and completed and submitted the last project of my workday, feeling grateful I'd met my Friday afternoon deadline. *I got home in the nick of time!* Tucking my laptop into the drawer, I glimpsed an old tide table partially visible beneath a file folder—a printout Francis had thoughtfully provided.

The day I had first discovered the tide tables, I had also discovered a new friend—one who was concerned about me canoeing alone. One month after I moved in, I had been sitting on my river-watching bench, leaning my back against the metal hummingbirds dipping their beaks into lily flowers. A round-faced man dragging his reluctant fluffy white bichon along behind him had smiled and tossed his Tilley hat down on the bench beside me.

"Hi, I'm Francis. I live three trailers over that way," he said, pointing to a blue-and-white trailer with a yard landscaped with a mathematical precision.

"Hi, I'm Ruth. Have a seat."

We'd both laughed, then begun a discussion that led us to discover that we were exactly one year apart in age, both excited about our pending retirements.

"I've noticed that you're having troubles fighting the tides sometimes."

He'd pulled a crumpled sheet of paper from his pocket and spread it on his lap. "This is called a tide table. You can print them off from www.tides.gc.ca."

"You mean I can know when the tides will change? Thanks, Francis, you may have just saved my life."

We had studied the tables and watched the eagles thermalling, then he'd dragged his dog toward home. I had solemnly promised to consult the tide tables before every canoe ride.

If I'd remembered my promise to Francis, today's canoe break would have been short and pleasant, and my last work project would have been finished with time to spare. While preparing supper, I thought about my promise to check the tide tables, and I wondered if I'd also fail to keep the promise I'd made to my parents to return their call with my decision. Would opening my home to Leah fit with my vision for my dream retirement years—canoeing and riding my motorcycle in the liberatingly beautiful and warm province of B.C.?

Reflecting on my previous seven years of corporate existence, I recalled how living in a central Alberta city shared with 80,000 others, how working full-time as an instrumentation draftsperson for DC Holdings, and how the two-hour commute had drained my energy and my time. In B.C., my timeline-driven, ideally flexible part-time job of estimating the square footage of granite for commercial construction projects, in a process called a take-off, could be done, with a high dosage of focus and concentration, from my kitchen table. Plus, the superior B.C. weather held greater allure for me than the prospect of sitting next to a wood stove in Alberta. Despite the burning star at the centre of our solar system radiating warmth and light throughout the year, it couldn't prevent the province from freezing solid all winter.

A few months earlier, on that humid day in May 2014, when I had first viewed my new modular house located near Maple Ridge, B.C. and looked through its sparkling picture windows at the unmarred, intensely powerful, concentric wave patterns flowing across the surface of the tidal Stave River, I knew I'd found my true home—a mere 400-square feet, and perfect for one person. By the end of June, I had learned that living close to nature let me draw on a source of strength that I'd sought—but not found—living in big-city Alberta. A natural ebb and flow happened freely: beauty and tragedy, good and evil flourished together, beyond the control of man, not overridden by man, giving overwhelming proof that in the country, someone else is in control. Someone with a power greater and wiser than man. The space where the tide meets the stream, known as an estuary, became my home, right there on the threshold between the wide, muddy Fraser River and the thundering Stave Dam: the space where the waters and my spirit mingled into one clear, fresh, vibrant body.

My alone times in my estuary became the part of my workday I most anticipated. Soaking up the sun's healing rays while listening to the trumpeter swans and red-winged blackbirds, and watching the lithe river otter—long and lean and auburn like myself—slide down the slippery bank, always recharged and refreshed me. After my exhausting day of work that had included battling the tidal river—its course as uncertain as my own—the weight of my parents' unexpected phone call added to my fatigue. I crashed into bed moments after finishing supper and lay still, absorbing the distant, sporadic melody of bird calls. *Now it's time to consider Dad and Mom's request.* Possible good outcomes and potential negative scenarios filled my mind, but I couldn't come to any conclusions. *How will my life change if I take her in? What will happen to my independence? Could I instill my love of nature into Leah to the point where she could find healing? What if? What if? What if?*

I folded my pillow in half, propped up my head, and stared at the ceiling in the dark.

If I don't intervene and her suffering increases, I'll feel guilty. What about the plans I have for me? Do I put them on hold? Or do I even have any?

Redefining the next phase of my life had consumed my thoughts recently. I recognized a deep void, a restlessness that made me feel like my canoe mired in the cattails, waiting out the tides. Whereas mature salmon fight the currents to return to their spawning grounds, I found myself idling, adrift. I longed for a push forward, to demonstrate to myself and my loved ones that I possessed the confidence to speak my mind. Before the Scotsman showed up, I hadn't entertained the thought of setting out alone on a grand adventure. When I'd first arrived in B.C., my goal had been to settle in and work. That all changed when my sister, who lived nearby, decided—possibly impulsively—to create a Warmshowers profile. When the Scotsman—who claimed to be cycling across Canada—contacted her about a one-night stay at her home, she panicked and gave him my phone number. The day the hulking, harmless Scotsman cycled into my driveway, I knew I'd met a kindred spirit. After an evening of BBQ, where he played his small pipes for my sister and me well into the night, the tales of his adventures on the open road planted a seed in my mind. The idea of cycling to California over a period of six months to visit one of my aunts took root that night. However, imagining how my family and friends would worry about me "somewhere out there" all alone kept my feet firmly planted. So, while my idea to travel sounded alluring, my cautious self continued to override my adventurous self.

Is the reason I can't say "no" to my mother's request because I haven't fully reclaimed the voice my marriage had stifled? Fulfilling my family's expectations to rescue Leah conflicts with my longing to care for myself first. I don't want to appear selfish and leave them with no peace of mind. Here I am face-to-face with my fear of disappointing them by not taking Leah.

The birdsong ceased; I fell asleep, entertaining muddled dreams that confused me even more.

Before making my decision, I knew I needed to consult family and friends. On the weekend following the "big call," I phoned my sister Wanda, my friend Helen in Victoria, and finally a daughter.

My daughter Lenora, who never minces words, said, "You can't let someone like Leah out into the world. You must help her, no matter how hard it is."

Wanda had another viewpoint. "You can't pander to Leah. She wants to leave where she's at because it's tough for her, but she'll have to learn to make her own way now. Did you give in all the times your girls wanted to leave home?"

"True, but I feel as if I should help somehow. I believe in the restorative power of love," I heard myself say.

"Good luck with that, Sis. Let me know what you decide."

Helen didn't agree that my parents—who were still together after fifty-five years and living in a beautiful home—would make better caregivers than I would as a single woman living in a tiny modular.

"You can't expect your parents to handle a teenager at their ages," Helen said. "Your mom was the classic housewife of the '50s, staying home to raise all you kids, so she has already paid her dues. Now it's up to you to help."

Another week passed as I pondered and prayed. The idealist in me began to envision saving Leah from a life on the streets; I would rescue her by surrounding her with unconditional love and caring; I would make a difference in her life. By the end of the second week, every hesitation had evaporated. Not one thought of the loss of my freedom, nor the obligation to share my personal space with someone who had suffered much in her nineteen years could now make me feel that the time I would invest in her would be wasted. Wasn't agreeing with my parents' request consistent with being an agreeable person?

That day I finally called them back. "Hi, Mom. If Leah is willing, I'll take her."

"That's wonderful, dear. You will need the patience of Job and the wisdom of Solomon. I love you."

"I... I love you too, Mom."

Mom couldn't have known any more than I how my life with Leah would unfold, or, more accurately, how my life would come to resemble my canoe bouncing backward, faster and faster, on the current of the Stave River, closer and closer to the danger-sign ropes.

On a sticky-hot Wednesday in the first week of August 2014, a fragile nineteen-year-old Leah walked up the steps into my always-green sanctuary wearing dated clothes and carrying a small canvas backpack. A pale nose, two quarter-moon eyes, and pouty lips appeared through a forest of frizzy, long red hair hiding slumped shoulders, all mounted on a frame thinner than a stalk of parsley in my herb garden.

"The poor thing leaves the footprint of a sulphur butterfly," I thought, and before she could shrink from me, I wrapped her in a warm, welcoming hug; her angular shoulders initially tensed, then relaxed into me. We sat together on my cast-iron and cedar-wood river-watching bench near the river; my eyes and ears focused on the sounds of the wind tossing the evergreens around, the surface of the water, and the scent of wild roses; her mind trapped somewhere in her recent past. Her eyes studied the long fingers of her right hand twisting the fingers on her left. Both hands pressed into her thighs.

Pointing to the bald eagles thermalling high in the sky, cackling in their eerie budgie-style calls, I said, "Here's an amazing fact I learned at the eagle festival last month: the white feathers in their heads are prismatic. They give off an aura-like signature that other eagles can recognize. Isn't that cool?"

"I wish I was like all the other teenagers," she mumbled into her lap.

"Look how the wind is tossing a bag filled with thousands of sun-scorched diamonds across the water's surface and making them dance," I randomly said, instead of trying to decipher her whispered fragments of garbled words that followed "teenagers."

"I hadn't noticed," she said, barely opening her mouth, staring down at her hands. "You know, I'd rather live on the streets than go back to live with her."

Once more I tried to refocus her on the present, on her surroundings in the here and now. "See those perfect, symmetrical wave patterns that the tide is creating? Can you feel their power?"

Her shoulders tightened, as if preparing a response taxed her entire body. Still staring down through her hair-forest at her hands, she said, "No. I'm hungry. They thought I deserved only one meal a day. And do you drink water right out of the tap here? I had to walk a long way every week to buy a certain brand of bottled water. I don't know how to live a normal life. Forget it."

Connecting with this poor soul won't be easy. I feel so ill-equipped to reach her. A chasm as wide as the Fraser River divided our lives.

Leading her into the kitchen, I directed her to sit while I took charge of preparing a meal.

A few moments later, staring at her plate heaped with colourful vegetables from my garden, deli meats, cheese, pickles, and freshly baked bread, she gripped a tall crystal glass filled with tap water, and slowly shook her head, looking up at me through her hair-forest.

"Leah, you can feel free to tell me anything that is on your heart," I said, "I won't judge you or your caretakers."

"I haven't eaten so much food for a long time." Her bony fingers twisted unkempt strands of hair around and around. "You're giving me hope. You don't understand how out of control my life was. I remember one time we went to some soup kitchen. They had all this amazing food for us but we wouldn't eat it because we knew they were trying to poison us so we snuck out and they must have called the police because they came to pick us up and it was about two in the morning."

She talked for a good half-hour, pouring out a stream of consciousness that she'd been unable to share with anyone for years. I couldn't imagine how terrifying those years must have been for her. Her stories made me feel sick to my stomach.

"I'm so sorry for what you've been through," I said, my voice soft. "But try to focus on that hope, Leah, not so much on the past. Think of that hope as a tiny flame and each day add a little stick of something else that gives you hope until you have a blazing bonfire."

We ate silently together; satisfying the one need we had in common.

Several weeks later, with my maternal instincts shining again and intending to expose Leah to nature's healing power, we hiked into the woods—she racing ahead of me along rickety, long-abandoned mountain bike trails high above the twig-strewn forest floor, laughing. Having fun! The seeming success of spending quality time with her satisfied me. *Could it be that this will be easy?* We danced a happy jig around a tree, then she took a spindly-legged leap across the moss-covered two-by-fours, tangled locks of hair flying behind her. On baby-dreams summer days, we picked chestnuts to roast over the open flames on my gas range. We gleaned emerald-green apples from abandoned orchards, making sweet, cinnamon-scented apple cider. Her eyes sparkled with delight—she'd forgotten she once mumbled and now spoke in clearer sentences. I could see she'd discovered some joy in life, some desire to heal, in the way she skipped up the stairs after being outdoors. *We are slowly, slowly making progress.*

September's arrival turned my thoughts toward the problem of Leah's education, or lack thereof.

"She pulled me out of school when I was thirteen. But I finished a four-month General Equivalency Diploma program last year. What do other teenagers do when they finish high school?" Leah asked.

My mind spun in neutral, trying to comprehend how Canada's modern educational system could have failed her.

"They go on to college. A General Equivalency Diploma qualifies you to attend. There is a college in a nearby town. I can drive you there in the morning and pick you up after classes are over."

"College sounds like hard work. I'd rather just hang out here."

"But, Leah, going to college and getting a degree is like having a plane ticket in your back pocket; a degree can take you anywhere you want to go in the world."

"Huh. I would love to go to Hawaii with my plane ticket. Well, I could try going to college, I guess."

The day she received her letter of acceptance to college in the next town, we celebrated by paddling my canoe to a mud island, where we turned into seals and romped in the muck. If Leah hadn't finally agreed to attend college, I may never have learned that speaking what one thinks is empowering. *I long to use my voice to express what I truly mean, to inspire, not destroy, others with my words.*

Following her initial day of classes, she announced, "That place is full of weirdos." Her retelling of her experiences delved more into the quirky personalities of her fellow students than the academic curriculum she had planned.

After weeks of driving Leah to and from college, I noticed a large chunk of time disappear from my workday.

"Leah, are you okay if I drive you to and from the Maple Ridge Library bus stop so you can bus to and from your classes?"

She nodded in agreement.

Did Leah's college experience entitle her to particular privileges? There she saw youth who had lived the same number of years—but kinder years than what she'd lived; youth she never spoke of as befriending; youth she still judged as weirdos. After classes, she would increasingly isolate herself in

her room to battle her migraine headaches—migraines that would not abate even using an assortment of drugs that doctors assured her would cure them. *Maybe I should pull her out, keep her here until she gains a stronger sense of who she is, what she wants to study. But if I do, would I be helping her future self?*

On the first day I had collected Leah from the Maple Ridge Library, I could see the red brick building receding from view in my rear-view mirror as I rolled down my car windows to let the breeze carry away the hot stuffy air. I looked at Leah sitting beside me, her stack of books, loose papers, and binders sliding around on her lap, reminding me of her determined effort to maintain her academic foothold.

"Leah, do you think you're ready for college? Are you finding class work too hard?"

"No. When I'm learning something new, I can forget about everything else."

Then silence. Her eyes stared at the road ahead as it narrowed from smooth city pavement to bumpy, dusty, country gravel.

"Okay. We'll keep doing what we're doing. Let's enjoy a breather and go to the lake above the dam this weekend."

Is she a risk taker or doesn't she understand how dangerous frigid water can be? In October, the lake's temperature hovered around zero Celsius. Too cold to swim, but not too cold for us to have a picnic. We spread an old Hudson's Bay blanket onto the gritty sand strewn with driftwood; and sat down to share a simple lunch, the lake before us reflecting the steely sky. Leah told me that she wore her bathing suit under her clothes in case she could swim. She said she wasn't afraid of cold water, because in her past life when no one left her enough hot water for a shower, she had turned off her feelings and showered with cold water.

After she finished her tuna sandwich, she stood up, unzipped her jacket, dropped her jeans to the sandy beach, flung off her shirt, pulled off her runners and socks, and rushed straight toward the lake, wearing nothing but her pink bikini.

"Leah!" I gasped. "What are you doing? The water is frigid. You shouldn't swim!"

The muscles in my chest and stomach tightened, preventing my breath from escaping as I saw her wade past her thighs, then vanish under the surface that looked as grey as the silver lining of the clouds. *Should I run after her and stop her, should I cheer her on, should I join her, should I call 911?*

A voice in my head screamed, "tell her to turn around!" yet the draw of the water's power over Leah also fascinated me. Caught between the urge to protect and the need to understand, I stood watching, waiting, her towel draped on my arm. Suddenly she emerged from the glacial water, shook like a wet dog, inched her way to the shore, then sprinted toward me.

"I almost died. I couldn't breathe!" she stuttered, shivering distressingly.

Draping the towel quickly over her shoulders sent water droplets scattering from her hair onto me.

"I turned off my feelings, but I almost died!" she repeated, struggling to pull dry, sandy clothes onto her wet body.

Working with Leah became increasingly difficult. I had invested months of my time into her, out of my love and concern for her mental health; but because she expressed no appreciation and gave nothing in return, I began to think I'd wasted my time. She refused to comply when I showed her that good manners meant clearing dishes from the table after a meal or taking her muddy boots off when entering the house, or even basic things like turning off lights when leaving. Each confrontation with Leah felt like stacking another building block onto the one below—creating an unstable tower, teetering higher and higher. Soon to topple.

Tucked between all the turbulent moments with Leah, a harbinger of hope arrived one dark, damp, cold evening in November as I sat in the library parking lot, waiting to pick her up at our appointed time. My phone pinged and I scowled as I read her text, "I had supper with a friend, I won't get to the library until late, not sure when." I'd loudly revved my engine, preparing to drive back home when I noticed the library windows shone with light and the red neon "open" sign flashed a welcome. Changing my mind, I turned off my car and decided to wait inside.

Wandering through the double doors, I spotted the discard rack, a library fundraiser, standing nearby. Craning my neck, I scanned the titles on the row of spines. Something about the seven simple words, *Extreme Landscape: The Lure of Mountain Spaces*—mere black text on white background and white text on black background—made me put my right index finger on top of the book, pull it forward, and slide it off the shelf. Randomly flipping through the book, I landed on an essay penned by Yvon Chouinard and Doug Tompkins, the visionary founders of Esprit, North Face, and *Patagonia*—the outdoor recreation stores they had established decades earlier in the '60s and '70s. Their love for the raw wildness of *Patagonia* leaped from the pages into my spirit, stirring a desire within me. The idea of travelling resurfaced with renewed vigour. In my reverie, I journeyed great distances to experience those primeval expanses for myself. The thought of climbing Mount Fitz Roy as they had, held a visceral appeal for me. My body thrilled, anticipating the accomplishment of travelling and exploring. Employing all the skills known to every intrepid explorer, I envisioned a strong and vigorous Ruth scaling Fitz Roy, living life to the extreme, battling and conquering nature.

This puts flesh onto the bones of my idea. I need to do this someday; this is my commission. An agency for reclaiming my voice.

I plunk my donation on the library counter and shove the book in my purse, where it will remain buried for the next three months. Yet, that book's fate is linked with mine—it is not destined to gather dust on a shelf. When Leah finally arrives, my thoughts are focused on the book and the intriguing distraction I hope it will provide for me. The car is filled with a dense silence during the drive home.

Over the next two weeks, the tension that first built in the car during our commutes, would begin to spill into my home. One night, peeking my head into her bedroom, I dangled a sopping wet bathmat in front of Leah, and explained for the third time why keeping the mat dry was important for hygiene.

"Leah, all you must do is hang the mat on the shower rack instead of leaving it in the tub. Then it won't turn mildewy."

"Whatever," she said, swivelling on her heel and slamming the door in my face. "You got more time than I got. Schoolwork takes a lot of brain power. You take care of that stuff."

Slouching onto the couch, I buried my head in my hands and the pounding pulse in my temples throbbed out the mantra, *I can do this. If I don't react, I can retain my peace of mind. I can do this. Think of all the good times we've had. I can do this.*

Two days later, her bedroom door flies open. From my desk, I watch her gather books, pens, computer, sweaters and shoes, and gulp down a glass of water.

"I slept in. Ya gotta drive me all the way to college today."

"Okay, sure, just give me a second to get ready. You go hop in the car," I say.

You think you're entitled to beckon me away from my work anytime, don't you? If I don't drive you, you will have a reason to be angry with me, won't you?

The following week, sitting with Leah in the bank manager's office, I felt uneasy. I sensed how the false ideas engrained in her brain to the point where she could no longer distinguish reality from her mother's altered perceptions of life had traumatized her.

"You have an allowance, Leah; and when you put that money in the bank, you can use a bank card to buy yourself a coffee at Tim Hortons, like the other kids do."

"No!" she said.

Her hands clenched in her lap; her eyes widened so that I saw an entire, white-rimmed eyeball through her hair. "If I get a bank card, they will implant an electronic chip in my brain. You know that is a sign that the end of the world is coming. People who do that will go to hell. And besides, money is cursed."

"What if we just open an account so that you could write cheques?" I suggested. *I will save explaining to her that money truly isn't cursed for when we're back home.*

Her agitation increased. Smiling at the bank manager, I pushed my chair back, and said, "We'll return later. Thank you for your time."

Okay, so I may never teach her basic social and financial skills, I will try another tactic another day.

One Saturday morning, I thought that by teaching Leah to sew, I would give her a valuable, lifelong skill. I suggested teaching her using my Janome sewing machine, but she frowned and said, "I don't want to learn to sew. I used to have a sewing machine. I wanted to make perfect clothes, but I couldn't, I just couldn't. Anyways I don't want to be different than other girls my age. I'm pretty sure other teenage girls don't sew."

My attempts to convey that normalcy is a subjective notion, merely a projection, went nowhere. Despite my desire to convince her of the benefits of acquiring a new skill, her closed expression warned me against disrupting our fragile balance. So, I remained silent.

"Sometimes I still don't feel like my life is worth living. Only where I live has changed. Except I do have that small glimmer of hope," she said.

I listened, because I understood. For a lengthy period, I, too, had once wondered if my life was worth living.

"Would you like to do some cooking?" I asked her.

"Why don't you just leave me alone? Quit already! You're trying to get me to do all this stuff. And learn stuff I don't want to learn. You were only a ticket away from the place I stayed after I left the hospital. I came here so I could leave there."

What? After all I have done for you and with you! That is how you feel about me? My shoulder's slumped, mirroring hers, as I left her in my home and tried to catch up with myself on a wooded trail at the base of the mountain west of my home. Months of attempting to teach her basic life skills had exhausted me. The trail stretched before me. Suddenly, I remembered Leah's mention of her temporary caregiver, her father. The need to call him now gripped me. The numbers on my cell phone blurred. Breathing deeply of the warm moist air, I lifted my red wire-rimmed glasses with my left hand, dabbed the tears from the corner of my eyes with my right forefinger, and dialled.

"Hey, this is Ruth. Oh, she is a... a challenge. Actually, that is why I am calling. Could you possibly give me some advice to help with Leah?"

Describing the recent months with Leah, I expressed, "I'm in need of some support."

"Ya, what more can you do? When you are around her, you just want to shoot yourself!"

"Well, thanks for your time. Bye for now."

That is so not helpful. As much as he's missed his daughter, she's proven too much for him to handle—likely why he seemed so grateful when I stepped in to help. I am truly on my own in this. The hopelessness of the conversation both fuelled my resolution to pull Leah up from the swamp of trauma onto solid ground and confirmed my desperation.

On Sunday evening, sitting on the couch and needing a distraction from my focus on Leah, I decided to clean my purse. *Why do I even keep old church programs and old tide tables in my purse?* From underneath an unopened first-aid kit, two wallets, my waterproof notebook, pencils and pens, two rings of keys, my sunglasses case and cheque book, out tumbled the little copy of *Extreme Landscape: The Lure of Mountain Spaces,* followed by three silver coins that disappeared behind the cushion.

Oh! The book I had bought from the library, while waiting for Leah a lifetime ago.

Once I'd cleared a space to sit on the edge of the couch, I scanned the book's index and selected the essay written by Yvon Chouinard and Doug Tompkins. Taking the time to read the entire essay evoked a torrent of long-forgotten childhood memories wrapped around mountains—Castle Mountain, the Three Sisters, and Mount Rundle—rising from a place in me where I felt most intensely alive. Those delightful memories brought a promise of hope to my soul. *What if I were free to travel to—escape to—Mount Fitz Roy? What if I could break free from the constraints and conflicts I'm experiencing with Leah? Could I possibly reclaim the voice and the joy that my anger and resentment toward Leah are extinguishing?*

Yvon and Doug's motto to commit first and figure out the logistics later absolutely fascinated me. Their philosophy eventually led them to scale Fitz Roy! Their essay recorded with vivid detail their drive from California to *Patagonia.* They described *Patagonia* as a loosely defined area that straddles *Chile* and *Argentina,* starting south of *Puerto Montt, Chile,* and *Bariloche, Argentina,* and ending somewhere before the Pacific and Atlantic Oceans mingle. There they scaled Fitz Roy—with full equipment—to the mountain climber's summit. They saw up close the peaks that clawed skyward like fragments of ice riven into splinters. An incredible adventure! The same power that I felt after a day of hiking in the wilderness now drew my imagination to the headlands of *Patagonia*. The black-and-white photograph on the soft cover of the book showed the majestic mountain, Fitz Roy. My finger traced its jagged outline, and I imagined myself at the trekker's summit. Given my moderate level of fitness, I knew climbing to the actual summit, in full mountaineering gear, possibly with a guide carrying three days' worth of gear, would not be an achievable goal for me.

Suddenly, the idea of travelling to *Argentina* to conquer Mount Fitz Roy flew from my thoughts like a startled chickadee when I heard Leah stomp into her room and slam the door. I leaped from the couch, sliding the book onto my bookshelf, and transitioning to caregiver mode. At our "lunch with family and friends" that afternoon, I'd ignored her. Last Sunday, her indifference toward me had made me feel invisible. We'd both silently asserted our woundedness. My intention to make her suffer had made me feel guilty. Determined to forfeit my right to give her a taste of her own medicine, and not wanting her to face rejection again, I knocked on her bedroom door.

"Leah, I'm sorry I ignored you today. I appreciate that you did the dishes today." I hoped for a word of appreciation from her in return, or a thank you for always driving her despite my pending work deadlines, but none came. Silence.

"Thank you for being on time today," I said, knocking again. *And do you think you could thank me for providing food and shelter for you for the past six months?*

My rational mind searching for solutions, I listened for a muffled answer from behind the door. None arrived. In that instant, I realized that her silence had scorched into every corner of my home, infecting every physical and emotional release of mine—canoeing, motorcycling, hiking—with negativity.

Leaving Leah behind her closed door, I sat down in my living room and stared out the window, and came face-to-face with how oppressed I felt; I simply waited, thoughts racing. *As much as I love this poor kid, I'm inadequate for the task assigned to me. By pouring my joy into her, I'm like the cracked clay pot; joy only leaves me to go to Leah; none stays to sustain me.*

Despite my attempts to shape her behaviour, she remains incapable of responding to life's challenges in a normal manner; therefore, I take the responsibility for her failures: I'm the guilty one—I failed her. I'd expected a positive outcome for her according to my timing—timing that could be doable for a normal person—but not for Leah.

The whole week has passed, and I haven't been out canoeing once! I'm absorbing the anger she has on a simmer beneath the surface. I want to leave my life and all my duties and dramas far behind. No wonder I am making annoyingly time-wasting mistakes at work. If I ask her to move out, I'll feel guilty because she has nowhere else to go; plus, I would be abandoning my commitment to myself and my parents. If I keep trying harder, I could reach her: but I don't know how to reach her. Do I continue helping her or do I pursue my Patagonian dream? Could my time with Leah be ending? I want to do a geographical and run away like Jonah. Oh, wait, a geographical hadn't worked for me before, why would it now?

A "geographical": the alcoholic arrives at the classic solution that moving to a new location, thus leaving behind his drinking buddies, will make the family happy once again.

"Why don't we leave the city and move out to a small town? I won't know anyone, and I can stop drinking. We'll make a fresh start!"

My ex-husband had spoken these words shortly after our second child was born, and I had talked myself into believing him.

"Sure, you'll make some desirable friends, and life will get back to normal," was my hopeful reply.

Within weeks, he had resumed drinking, and I had realized that the woman without a voice still lived in my skin—she had followed me to our new home.

Doing a geographical now, with Leah, would be pointless. *Though unprepared, I'm willing to help Leah—to do the honourable thing.* One in need of rescuing came to me; I had extended my love toward her—aligning with my mission to help—but had inadvertently enabled her destructive behaviour by taking over her tasks. But abandoning her could twist her up into her mind even more, could disable her for life. *Travel will have to wait; I won't say anything to Leah about this.*

Moved by compassion for this young woman who felt she had a right to punish me with silence, I walked to my bedroom past her still-closed door, a physical symbol of the emotional chasm between us. I decided that I would be the one—given enough time—who could change her, fix her, direct her onto a new path. Moments after, I fell asleep determined to make a difference in Leah's life, make it better, make it whole.

CHAPTER 2

The Buttercup: Reflections and Resolve

NOTHING MIGHT HAVE BEEN DIFFERENT ABOUT THIS JANUARY DAY AND countless previous January days, except for the drive home. I might not have gone canoeing, or Leah might have had a better day at college, but we both got into that car. Canoeing always calmed and centred me, so that afternoon, I had decided to put in for an aquatic excursion during my work break, but, regrettably, without consulting my tide tables. When troubling thoughts tumbled around in my head, I'd sometimes forget to do the important thing, like being properly prepared to go onto the river. Going out brought me pleasure, but once again, returning home, I found myself struggling against the brisk, cool wind and insistent waves, fighting to guide the *S. S. Stallard* as it teetered toward spinning out of control. Plowing my paddle deep into the frothing ripples had no effect. The surging current gained its power over me by behaving in an un-river-like fashion-flowing uphill! It perplexed me. Once again, I found myself bobbing toward the red danger-zone ropes at the base of the dam. Once again, I steered into the cattails, stopping near enough to the roaring, foaming cataracts for my spent muscles to feel the cold spray infused with the smell of dead salmon. My classic fix—to back paddle, then continue forward, steady and strong—only set me further back, closer to the dam, and piled my canoe into another cattail marsh. *I don't have an ounce of strength left for me. I've given all my resources to Leah. Is that why I let the tide trick me again? When Mom hinted that I'd need the patience of Job, did she know I'd come to find myself as powerless over Leah's life as I now am over the river? At least I can stay in this marsh and won't end up near the base of the dam. Stuck.*

My focus shifted to Leah. When she arrives at the Maple Ridge Library bus stop, I won't be there to pick her up. Leah, the picture of entitlement, will fume. She'll think I'm purposefully spiting her. *Once again, I really, really need to get home.*

From my hard, wooden canoe seat, I could see sunlight glinting off the window of my home one kilometre away, perched on the riverbank; so close, yet so impossibly far away.

To test the current from my cattail-mired position, I ripped off a gone-to-seed cattail top and tossed it into the river behind me. My marker quickly disappeared, tumbling, swirling, disintegrating, toward the red ropes. Still stuck.

Shifting on my uncomfortable seat, I watched—spellbound—silent bald eagle rhapsodies, as dozens of them spiralled skyward, while dozens more dove earthward to devour the spent salmon littering the pebbly riverbank. The reeking stench of death reminded me that those salmon had fulfilled their destinies. Mere weeks earlier, I'd watched a run of them fight the currents over great distances upstream where they would gather to spawn. Before Leah came into my life, I too had been able to travel against the tide. Why could those miniscule fish succeed, yet I couldn't? Tide had overpowered me; so had she.

Ankle-deep in brown, brackish water, my feet appeared enmeshed in an alien, aquatic world. *Worse than the thought of waiting out the tides is the thought of facing Leah. I shouldn't have gone for a canoe ride so late in the day.* Apart from temporarily abandoning my canoe, slogging through the oozy mud surrounding the cattails, climbing the slippery, rocky bank to the road, and walking the forty minutes home, I had no other choice but to wait for the tide to turn.

Failing to find a comfortable position on my canoe seat, I lay back on my fluorescent yellow-and-red life jacket; and allowing my muscles to relax into the rigid foam, I gazed up at the calm blue sky, saw the fluffy white clouds suspended motionless above me, and felt the humid warmth wrap around my bare arms like a soft velour blanket. A rare calmness washed over me. Those dance partners, Moon and Tide, must be tangoing passionately right now. *Let them. Yes, I can be at peace with the waves Moon flings upon the shore and then withdraws. Just as Moon and the waves are in this turbulent yet constant relationship, so, too, my life is free to ebb and flow.*

The moment my eyes lifted from the churning waters, I saw a different world, that space where calm reigned. A deep-felt connection emerged as I gazed at the shifting forms of clouds high above, and love flowed between us. Imagining life amidst these clouds sparked excitement, a sense of fulfillment, and the joy of a worthwhile existence. Breathing a deep sigh, I glimpsed the possibility of having joy despite my suffering: even though all the joy I'd tried to pour into Leah had dribbled out the cracks in her nature—leaving nothing for me.

Testing the current's direction a second time, I tossed another cattail head into the water and watched as this time it floated toward home, away from the thundering spillway. Using my paddles to push against the reeds, I maneuvered the canoe into the river, pointed my bow south, and ten minutes later I'd clambered up the riverbank to my place.

Since the sun had already set behind the mountain, I changed into warmer clothes before getting into the car. I'd discovered that just as the river's temperament could shift from friendly to furious in moments, the temperatures could also plunge rapidly, transforming a sunny afternoon into a frigid evening. *Here I am, driving to the library again.* I hadn't wanted to go back out in the biting cold to retrieve Leah, for I had another work deadline looming. As I drove, I prepared my "sorry I am late" speech.

At five o'clock, half an hour past our appointed meeting time, I pulled into the library parking lot in my compact, black 2012 Echo, my eyes searching for Leah on the steps. Not a soul. By the time I'd shut off the engine, the dampness had already begun to seep into my bones, making my decision to check inside easier. Still no text from her. A quick survey of the desks and cubicles inside the library told me she wasn't there. *At least I am not the late one.*

Back in the cold car, I waited for another half an hour, thoughts swirling. A knot formed in my stomach when I recalled her wicked laughter, her mocking eyes, her cruel, rude comments—all her behaviours reminding me of being trapped in an alcoholic marriage. My memory of the cruel words coming from a man I had once loved back in the late 1970s often drove my responses to Leah. Then, I had believed divorce wasn't an option because scripture forbade it. Spinning around on the anger-fuelled merry-go-round of alcoholism, I had stayed in my assigned role as a co-dependent spouse. To stay in a place where he constantly demeaned and corrected me, where I was ridiculed, threatened, and punished, could only have been wrong, even evil; yet I didn't trust my opinions or follow through on my perceptions. The alcoholic had come home drunk late on an evening when I sat in my rocker, nursing our firstborn, and reading my Bible. He flung the bedroom door open and yelled, "Why do you have to read that disgusting book all the time?" When I had jumped, our daughter jerked her head up. My jaws clenched shut, I rose to leave the room. Fuelled by his explosive anger, he drove his fist right into the door. Our baby's body had stiffened against my hip and arm as she cried, terrified at the wrenching sound of splintering wood. This formed a brief, forever-imprinted memory in my mind. Yet, despite this, somehow, he had made me believe I was the inconsistent and unreliable one.

Just as I hadn't found serenity or maintained an appearance of normalcy in the insanity of my alcoholic marriage, I saw that now my family must realize that Leah and I were not making progress. Just as I had once pushed people away from me—not allowing them into my violence-ridden life, trying not to impact others—I couldn't prevent my anger toward Leah from building.

Finally, Leah stepped down from the last bus of the day. She would be late for the last time.

Then, with my dread of a confrontation mounting as she strode toward the car and thinking of my repeated attempts to teach her proper social mores, to steer her back to a normal life, and show her constant love, I unlocked the door for her.

She glared at me; her chin lowered; no apology left her lips.

"Look, Leah, when you don't let me know that you are going to be late… Oh, never mind. I'm sorry. I'm just glad you're back safely. Let's go home."

"Home! You think I like being stuck out at your place in the wilderness? Why do I need to finish school anyway?" she yelled. Not one word had been mumbled or spoken indecipherably softly—she had found her voice.

"I think you might need more extensive counselling," I said, trying to remain calm, trying to avoid conflict.

"Why do you always have to interrogate me? Teenagers are supposed to be rude. Can't a person have a bad day once in a while? You have no idea what I go through every day and the torment I lived through!" She raged on.

Out of thin air, out of nowhere, as unprepared-for as a sudden snowstorm, Leah had ignited the quarrel she sought. Flaring tempers, words flung carelessly, poison. Wounding our hearts. I exploded.

"Can't you have a good day once in a while?" I yelled back, distancing her further from me.

Seven bittersweet months of effort left me feeling, in that moment, as if she had two arms wrapped tightly around my waist as we both slid down a bottomless slide together. Faster and faster. Tension filled the small interior of my car, threatening to blow the roof higher than the mountains flanking our route. If I'd always expressed my thoughts, I may not have exploded into the uncontrollable rage when I felt the seething venomous wall of hate between us. That day I landed with a bone-crushing thud at the bottom of the slide. The passive-aggressive hit bottom. All did not bode well.

When we arrived home, she leaped from the car before I'd come to a complete stop, raced up the stairs, flung the front door open, and ran to her bedroom, slamming the door behind her. Two light steps took me up the four steps on my deck. Swinging wide her permanently closed door because I no longer wanted it separating us, I stared at her sprawled on her bed, and realized in that instant that I must tell her to leave, to get out of my home. Not offering her another second chance, on January 19, 2015, at 10 p.m., I yelled, "Leah! You are taking everything, you are gone! Someone will be here soon to pick you up. Now!"

Harsh words left my mouth making a sound like nettles stinging my ears. Reaching out to snatch them back seemed as impossible as breathing life into the brittle bones of the salmon on the mud flats. *God forgive me for failing in my duty.*

Steadying myself against her bedroom door frame, I asked, "I'm so sorry, Leah. Can we at least part as friends?"

"Maybe, if I ever stop being angry with you."

The car had contained our verbal battle, but the thin modular walls of a home designed as a summer getaway formed no barrier for our shrill and shriller voices leaking out into the humid air. As our conflict continued, I could see my neighbour Sue's face peering through the curtains of her kitchen window; curious about the uncharacteristic escalating noise level; listening to our outbursts; watching the unusual activity. At last, Leah maneuvered her way past me and charged out the front door without a glance back, laden with backpacks, boxes, green garbage bags, loose blankets, and toiletries, leaving me feeling worthless and used.

Moments later, headlights flashed in my driveway, temporarily blinding my already tear-blurred eyes. Standing alone on my porch, I stared blankly at the vehicle taking Leah away until the tail-lights were swallowed by the dark. Restoring the sanity of one thin nineteen-year-old should have been simple, possible; yet I didn't complete my task; therefore, I had failed. *I feel so tired! I am gone. I am nothing, I feel nothing. No wonder I'm making mistakes at work, no wonder I have so little energy and so much desire to sleep, just sleep. Who paddles a canoe alone anyhow? Only a motorcycle is designed to be ridden alone. I'm no different from the sulphur butterfly named Leah. She broke me completely.* The one who planned to rescue a frightened girl and guide her to a career she would love passionately, ended up destroying any hope of a positive future.

For a split second, my anger burned toward Vicki. *If only you could see your daughter now—oh, how messed up she is, how fractured in spirit.*

After several days of crying, I phoned my eldest daughter Annie on a Saturday morning.

"Nicely done, Mom. After breakdowns come breakthroughs," she told me—a wise, bold, positive voice of affirmation and faith that I listened to with gratitude and hope.

No sooner had I hung up after my daughter's call than my phone dinged twice. Doris's first text message read, "Interrupting blastoff stuff alert. I'm coming over for tea." Her second message: a row of hearts and smiley faces.

Doris and I had met at an outdoor church service several months previously. Doris, her sandals crackling along the gravel path toward me, had commented first on my willowy form, then said, "You have a shining white light above your head."

"Hi, nice to meet you too, I'm Ruth." I had rolled my eyes upward in hopes of seeing the mentioned light and extended my hand. "Just mere mortal Ruth." Unwavering, she kept focusing above my head, glimpsing a realm that eluded me, with a reverent smile that made her look angelic. Not your typical introduction, but Doris proved not to be a typical fellow churchgoer.

"I'm Doris. We are going to be friends. You need to guard your life."

How could she have known? We had met long before Leah entered my life.

Now I needed Doris to help me guard my life.

"Sure," I texted. "Please come over, I'll make the tea. P.S. My job is doing take-offs, not blast-offs. Thanks, Doris."

Doris sat cross-legged in her favourite chair, holding her teacup on her knee.

"Leah's so shattered; she needs professional counselling." Doris's voice soothed me. "You do realize that you're pleasing everyone around you, but you're losing your own voice. You tried so hard with Leah. I don't blame you for asking her to leave," said Doris. "Did you see that spectacular sunset last night?

"No."

Of course, I hadn't asked Leah to leave—I had demanded that she leave, but I didn't have the courage to tell Doris the truth.

"And today was such a beautiful day!" Doris continued.

"Was it? The rain here never stops pouring from skies the colour of lead. That's all I see."

"You should sign up for the 'Learn to be Assertive' classes at the clinic. And you should talk to Pastor." Doris sang in her thin melodic voice, "Learn to fly even if your wings are broken. Learn to live so free, la, la, la. Or something like that."

"My broken wings are feeling stronger as we speak. You're right. I long for some me-time, and to have the luxury to relax and catch up with myself. To find my joy. But how?"

"Open the windows of your soul and let the joy shine in," said Doris as she skipped down my front porch stairs into the sunshine.

Solitude settled in my home the instant Doris departed. Contemplating a canoe ride—a unique possibility in winter in B.C.—to reconnect with nature and regain focus, I untied the *S. S. Stallard.* Still, I struggled to concentrate. The tidal river's retreat forced me to walk a long mucky way to the water's edge, dragging my canoe behind me. The furrow my canoe etched in the mud reminded me that my heart, too, felt deeply etched with furrows.

The tide had favoured me with an uneventful trip, but not so the wind. He tossed all my uncertainties back into my face and blew the stench of salmon remains into my nostrils. Returning home, I dragged my feet through the mud flats along the shore, leaving the *S. S. Stallard* half-hitched to a tree, slipping on slimy rocks, mincing my steps around dozens of fish carcasses lying where Tide in her wise understanding of the food chain had left them for the eagles. *Maybe I should just lie down in defeat among the dead.* For the past year, I had been gracious instead of using my voice to express what I honestly thought. By diverting all my resources toward Leah, I ended up carrying a load too heavy for my heart. By evicting Leah, I had set up a dismaying dissonance within myself, as I hadn't taken the compassionate and forgiving path that I believed a true Christian should tread. Salmon, on the other hand, seemed to me to exemplify Christianity at its finest; they pour every last ounce of their life essence into returning to their spawning grounds. They catch only a fleeting glimpse of joy before silently sacrificing their lives for the next generation.

My downcast eyes took in only their skeletons, each delicate yet strong bone intact, each tooth jagged, white, and sharp. My peripheral vision noticed a sliver of yellow among the greys, browns, and blacks at my feet. *It figures, someone's garbage.* Yet when I looked directly, I saw, growing through the dank January mud—a buttercup, a thing so out-of-place, so resilient, so wondrous here in the carnage of the salmon that I cried, "Oh, wow, look at this."

Leaning down, I gently cradled the flawless yellow flower in my palm. As if its presence granted me a renewed perception, I returned my gaze to my lovely world of clouds suspended motionless in the stratosphere. Inhaling deeply, I sniffed the buttercup. A faint scent of sweetness and spring, a slight smell of life that maybe, just maybe, could be enough to cover the sickening scent of death.

The following Monday, after finishing my last estimate, I looked around my home, the home so recently filled with negative energy, the home I took refuge in. A feeling of despair at how uncontrollable my life had become, settled on me. Not even the sunshine pouring into my living room could make me accept how I had exploded at Leah. *I lost my way. Actually, I lost me. What is keeping me here?*

"I'm ready to sell my home and move back to Alberta where the rivers are always friendly. Leah's negativity is everywhere. I should have kept trying," I told Doris, in despair.

"I'll come over and pray that old negative energy right out of your sweet little home." Doris arrived, and miraculously after she prayed, a new-found peace fell on me. Her mission completed, she curled up in her favourite chair in my kitchen, cradling a mug of steaming chamomile tea. "You are attached to that computer with a ball and chain. Look how sugar-dust-white your skin is. You should be outside enjoying the sunshine and the chirping birds and your herb garden. Or travelling just for you; instead, you're inside your sweet little home working."

"I'm so grateful for my job," I told her. "It pays my bills. Imagine, I get to live in this tiny modular home on the edge of nowhere doing take-offs for an international granite company's estimating department. Besides, I'm usually finished by noon so I can still canoe and hike."

After Doris had bounded down my steps, I thought about her words. Not long after her visit, I noticed my interest in—as well as my energy for—work, began to plummet like a thermometer during an Alberta winter. My heart started taking a dim view of sitting in front of my computer alone all day.

Over the next seven months, I pondered the questions, "What can I do to reset my life?" and "How can I acknowledge the pain, anger, lack of respect, and entitlement?" My classical approach to problem solving—making lists—usually helped me formulate a concrete plan.

Number 1: Run away from my failed attempt to mother Leah. But I would need to run away more successfully than Jonah. And I had an idea of how to do so. My Bible College degree had qualified me to pursue full-time missions work; I might have been successful in fulfilling my duty to share the gospel if Garth hadn't conducted my third interview. The first two interviews with other agencies hadn't been inspiring, yet I'd kept applying. Garth, the manager of a reputable overseas agency, agreed to a one-hour call to assess my eligibility to serve with a global workers team in Sri Lanka. I could almost see him sitting in his office looking at the porcelain framed picture of his wife with their white poodle on his desk while he leaned back in his leather chair and said, "I can tell you, since I have been there, being divorced would be a problem in Sri Lanka. They struggle with that. Plus, and this is important, I am not sure you know where your heart-place is since your divorce."

Before I could ask him to explain heart-place, he said, "After listening to you, I don't see where your sending-place is. All these things muddy a call: lack of family connections; transience, because moving around so much just is not healthy; part-time job; no deep connections with your home church; and no financial support base."

"Where else can a divorcee serve?" I said, cringing at the label.

Does everyone who is called need to be able to define their calling? What exactly are a sending-place, and a heart-place? Where can I apply to be a rogue missionary who simply offers a cup of cold water?

"Actually, the only overseas experience you have is that short-term mission you did in Cuba in 2012; plus, you are lacking in specificity. I feel like getting a full-time job is the best thing for you to do right now."

Even before I hung up, hot tears stung my eyes. My feet carried me by instinct to the refuge of my room, where I flung myself onto my bed. Those tears spilled out until my pillow had absorbed enough moisture to fill a rain barrel. I yelled, I pleaded. *God, get me out of this confusion—that man made me feel like I am valueless—because right now I feel so alone and disconnected and so sullied for being divorced, nor do I fit the model of the perfect global worker. Garth makes me question both my ability to hear God and where I got my idealistic, vague ideas about His will for me. God, why don't you just take me home? Why do I need to be here anymore? I couldn't help Leah, and I can't find my place.*

After what felt like hours, I forced myself to step out into the cool evening breeze and hiked into the cedar forest. Surrounded by the quivering cedar shoots, my spirit lifted from feeling like I sat troubled on the earth to flying free of all my burdens. Pulling my cell from my jeans pocket, I phoned Doris to tell her about my interview with Garth.

"Missions work isn't everything. God uses us wherever we live. All you need to do is refresh your vision; you are not the type of person to sit around; that isn't you. You have an adventurous spirit," she said.

Running away from my life to a life of missionary service could now be crossed off my list.

Number 2: Sign up for those assertiveness classes. Enrolling is crucial, as being more assertive would have greatly assisted me with Leah. Shortly after she'd arrived, two incidents with Leah had made me draw in my anger and stay silent. For the first, I'd heard the bear-proof garbage lid slam. Without having to look, I knew what she had done, something so illogical I could scarcely believe my ears—she had tossed piles of feather-soft, nearly new bedding she'd been gifted into the dumpster because they reminded her of the past she couldn't seem to shake. The computer incident came next. It began with the shattering of the crystal drinking glass, the splash of a large volume of fluid, and ended with the shriek, "Oh! Now I need a new computer." She should have valued, appreciated, and taken the best care of her expensive gifts; but I realized that in her case, living on welfare had taught her instant gratification instead of the discipline of trading time for dollars. These items had cost someone else hard-earned dollars. *Such a waste!*

My anger burned below the surface since I knew that speaking to her about it would only spark her indignation.

In the assertiveness classes Doris had recommended, we role played. A woman with zero makeup and uncombed hair played me, the timid caregiver; and across the table from her, I acted as Leah, the entitled victim, practising exercises designed to convince me that the world wasn't an unsafe, scary, dangerous, or unfriendly place. Week after week for several months we honed our skills until I realized that diminishing oneself, so others won't feel insecure, is not enlightening. After that, everywhere I went, I spoke my truth, instead of what I thought others wanted to hear. My lessons rang in my ears. "If you think it, speak it. You need to stand up, create things, do things! You have the right to make good-for-you decisions. Make time to take care of yourself." Idea number 2 got a check mark.

Number 3: That talk with Pastor. Seeking out Pastor—whose nose ring had initially belied his wisdom—became my priority. He told me to process my disappointment in Leah slowly and provided me with the "Ten Steps to Forgiveness" workbook to guide us both toward eventually forgiving each other.

"Look at your reactions to her," he said, "And ask why you reacted the way you did."

Just the mere memory of my past experiences made me feel maggots crawling on my skin. I should have ignored the mint-toothpaste-tinted water droplets dried on the mirror, the water that dripped off every edge of the counter. *Why didn't anyone teach her how to tidy up after herself? "Why does it bother me so much?" would be a better question.* The contrast between my formerly spotless bathroom and the water-deluged bathroom Leah created reminded me of a time when my obsessive cleaning habit first served me well; it had been my attempt to find serenity and appear normal to the outside world in the chaos of my alcoholic marriage. Watching both the alcoholic and Leah—people I loved—disintegrate into frightening, angry people made me wonder: Am I the common denominator?

Back in the 1970s, before we'd started our family, my ex-husband had stood behind me at the kitchen sink, set his chin on my shoulder, and pointed at the sink. The scent of rye whisky slurred in the air. *Please let him be in a decent mood today.*

"Look at all that junk you left in the drain. How will you ever make a good mother when you can't even scrub a sink? You're a lousy housekeeper. If you kept it cleaner, I wouldn't drink so much."

He drank, I had believed, because of my careless cleaning habits. Moving out of his way and wiping my hands on a stained tea towel, I made a silent vow to keep the sink, the counters, the floors, the bathroom—everything—as shiny as possible, as I wanted to have kids, four of them. Being the best mom had been on my heart for the past three years. He trained me to be sensitive to the need to maintain a spotless household. No matter how clean I kept the house, though, he still drank; I still felt trapped in a marriage I thought I had the power to save. When Leah hadn't met the same level of cleanliness that I expected from myself, I got angry.

Another negative reaction to Leah would be triggered by the wadded mounds of toilet paper and Kleenexes spilling out of the bathroom garbage can onto the floor in our shared bathroom. Seeing the waste made me so angry. *Why did I get upset?* Again, my answer came from deep in my past when I lived only on the love of my children. The alcoholic had enough money for the basics like alcohol but neglected to provide for the extras, like food and toilet paper.

"You're useless because you can't even contribute to the family finances. If you were a better money manager, we wouldn't be in this situation. You need to get a job."

"Okay, I will go back to work," I had said. Returning to work and leaving my young child with a sitter seemed to make sense at the time.

"Bring home some toilet paper from work," he had told me.

"Isn't that stealing?"

"No, they don't pay you enough and besides, who will notice?"

But going back to work wasn't the answer. One day when I had picked up my daughter after work, the sitter gave me a picture of her propped up on the couch, leaning into the shoulder of the boy to the left of her, her fingers twirling her hair so that her elbow covered the arm of the girl to the right of her. The eyes staring at me looked so bewildered, so sad. Sitting on someone else's couch. The next day I quit my job even though I knew doing so would throw us into financial difficulties and incur his wrath and the withdrawal of his love. The negative memories churning to the surface showed me that I had no reason to get angry at Leah. *But it's too late now.*

From my marriage, I'd learned a coping mechanism that had trained me to use my voice to lie and enable, instead of addressing Leah's disrespect for me. Back in the early 1980s, when the children were small, the alarm clock would ring, I would reach for the phone over the alcoholic—still sleeping off another bender—and dial his boss.

"Good morning, Mr. Jones. Bill won't be at work today; he has a very contagious flu." His snoring form never moved.

I should have told Leah that her habit of leaving her space heater running day and night showed a careless disregard for the extra costs I bore. She seemed indifferent to the burden she placed on me. Instead, I lied, "It's okay, you can keep your space heater on, our Hydro bill isn't that much higher than normal."

Years back, whenever the alcoholic drank or became abusive, my sole focus was on expelling him from our lives to ensure the safety of my children and myself. Instinctively, I adopted a survival tactic—inflicting pain on others before they could hurt me and withdrawing before they could abandon me, a behaviour forged by his recurrent disappearances during times of strife. I had to explain things to our friends and family. This became my dysfunctional coping mechanism. People avoided me when I got angry. If they got too close, I feared they would see the worthlessness the alcoholic had forced me to feel. The lie I believed—I am only lovable if I behave a certain way—I projected onto Leah. If she behaved a certain way, I could love her; if she didn't, I couldn't be around her and had to abandon her when she needed me most.

No matter how hard I try, I still can't keep my life within the rails of "Thou Shalt" and "Thou Shalt Not."

The feeling of hope for freedom that could come after delving into the reasons why I reacted to Leah the way I did, made me grateful I had talked to my wise young pastor. Another check mark.

Number 4: Sleep for a year. Something I had once longed to do. Many years past, in my marriage, I had thought I, too, had fulfilled my destiny; to bring two wonderful beings into the world, and then just die like the salmon. The depression that had settled on me swathed me in sleep. To awaken was too painful, to sleep forever was preferable.

"Mommy, wake up."

My children's presence had filtered into my awareness; they tried to shake me awake, then leaped onto the bed with me. My mind had drifted back into my dream.

"In a second, I'm having fun here. I'm running barefoot on the sandy shore of a Caribbean Island. See the palm trees swaying in the breeze? I'm holding hands with this handsome man. He's so nice. He is nice to us."

"Where Mommy?"

The line between fantasy and reality had blurred as I had struggled to wake up to nurture the two reasons I still wanted to live.

Despite my present low energy levels tempting me to choose sleep as an alluring alternative, I knew a year-long slumber would not solve anything, just as it had not in the past. I crossed it off my list.

My lists helped me deal with my conflicting emotions but left me wondering how to reset my life. Until the hailstorm struck.

CHAPTER 3

The Art of Farewell: Preparing for Patagonia

EIGHT MONTHS TO THE DAY AFTER I KICKED LEAH OUT, AN INTENSE hailstorm made me realize that clarity can come from within a tempest. Stepping outside my home after the hailstones had stopped ricocheting off the grassy riverbank and pavement, I breathed in the scent of the ozone that freshened the warm, humid air. Against a dark grey, immobile sun-hider, a plume of swirling white clouds surged upward, unmistakably conspicuous. From the top of rising ivory wisps, as though released from a bottle like a genie, an "angel" materialized. Her exquisite body had two firm, smooth, outstretched pointed wings, a round head, and a gown floating on the air currents. She flew freely.

Unlike most clouds that slowly morph from one shape into another and into nothingness, she kept her perfect form as she ascended swiftly. Eyes riveted on the "angel," enthralled, I watched her thermal, heaven bound, like an eagle. She compelled me to accompany her, to reshape the contours of my existence—she seemed familiar to me. Then she dissipated. *Patagonia! Now is the time for me to go to Patagonia and climb Mount Fitz Roy!* The cloud angel had cracked open the dream locked in the storage vault of my heart. *I am powerless to change Leah, but I can change my life.*

Springing up my steps two by two, I dashed back into the house. As if waiting for my return, *Extreme Landscape* still stood on my bookshelf between my Bible College textbooks *The New Greek-English Interlinear New Testament,* and *Freedom, Authority, and Scripture* by J.I. Packer. After re-reading the essay, I surfed the internet for ideas. A short trip to *Patagonia* for a week-long trail ride in the *Andes*? Pet-sitting my way across *Argentina* until I arrived at Fitz Roy? My index finger stopped scrolling when my eyes caught the words "Help Exchange." I discovered that in the typical Help Exchange arrangement, the helper works an average of four hours per day and receives free accommodation and meals for their efforts.

Pondering the Help Exchange idea, I became entwined in thoughts of travelling unimpeded, the promise of enough funds to extend those travels, the chance to immerse myself in a foreign language, and the prospect of doing life side by side with nationals, absorbing their cultures—in effect, the perfect blend of adventure and personal growth. Nothing might have been wrong with the concept, except for Gertrud. Four hours of work per week might have sufficed, the savings may have been worth it, but I would find out that The Lodge didn't operate that way. Yet, much later, I would be thankful for Gertrud.

To narrow my online search, I used the keywords "horses" and "*Argentina*," as I had a passionate, unquenchable love for the noble creatures. Weeks later, after submitting dozens of Help Exchange applications, I'd received only one response—from a German woman named Gertrud, who, with her Chilean husband Antoine, owned The Lodge, in *Chile*. On Tuesday, September 29, 2015, Gertrud and I chatted for the first time via WhatsApp—I feeling as though she lived just across the river and we'd shared many a cup of tea; and she sounding confident that my riding skills were polished, and that my maturity would ensure I'd fulfill a three-month commitment. Gertrud's positive tone, softened by her beguiling German accent, reassured me.

"Based on my gut feeling, I'll have no problem if you come to help us out from January 22 to the end of April, ja. Your job will be to lead trail rides and muck the barn. I have you booked in, ja. And remember, I am depending on you to stay with us the full twelve weeks. I've hired so many young students who don't keep their word, but I trust you will, ja," Gertrud said.

"You can count on me. I'll be there!" My words floated in the air even as I hung up, leaped from my chair, skipped around the kitchen table, and yelled, "AAAAAAAAAHHHHHHHHH! Gertrud's response just solidified my decision! This is going to happen! Twelve glorious weeks riding horses at a ranch in *Patagonia*!"

Racing into my bedroom, I snatched *Extreme Landscape* from the shelf and once again traced my finger along Fitz Roy's jagged outline. *I'm committing three months to working in a specific location, aligning it with a journey toward self-discovery. But to accomplish my goal of climbing Fitz Roy in*

Argentina, I'll need an extra three months in South America. Our government permits a maximum absence of six months from Canada without losing health care benefits, so I'll travel for the full six months! I'll figure out the "how" when the time comes!

Whenever I had vacationed in the past, I took The Shepherd with me, but since my trip to Scotland with my cousin in 2012, I had found another travelling companion—a sheep. Only Hatchi would accompany me to *Patagonia*. From the moment I had seen him on that shelf in the sheep farm's gift shop, with his outstretched brown hooves, his small black-bead eyes, and round beige ears, I knew he would return to Canada with me. He was the physical shape of love: soft, tan fur covering a pear-shaped body, soft as my newborn's skin. The perfect name had eluded me until my cousin took me to her neighbour Hatchi's sheep croft later, where I watched the tall, stooped farmer, his thin wisps of white hair sticking out from under his Harris Tweed cap, feed an eager, orphaned lamb with a baby bottle. In that moment, the farmer's compassion spoke to me of nurture and care, and I connected his name to my sheep. Like the landscapes Hatchi has seen from the back of my motorcycle, he embodies my travels—unexpected moments, softness amidst rugged terrains, and silent companionship that transcends language.

As I mulled over how I could integrate into a new culture without understanding its heartbeat—its language—I recalled that I knew someone who spoke Spanish. When I shared my plan with my hairdresser, who had recently moved to B.C. from Ecuador, her concerns echoed a deeper truth—I will need to be able to communicate to survive.

"How are you planning to communicate in a foreign country where not many of us natives speak English?"

"I was hoping you could teach me Spanish."

"You are better off to watch lots of Spanish movies with subtitles. You must learn how to listen in order to master the vocabulary because we talk so fast. The movies will show you to listen to the flow of the language," she said, snipping my hair shorter than I had desired. "You won't learn by getting someone to tell you that *perro* means dog. Watch out when you are in *Chile* because everyone will want you to teach them English but don't let them, get them to teach you Spanish instead."

The melody and rhythm of the Spanish language captivated my senses. Each word tasted like caramel, each phrase danced like crackling, burning pine, and each sentence pulsed like a beating drum. I breathed in the words; with delight and fascination; I dreamt them. Why say "then" when you can say *entonces*? Why say "spirit" when you can say *espiritu*? After watching multitudes of movies, building on the few phrases I had mastered during my mission trip to Cuba, I could understand basic conversations.

On a chilly, early October evening, during the time between letting my body relax into the comfort of my mattress and surrendering to sleep's sweet invitation, the honking of the Canada geese spoke to me. "Get ready. Come south with us. Spend the winter in *Argentina*. Being safe, sticking solely to the beaten trail, prevents you from choosing abundant life over duty; you need to embrace and live out your dream instead. Get ready and come." *I'm ready to leave with the geese. But how do I twist my thoughts—my dream—into action?* Filling in the space between my thoughts and action would happen as organically as the high tide filled in the spaces between the exposed rock and debris of low tide to create a watery expanse of dancing sun-scorched diamonds.

As I navigated the days leading up to my departure—surrounding me, supporting me—the voices of those closest to me echoed in my mind. My pastor, one daughter, and one aunt were among those who wholeheartedly supported my intentions; yet they were in a minority. They could see my journey as a bold-spirited step toward self-discovery, and their faith bolstered my gumption.

While I explained my plans to my pastor, he listened with his intense golden eyes glowing as brightly as his red hair.

"God has things he's going to do through you that will rock your world! If you look for him, you will see God all along the way to *Patagonia*. Blessings on you as you receive the calling God has invited you to respond to."

"Thanks, Pastor."

He suggested transforming my journey into a spiritual quest, framing it as ministry research. His guidance led me to create three practical checklists: one for travel logistics, another for moving and preparation, and a third for potential research-paper-turned-book ideas. Using TravelPod, I established a blog to consolidate my notes online. These checklists embodied my lifelong learning approach—urging me to appreciate and be curious about God's creation, fully engage in the world, and share the love of God. Working at The Lodge might have been just a holiday, travel for the sake of travel;

but Pastor's charge to "thou shalt evangelize" elevated it, transforming my journey from a simple escape to fulfilling a Christian duty.

He gave me a series of questions to help frame the diverse beliefs and experiences awaiting me. I intended for these questions to guide my interactions with everyone I met: What is your belief system? Whom do you worship and why? What would it take for you to change your belief system? What do you believe happens after you die? Also, I turned these queries inward, pondering how I could serve God meaningfully, leave a legacy, express my true self in myriad ways, and cultivate a sense of belonging in this vast world. As it turned out, the spontaneous nature of my travels often led to forgetting to ask these questions of everyone I encountered. Sorry, Pastor.

My youngest daughter Lenora, whose voice had always sounded confident with a delicious helping of mischief, as if she knew or could invent the answer to any question, said, "You're so cute, Mom. Do it!"

"Thanks, sweetheart."

My Aunt Sonja maintains that you can't have a voice if you don't take risks. Life is all about venturing outside your boundaries.

"Ruth, you can do this. I know you can," she said. She poured green tea into a china cup. "Now have some tea with some of my world-famous shortbread."

"Thanks, Aunt Sonja."

Conversely, my well-meaning parents, boss, brother, old friend, and gliding instructor couldn't see my vision. They only felt the fear of the unknown; and these fears, concerns, and objections, all stemming from a place of love, tethered me to the ground. Using reason, they disapproved of my "commit first, figure it out later" approach. Their responses reminded me of a quote I'd read somewhere, "The very voice of love tempts us to stay by asking, 'Have you no pity on our loneliness?'"

Beside me, my parents sat in silence. The table, set with their gold-rimmed dishes and sparkly silverware for supper, had a familiarity to it, a stay-here draw about it.

"I know six months is a long time, Mom, but I've been saving for a year, so I know I won't run out of money."

"What if you hurt yourself out there? How could you get assistance? And what if the different climates or different grasses or dust triggers your asthma?" Dad asked.

"Don't worry, I take my inhaler every day so that will protect me from different humidity and allergens. And I have a six-month supply I will take with me," I reassured them.

"Are you certain it is completely safe to travel alone?" Dad asked.

Of course, I'd thought about the safety of travelling alone all that way, but I would rather live and do this than stay safe and not live. In a minute, I would start feeling that tether tighten around my ankle again, so I drew in a cleansing breath and, changed the subject.

"Do you have any of your yummy oatmeal cookies in the kitchen, Mom?"

Resigning from my job to embark on this six-month journey, effectively stepping into early retirement, weighed heavily on my conscience. Few employers would keep a job open for that long, intensifying the difficulty of my decision. As I dialled my boss's number, the weight of my choice pressed down on me. Breaking the news to her felt as difficult as I had anticipated. After our goodbyes, the line stayed open for a moment longer, letting me hear her resigned sigh. This unintended eavesdropping only amplified my guilt. Despite the pang of regret and the uncertainty that severing my income stream induced, a deeper conviction assured me that this journey comprised a necessary step in reclaiming my life.

My brother's eyes, normally calm and blue, looked perplexed, yet as pragmatic and intelligent as always.

"Have you thought about cash flow? When you return home and have no more job—what then? What if your tenants in your rental property in Alberta decide to vacate? Plus, you will need health insurance. Once the dream fades, you will find yourself alone again, your connections to family and friends will be stretched thin by time and distance."

My eyes groped for his, they slipped, I looked away, I had no answers. Then he mentioned a crucial point.

"And your peanut allergy...it's a critical concern, Ruth, especially when you're travelling alone. Remember the Bible College incident? You can't afford to take such risks abroad."

"How could I forget?" I said. "That mistake will make me extra cautious on my journey. I know everything I eat carries the potential to trigger a reaction, so I promise I'll travel with a new EpiPen and read ingredients. Peanut is *mani* in Spanish. See, I've been doing my research."

A close friend, one whom I'd treasured since she'd greeted me on day one of Bible College, sighed deeply into the phone, her breath caught and magnified by the microphone.

"What are you searching for? Why can't you be content with where you are at right now? What ARE you running away from?"

"I'm not in flight, I'm on a quest." She sensed the determination in my tone. "I'm not willing to shrink back and let the 'what ifs' make me miss this opportunity, I will go, and I will go alone, but I won't be alone, God is with me."

"You'll need him." Her last words to me for six months.

When I called Tom—my former gliding instructor whom I dubbed "the voice of reason," who could fly a glider to a destination and only sometimes land out in a wheat stubble field—he asked a logical question. "Make your checklist. Book your hotels, organize your flights, and map your route. A significant task. Do you have control?"

"Yes, I have control." This answer, the rote answer given when passing control from teacher to student, is designed to prevent a crash. *I hope.*

I hope their fears are unfounded and I hope I know what I have committed to! Yes, I learned how to fly a glider, so I am sure I will manage to figure out the details, one detail at a time.

Reclining on my favourite bench above the river, I heard Francis's bemused voice.

"What on earth are you doing?" he asked, looking down at me from under his creased Tilley hat. My neighbour Francis had become a reliable walking buddy, always ready to enjoy the mellow artistry of this spot with me.

"I'm looking for the corners, or handles, so I can pull down Sky and ask her the source of her deep blue peace," I said, sitting up.

"Good luck with that. Question about your wild idea to go to South America: What if your water pipes freeze while you are gone? Have you thought about that?"

He tossed his hat on the bench, scooted me over, and sat down, his fluffy white bichon tugging on her leash, barking insistently, willing him to rise. Beyond and below us on the river, I watched the passionately paddling mergansers and wondered if they would soon be eagle food.

"That's something I hadn't thought of," I said. The ducks disappeared beneath the surface of the water, leaving concentric circles in their place. "But I have an idea: I'll find someone to rent this place while I am away."

He laughed. "What is the probability that you could find anyone to rent your place way out here for the exact six months that you will be gone?"

I had no answer.

I needed a way to sever the tether that my loved ones used to anchor me to the ground. My plan to change, to step away, like I stepped out of my motorcycle gear after a scoot, could only be done by spending those six months away from my circle of influencers. The eight years since my divorce marked my first experience of living alone; yet I remained closely connected with friends and family, seeking their affirmation for my ideas. I walked past the salmon graveyard on my afternoon stroll, with only the odd bone now poking through new green grasses and red-and-yellow flowers. The new life concealing the reminders of my long season confined by Leah—the season my anger drowned out my voice—brought new views.

During our last Gospel Riders scoot, I caught wind of some unexpected news—Crawford planned to drive to *Mexico*, delivering donations for a woman's shelter. The thought of travelling that first stretch with him seemed like the perfect way to sever that tether, plus ease into my own journey to *Patagonia*. I trusted Crawford, my steadfast confidant, my source of encouragement; the friend who had shared many a motorcycle and bicycle ride, and canoe paddle. I invited him for a cycling trip along the river the next weekend, hoping this would be my chance to broach the subject with him.

"Thanks for coming, Crawford," I said when we met at the trailhead. "I have a question for you."

His ears muffled by his helmet, he pedalled on ahead of me, crunching on the loose shale. *My question will have to wait.*

As I struggled to keep up with Crawford, my lungs wheezing from the exertion, memories of my treasured *Pegasus* floated back, mingling with my current jumbled thoughts. A week before I had moved to Maple Ridge I'd sold *Pegasus,* believing I couldn't make the two-day ride from Calgary to Maple Ridge alone. When I got home from the dealership, I'd lain in the fetal position for twenty minutes—processing the emotional weight of parting with a motorcycle that had brought me freedom and joy over the previous five years. I thought I'd never ride again—until Josie came into my life. Since I'd been a member of Gospel Riders in Alberta, I sought out an event put on by the chapter in Maple Ridge. There I met this spunky, seventy-five-year-old, Spyder-riding prayer warrior and her Harley-riding husband. Josie welcomed me as the only official motorcycle-less person in their Gospel Riders group and made it her mission to get me back on the road. At each meeting I attended, Josie would end her prayers with, "And Lord, don't forget Ruth needs a beautiful new motorcycle." Her prayers were answered three weeks later when the president of the group mentioned that a friend wanted to sell her Yamaha V-Star 650, as she'd bought a larger bike. At first, I doubted that a 650 would be powerful enough to keep up with the group; but after a test ride, the sleek lines, the shiny blue-and-silver tank, the way it handled, and the sheer joy it brought me, made me fall in love. Naming her *Angel of the Winds*, after a passage in Scripture, felt fitting as I knew she came from on high. Divine intervention had brought me back to the road! Maneuvering a bike after so long would prove to be more challenging than I'd anticipated. Being able to ride with the group as a full-fledged member filled me with a deep sense of belonging. For the next five seasons, I rode that motorcycle—cherishing the wind in my face—every ride fusing power and grace, control and surrender.

At that first meeting, Josie had introduced me to Stretch and Crawford. Stretch, Crawford, and I had become like the rungs of a ladder—starting with the oldest, shortest Crawford and climbing past me to the youngest, tallest Stretch—since I'd joined the team. They also shared my belief that you shouldn't enjoy motorcycling just for the pure fun and thrill of feeling the wind in your face; you should tie your activities to a mission-oriented group. Wearing our Christian patches, we didn't just ride; we ministered to others, spreading the gospel—lending a higher purpose to our love of riding.

Reflecting on my recent trips, I recalled my first Tuesday evening ride with Gospel Riders, when Crawford had watched me crawl around corners, drop my V-Star at intersections, maneuver so close to a gas pump that I'd bumped into the curb, and barely miss colliding with an oncoming Ford F250 while trying to avoid a blown tire on the highway. In Alberta, I'd ridden the straight and level roads with passion and confidence. But handling the twisty, curvy, hilly roads surrounding my new riverbank home in B.C. both thrilled and terrified me. That ride ended at Tim Hortons, as would all our weekly rides. Pulling up into the last space in the row of eight motorcycles,

I had kicked down my motorcycle stand and shakily removed my helmet. Crawford had been waiting for me.

"Isn't your motorcycle named *Angel of the Winds*?" he had laughed. "Then why do you ride like you are crippled?"

"I...."

Asking myself why I rode so slowly, I saw that beyond my fears of crashing into a tractor-trailer, riding off a cliff, injuring someone, or plain getting lost, lay the fear that my family and friends would deeply grieve my death, a death they would deem avoidable.

"Ride like the wind, Ruth, ride like the wind!" he had said, putting his arm around me as we walked into the coffee shop. "I'll buy you a tea."

The absence of the sound of bicycle tires crunching shale cut through my nostalgia. Noticing that Crawford had stopped and leaned his bicycle against a mildewed wooden bench, I parked mine and sat on the bench a respectable distance away from him.

In his pragmatic way, he turned to me and, using my motorcycle name, asked, "So, Squid, what is this question you want to ask me?"

"Remember how I told you that I've decided to go on this trip to *Chile* and *Argentina* alone?"

He nodded.

"Well, Stretch told me you're going to drive your truck with a load of donations to a woman's shelter in *Mexico*. For me, the idea of just up and leaving alone is—well—a tad scary. So, here's my question. What if we travel as far as *Mexico* together? You know, to ease from travelling with someone to travelling alone," I said.

Crawford, his eyes sincere, each hair individually smoothed into place, hair that only ever looked askew just after he removed his helmet, said, "No. You are a tall, attractive, single woman and I am a short, dapper, single gentleman; you know what I'm saying? We're both Christians, right? It's fine to cycle together, and fine to ride with Gospel Riders together. But driving to *Mexico* together, that's different."

The research I'd done in preparation for our talk, should persuade him.

"You're like the Ancient of Days, Crawford. No one is going to judge two friends who go on a trip together. I'll help you load the trailer with all those baby carriages, and clothes, and diapers and stuff and unload it on the other end. Besides, I checked their website; the shelter needs house mothers.

I believe in their ministry, and I could volunteer to help them once we got there."

"No."

The cycle home seemed as long and as quiet as the time my daughter spent her first full day at school.

Four days after my ride and talk with Crawford, someone knocked at my door, disrupting my swirling thoughts. I opened it a crack. My eyes tear-reddened, my pilled grey sweatpants already on day four, my sink piled with dishes like a Tetris game, all made it look as if I'd lost a battle with the Philistines; I felt unprepared to have a visitor.

"Doris. Oh, Doris. I can't do it, Doris, I just can't. I thought travelling as far as *Mexico* with Crawford would help, but he won't take me with him. I want to travel solo to *Patagonia*; I feel I'd be doing what I need to. To find my voice, to find me. I put forth considerable effort to alter Leah's perspective and give her a brighter outlook on life. I've come to realize that all my life I've surrendered my joy; the truth is—I can only effect change within myself. Yet I don't have the energy or the know-how to solve all the problems and attend to all the details my friends and family bring up. Plus leaving on my own overwhelms me," I blurted in a stream of consciousness.

"You look terrible. May I come in? Awh, Ruth, my heart is sad."

She pushed the door open and headed for her favourite chair, patting the seat beside her.

I sat.

"This will be a liminal journey for you." Then Doris's face flashed a smile that created two impish dimples. "Don't you think you deserve an epic adventure like this? Oooh, just think! What if this is how you'll meet someone? Maybe a fellow traveller in a hostel or on a bus. A romance of the century! Just stop all this busyness and just do it. After all, you can't hold a moonbeam in your hand." She placed her hand gently over my upturned hands lying in my lap.

In awe, I watched Doris actively engaging in my life, sharing moments with me, and encouraging me with the persistence of a snail boring through a clamshell. My lifeline.

"I feel as though I am in a dream where you can't run no matter how hard you try. I look at my daily workload and see only another deadline, another day. I feel mired like I'm reaching for—yet not reaching—*Patagonia*."

"You'll get there!" she said.

Her optimistic prediction held a truth—my arrival at that place would come sooner than either of us could have imagined.

The following Tuesday evening, despite my inner turmoil, I forced myself to join our weekly ride. *I know Doris would want me to go*. Helmets, black leather gloves, tank bags, and Gospel Riders-patched jackets covered the table and chairs next to us at Tim Hortons during our pre-ride get-together. I sat with Stretch and two others, noting Crawford's absence.

"The ultimatum has landed. Gerty advised me that if I don't spend the fall with her, our engagement is off," said Stretch, his face as long as his long legs sprawled into the aisle.

Attempting to focus on his conversation among several others, I said, "I'm sorry to hear that, Stretch. I thought you two were perfect for each other. Well, you know Crawford is driving those donations and his motorcycle to *Mexico*. He could use some help."

"I understand. That's why I informed her that our engagement is null and void. I made it clear that I'm heading to *Mexico* with Crawford!" His boyish grin illuminated his face from behind the latte. "I'll bring my V-Strom, and we can turn it into a two-month scoot."

"Really?" I exclaimed in a high-pitched voice, trying to conceal my anxious desire to talk to Crawford. "Let's ride."

Later that evening, after a ride infused with a buoyant surge of energy and hope, I dialled Crawford, eager to ask him another question.

"Crawford, Stretch told me..."

"Yes, Squid, you can come. We'll be a three-person missions team. You can accompany Stretch and me to the shelter in *Mexico*; then you are on your own. You know what I'm saying? I am leaving October 20. Be ready."

"Thank you, Crawford. Thank you. I'm already ready."

As my cell phone clattered onto my counter, my face flushed with the same excitement that suspended my breath during every canoe trip or motorcycle ride. Slowly settling down on my couch, I sat for the next four hours speaking not a word. How deep is my awe at God's plan—that he should open this door using the four supportive hands of my Christian brothers. And to think that he had set that plan into motion eleven years earlier using Deb's long red hair.

Back in Alberta, during our shared volunteer duties, Deb, a young grandmother, and I had chatted as we sauntered out to the parking lot. I walked to my car. She walked to a red Honda Shadow motorcycle, pulled her leathers from her bags, tightened her helmet strap under her chin, swung her leg over the seat, waved a leather-fringed gloved hand at me, and peeled out of the parking lot, her auburn ponytail flapping against her back. She exuded joy and freedom. *That looks like fun!* Watching her form grow smaller and smaller, I found myself unable to turn the key in my ignition. My thoughts cast back to the joyful feeling of the wind blowing in my face during the times I had canoed with my dad, and for our college canoe team, or when I rode my bicycle. When I finally turned the key, a seed had been sown—*I want to feel that wind again! I want to ride a motorcycle, too!*

The commitment I made to Crawford confirmed that the tether around my ankle had snapped, preparing me to embrace travel as my agency for change. October 20, 2015, would arrive in three weeks. Shaping my dream into reality depended entirely on my forming tangible plans. The prospect of my soon-coming journey thrilled me; and with more zeal than I had felt in the past year, I tackled the practical logistics of leaving my home.

Despite Francis's skepticism, I must find tenants to stay in my home while I'm gone to generate income for all my expenses—a challenging feat.

Two weeks of telling applicants that "no pets" actually meant they couldn't bring their pet; that four kids probably wouldn't fit in my 400-square-foot modular home; that I did indeed expect them to rent for only the full six months; as well as suffering through lengthy periods of no responses, frustrated me.

Should I pick the best of the worst, or forget about the whole rental plan, or keep waiting?

One week before my departure date, the call came. The couple who understood all my conditions arrived on my doorstep to view my home and sign the lease.

"Thanks so much! I know you will take diligent care of my place while I'm travelling. Any questions?" I said to them, feeling delighted with the arrangement and the income.

"Just one. Can we use your yellow canoe while you are gone?" asked the husband.

"NO! I mean no, it's not included in the rent, sorry," I said, sensing how his question had disrupted my harmony.

"Just asking, that's all. No problemo."

As my prospective renters walked away, I pondered the strangeness of my response, and eventually traced it to the unusual arrival of my beloved canoe. Weeks after I had settled into my modular home, while gazing out my living room window, I had thought that if I had some type of boat, and could float down that river just before dawn, I could have an unobstructed view of the sunrise. The desire to witness the sacred miracle of a new day, watching shades of reds, pinks, and blues display the glory of that time between times—the handoff from night to day—wouldn't leave me. The problem of paddling a canoe solo led me to consider the superior manoeuvrability of a kayak. However, when I slipped into the narrow vessel for the first time, my heart began to race. The confined space felt claustrophobic, and the fear of capsizing gripped me. In my vivid imagination, I saw myself trapped, struggling for breath under an overturned kayak, weighed down by leeches. Back to canoes. The ones I found on Craig's List were beyond my budget. I had contented myself with watching the sunrise from my living room window—until the day Francis and his dog walked past my rock garden one blazing hot summer's day.

"Hi, Ruth, wouldn't this be an enjoyable day for a canoe ride? You have been talking about getting one. I saw a canoe moored on the south end of the river near one of the trailers. Why don't we see if we can find the owner and see if they want to sell it?"

"I'd love to," I said.

At the third trailer door we knocked on, a man wearing nothing but navy-blue sweatpants answered.

"Yup, that's my canoe. Give me twenty bucks and it's yours."

Only twenty dollars? "Could we view it, please?"

"Go for it," he said, pointing a nicotine-stained finger toward the riverbank, and slamming the door on us.

Francis and I had made our way down the overgrown path. Peeling red paint, a missing bow seat, mud and leaves caked the bottom, and a cracked fibreglass floor and gunnel made the canoe look unappealing and downright unseaworthy to me.

My eyes bored into his.

Francis lifted his shoulders to his ears, spread out all ten fingers, smiled innocently, and said, "Looked okay from a distance."

"Maybe my carpenter friend could fix it for me. It does have potential," I said.

The day I returned to the trailer with a twenty-dollar bill fresh from the ATM, I thought for sure I'd made a mistake. The paddles, though in decent shape, couldn't take me across the river to my modular fast enough. Bailing, paddling, bailing, paddling. No amount of effort could prevent the bow of my new canoe from swinging wildly from left to right with each stroke. Zig, zag, wobble, zig, zag, wobble. Long minutes later, I pulled in near my home, where my friend whisked my canoe—sloshing with enough water to sustain a dozen large goldfish—away to his workshop. Observing the canoe vanish into the distance, I considered that I wouldn't be upset if it fell off his truck.

During my canoe's absence, I never once missed the thing; yet for some reason, I watched one YouTube video after another that made solo canoe paddling look easy. My bookshelves filled with books written by Bill Mason, the well-known canoeist. The J-stroke appeared to be the method solo canoeists—so I am not the only solo paddler—used to paddle and arrive at their destination before everyone else has packed up for the day. Putting the J-stroke into practice would take me a long time; but once I had mastered it, I would marvel at the effectiveness of the stroke.

Weeks later, when I saw the miracle of transformation the fibreglass patches made and how, where once an empty bow had been, a rich oak bow seat stood, I fell in love with my new canoe.

"Thank you! I'll pay you in cookies." I danced around my friend, then gave him a bear hug.

"Deal. But I ain't painting it. We'll stop at the hardware on the way to your place."

"I'll take the Lemon Mivvi," I had told the clerk at the paint store.

My friend left me with an upturned canoe on two sawhorses. The sun beat down on my bare back while I painted my canoe a vivid yellow. Using an exacto-knife, I cut out the letters *S. S. Stallard* into a sheet of durable plastic, painted over my stencil with white paint, and slowly peeled it off. My canoe had been christened. The following day, Francis had come to see me off for my maiden voyage—I could still see his thumbs-up and his grin from the opposite shore.

No stranger shall paddle the S. S. Stallard—my exercise partner and fellow explorer, the one who allows me to interact fully with my aquatic surroundings.

Over the next few days, I talked with Sue, the manager of the woman's shelter somewhere on the Pacific coast of *Mexico*. She said she would be eager to have me volunteer as a house mother after we dropped off the donations. One rainy morning, Crawford and I packed his trailer with shoes, maternity and baby clothing, strollers, tricycles and his V-Strom, and I borrowed a canvas backpack cavernous enough to hold four seasons' worth of attire plus my daypack and Hatchi. The idea of navigating a foreign country alone both thrilled and intimidated me. *Am I ready for this adventure? Will I find the courage to open to new experiences and people?* Within days I completed a whirlwind of final items on my list: I visited, hugged, called, shed tears with those closest to me; I surprised Doris by laughing when she told me to skedaddle; I paid all my bills six months ahead; I had my hair styled in a pixie-cut; I parked *Angel of the Winds* in a friend's garage; I handed my house keys to my seasonal renters; and I left. My journey—destined to indeed rock my world and unveil life from a grand perspective—had begun.

By 7:00 a.m. on October 20, 2015, Crawford, Stretch, and I were already rolling south in the big red truck, our mission clear—deliver a load of donations to the woman's shelter in *Mexico*. A peculiar sensation stirred within me. We were outwitting the seasons by traversing south through Washington, Oregon, and California; journeying backward in time from fall to summer. Leaning my forehead against my back-seat window, I observed the California sky: it looked bluer than the sodden black, pre-winter skies I had left behind that morning, its clouds whiter and lighter. The memory of those dark clouds in B.C. still caused me to tremble in fear, as if Nemesis herself rumbled like thunder, ready to dole out her just punishment to me. Those clouds that had blotted out the sun were more than meteorological phenomena; they represented the darkness within me, the part that hindered Leah's ability to fit in and thrive. If only I had asked Leah why fitting in mattered to her, rather than imposing my ideas of individuality on her. In trying so hard to stop Leah from pursuing what she wanted—to fit in—I had exhausted myself until I almost couldn't muster the strength to embark on my *Patagonian* trip.

As Big Red rumbled forward, my mind wandered backward through time to Leah's first day of college. Leah and I had driven through the campus populated with more brick buildings and roads and stop signs than our trailer park—bumper-to-bumper with more traffic than I dealt with in a week—looking for a place to park. By the time I finally found a space, I noticed Leah twirling the tips of her hair around and around her fingers. My eyes followed her gaze at the other students filing past in a silent parade, all kids her age, similar but not similar. The similarity ended when she saw their shoes. They were wearing spiked heels, blinding neon-green sneakers, pink flip-flops, mauve sandals. Her shoes were plain, brown, practical, ugly. She looked at the girls' brightly coloured dresses; she looked at hers. Her plain grey sweater, suitable for this autumn day but lacking any style at all, draped loosely over her shoulders. The hairstyles most clearly indicated that she had come from a different time, a different place. She'd been unable to cut her hair for six years: the long strands glowed red; she loved her hair—I loved her hair—yet she hated it. The other girls had short bobs with wispy bangs. They probably cut and styled every six weeks.

"I don't fit in," she had sighed. The look on her face said, *I am afraid to get out of the car.*

"Leah, being an individual is more important than conforming. God made you a unique human being."

"Will you take me shopping to buy some new clothes and shoes?"

"Leah, I've already bought you a lot of new things."

The period between turning off the ignition and opening the door had seemed like a suspended breath. Time to blend into the throng.

"I will come with you," I had said. Guiding her arm while heading to the main registration building, I reflected on her admirable courage and tenacity. "Leah, you can do this."

The moment she sidled out of my embrace, I had noticed that none of the other students walked with a parent; instead, friends clustered in groups of twos or threes, or walked alone. *She doesn't have a friend in the world.* She pushed through the heavy glass doors without a farewell hug.

When I had returned for her later in the day, she climbed into the passenger seat, and asked, "Now, will you take me to the mall for my fresh look? I want to change; I want to look like all those other teenagers. Out in the boonies where you live, I'm okay; but look around, do you think I fit in here?"

Glancing at her, I had distractedly dismissed her request, and, trying to reassure her, I said, "I think you're already beautiful, Leah."

The car rolled on; but as the distance between us and the potential for her shopping spree grew, regret wove its way into my thoughts. Upon our return home, she had gone straight to her room.

Weeks later, while waiting for her at the transit stop in Maple Ridge, I had scanned the flow of students, businesspeople, and the ever-present homeless as they poured off the bus. Leah was typically easy to spot, with her hair-forest and colourless clothes, but not this day. I glanced at a young woman with a fresh new hairdo stylishly shaped around her ears, framing a gorgeous face. She wore a sheer white lacy blouse, high heels, and tight jeans that accentuated a lovely figure. I wouldn't have believed this could be Leah if it hadn't been for the slight stoop of her shoulders. To blend in with her peers, she must have poured her entire government assistance cheque into clothes, makeup, and hair styling. I had imagined her racing through the streets, catching a maze of buses, perhaps even skipping classes in her determined pursuit to fit in.

Hindsight plagued me with guilt. *Why couldn't I have taken her shopping? Why couldn't I have at least driven her to get a haircut*?

Regret over Leah's past struggles loomed; but the landscape outside Big Red's rolled-down window settled the memory, and whispered to me, "Nothing within my control could have changed Leah's outcome."

From the dusty roads of California, the winds blew warmer; the soil looked rockier than back home; and the neat squares of green peach orchards and brown stubble fields extended farther into the distance but faded into familiar mists, reminiscent of the mists that had often blurred the boundaries of my estuary home.

The journey took an olfactory turn inside the truck when I detected a suffocating aroma, prompting me to ask, "What is that odour? Smells like wet dog."

"It's Crawford's cheap aftershave," Stretch joked. He craned his neck and winked at me from the front seat.

"So, are you good with Sue at the shelter?" Crawford shifted the conversation toward my personal plans.

"Yes," I raised my voice higher than the sound of the diesel engine. "I'm ready to be their house mother until I leave for my Help Exchange at The Lodge in *Chile* in January."

Through my preparation, and later the freedom of my first days of early retirement, I moved eagerly with my dream before my eyes; but despite my focus I kept thinking, "I should be working." However, the thought that I would be making better use of my time than the guys, riding their bikes randomly across the *Mexican* roads, gave me comfort; my Christian duties would be met.

As we drove down the highway, the anchor of a feminine touch in the conversation soon got dragged on board, and although I'd wanted to be included, the discussions drifted toward masculine interests. Somewhere between, "What do you think the best transmissions will be for *Mexican* terrain?" and "That was my all-time best prank I ever played on my co-workers," and "I've noticed a rattle in my engine—what do you think could be causing it?" I lost consciousness, grateful for my ability to sleep in a moving vehicle. Even in my dreams, I couldn't have envisioned how my stay would unfold, how my faith would be shaken.

CHAPTER 4

Purposeful Paths: Encounters in California and *Mexico*

We navigated across Seattle, and later Portland's spindly skyscrapers and multi-lane highways. A sense of freedom and adventure surged through me, fuelling the hope that once I'd embarked on my solo journey, I'd connect more with my authentic self. The long monotonous days of driving that followed, with the wind blowing in from our open windows getting hotter and drier, seemed unfruitful to me, stirring up a pang of conscience about being a "non-productive" member of society.

"Do you ever feel like we should be doing something more meaningful with our lives?" I asked from the back seat.

Stretch put his elbow on the console, turned toward me and said, "We've all been in family responsibility mode for an extended duration. I believe resting now is acceptable. Remember, all is well as long as we do a minimum of one thing every day. If we accomplish ONE task every day, we can be productive."

"Makes sense to me," I agreed. "After all, isn't working less boring than pleasure?"

"I concur with you, though, Squid. When I was working, I hated it, detested the demands on my independence, and wanted to be free; but now that I'm retired, I have a strong conviction that I need to work," said Stretch.

This discipline sounded so familiar to me: "accomplish" meant one thing—to grind a limitless number of tasks into the hours between opening one's eyes in the morning and falling exhausted into bed at night. *When we were trading time for dollars, when did we ever make time to think about what would truly rejuvenate our spirit?*

"You have been walking through a deep valley with Leah lately, haven't you? Sometimes, rest is the first step toward healing," said Stretch.

"I agree," I said.

Whenever my mind drifted back to the challenging months I'd gone through with Leah, I recalled the physical weariness, acknowledged that my emotional turbulence had begun to lift, and that this enforced rest would be healthy for me.

Crawford, one finger on the steering wheel, located my eyes in the rear-view mirror and said, "I am working right now. I am working on waiting for something to develop."

"That's the spirit!" Stretch said, and we all grinned.

Another day on the road led to another day of inaction. However, I saw that Crawford, in his quiet manner, must have internalized my musings on meaningful work.

"Hey guys, Gleanings for the Hungry is not too far out of our way. It's near a village called Dinuba, California. What if we stopped there and helped out for a while?" Crawford's question woke me from my lurching sleep.

Torn between the comfort of rest and the appeal of contributing, I said, "Let me get back to you on that."

Since my "Christian duty" sensibility told me volunteering with Gleanings, a ministry that shipped freeze-dried peaches and patchwork quilts overseas, would be something my parents, siblings, and kids would approve of me putting my hand to, I overrode our previous decision that we were currently in resting mode.

"For sure, I agree we should help out for a week or so," I said, buying into Crawford's suggestion.

Stretch used his voice to let Crawford know he had a different plan in mind. "Wait a minute, didn't we just agree that we can be justified in enjoying our freedom for an extended period of time? Besides, stopping there will negatively impact our motorcycle riding adventures."

I could learn something from Stretch.

"If we do stop and help, well, isn't that a good Christian thing to do?" Crawford asked.

Giving freely of our time tugged at my sensibilities. "Sorry, Stretch, I have to say I am with Crawford in this. Volunteering for a bit seems right."

We both stared at Stretch; my eyes bored into the back of his head, Crawford taking his eyes off the road to briefly glare at him, as well.

"On the other hand, volunteering positively impacts society as a whole. That makes it unanimous," Stretch said.

We rolled onto the Gleanings property after nearly twelve hours on the road, with the evening sun casting irregular shadows across the peach and pomegranate fields. The atmosphere still hummed with purpose, in stark contrast to the inactivity during our travels. Although he hadn't wanted to stop in California, Stretch knew after the first day of setting up a computer network that we'd all be grateful for our time spent helping the less fortunate. Crawford's mechanical skills shone as he drove peach trucks and repaired forklifts. For me, the act of cutting fabric and piecing quilts together in the spacious craft room, combined with deep conversations with three feminine vessels of grace, provided me with a new-found piece of myself. *Staying here isn't a detour; it's a valuable chapter in my journey, a step toward understanding that I am exactly where I need to be.*

After a week of sewing quilts, eating pomegranates, and laughing with the other volunteers, I looked forward to heading south again, to begin supporting the women and children at the shelter. Yet, on November 1, no sooner had fields of dust and tumbleweed replaced the peach orchards than I heard myself say, "Maybe we should have stayed longer at Gleanings. There we did one thing every day."

The guys' eyes widened and locked on each other; they shook their heads and smiled at me.

Smoothly and slowly *Los Angeles,* then *San Diego,* then *Tijuana, Mexico,* slid across our field of vision from the front windshield to the rear-view mirror. Each cityscape we travelled past shifted my vision from the narrow confines of everyday life to a broader, more panoramic view of my inner scape.

Several hours south of *Tijuana,* Crawford yelled, "Something just developed. This town is *Ensenada*. That means that we are almost at the woman's shelter. From here, it's a two-hour drive out into the boonies. I'll be glad to unload all these donations and switch into motorcycle mode."

Sitting farther ahead on my seat, I willed Big Red to devour the seemingly endless roads—roads even flatter and straighter than in Alberta. Eight hours south of Gleanings, early on the evening of October 26th, I saw the woman's shelter—a lone structure in a vast, empty landscape; a solitary presence that reflected the desolation of the clients' lives. It stood far removed from the problems they'd fled in their urban existence. Its chain-link fence topped with three loose strands of barbed wire, rambling adobe buildings, and one out-of-place flower garden caught my eye. A woman with long black hair covering her eyes knelt on the baked earth, pulling straggly weeds from the garden. I watched from the window, seeing how the thick, dusty earth had trapped and put on display a criss-crossed network of children's bare footprints, chicken scratches, cat-and-dog trails, bicycle-and-car tire tracks; how the bright blue-and-orange dresses hanging from a clothesline were weighted down with dust; and how one palm tree and several large cacti struggled to survive. As would I.

We stepped out into the heat; we could feel its intensity radiating upward from the golden soil and beating downward from a cloudless blue sky. If I had stood beside God on creation day, if I could have asked him a question, I would have asked him what he gave the people who lived here to make them love and thrive in this desolate, flat land, shimmering with distant heat waves.

Sue, her white hair and pale skin in noticeable contrast to the jet-black heads of women and children running or plodding through the dust, met us in the yard. Sue, hailing from B.C. and a survivor of domestic violence in her youth, believed God had guided her to establish this ministry in *Mexico.* For the past six years, she had operated the shelter, which churches in B.C. financed.

"Thank you so much for bringing all these donations to us. These gals will appreciate everything. Darkness surrounds their lives, but God wants them to know they are treasures. Wouldn't they want to serve a God who treats them so lovingly? We show these women love so they can understand how God loves them. And that is what you are here to do, show them love. You must be Ruth."

"Yes, pleased to meet you," I extended my hand and introduced the guys.

Crawford wiped his hands together, no doubt glad the adventure we had getting all the items across the *Mexican* border and unloaded had ended. Stretch wiped the sweat from his forehead.

"Are you really sure you want to stay here?" Crawford asked me later. "If something bad develops, you could ride with us to *Loreto*. We'll be back in a few weeks, though, to drive to Canada again."

"Thanks for the offer, but I'm staying until I go to The Lodge in *Chile*," I said. *I don't need to depend on you guys to keep me happy. Hopefully, all the times we have laughed and swapped stories together have prepared me for my liminal solo journey.*

Despite their fear of girl fleas, we hugged all around. Then they unloaded their motorcycles—revealed once we had removed all the donations—left me making my imprints in the dust, and rode south.

In a heartbeat, a dark-skinned child no more than four years old, balancing a baby on her hip, passed the youngster to me before darting away into the yard. I sat down on a bench. Two chubby fists rubbed against naked gums; the brown baby—wearing only a white diaper—lay on my lap, drawing untapped grandmotherly feelings up from a space deep within, desires I'd likely never fulfill in my real world. Smiling into the precious little face, I thought, *I will do well here. I don't even miss the guys.*

The next eleven days passed in a whirlwind of activities commandeered by this bold, solidly grounded Christian leader, whose mandate to provide a temporary, safe place for battered women seemed right.

"Today, we have a lot of work to do before the water baptism. You will help set up the tank and the chairs tonight," Sue told, rather than asked, me.

Watching these women and youth get baptized made me feel proud that I had a part in their commitment to an alternative lifestyle. Each day brought a new challenge as I attempted to follow Sue's directives, usually while playing hide-and-seek with a gap-toothed little boy. The search for fresh drinking water for him posed an even greater hurdle.

Finally, I located Sue cutting a young mother's hair and asked, "Where is the potable water?"

"Grab a bottle from that fridge then let's get busy putting these donations away."

One day continued to roll into the next in a blur.

"Your task for today is to teach the moms how to sew a diaper bag. These are the practical ways we show God's love." Sue's list for me far exceeded one task per day.

The women, one with a swollen black eye, and most with distant looks of sadness on their faces, gathered around me, smiling shyly, each with their new bags in their arms, waiting for their turn to hug me.

"Today we must beautify this spot for our picnic." Sue directed me throughout the day as we prepared for our outing by the campfire.

Later that evening, the leaping, crackling flames flickered in the fire-pit, their light casting shadows around us. Sitting quietly by the fire gave me the opportunity to hear the women's stories. A hand on a knee, an arm around a shoulder. *I care.*

"Today we go to church in the next town." The next morning, Sue told me to make sure the twelve children and five mothers were ready by nine o'clock sharp, confusing me for a moment. *How could it be Sunday already?*

The trip involved holding two children on my lap, balanced on a springless seat on the shock-less bus, and taking them by the hand to their Sunday School classes.

"You're safe here with us," I said to each family I signed into the shelter. They'd likely phoned first, but their random arrivals took me by surprise. Most appeared under the cover of darkness, late into the night. Those words about safety had comforted me during the three long weeks my son and daughter and I had spent in that shelter in Northern Alberta so many years ago. Assisting with the operations of this ministry allowed me to repay the women who had spoken into my life during my prolonged stay, beautifully. *My heart goes out to these women. By pouring all my resources into these suffering ones, I am growing spiritually, I have a purpose—a mighty one. Maybe this is where I am supposed to be. I'd rather be here than anywhere else right now.*

After a week in *Mexico,* a fellow volunteer told me how to get to a nearby beach.

I thought we only had dust in this place. That evening, I walked away alone to explore the shoreline. A splash of moonlight etched a luminous path across the burling surface of the ocean, the lines on either side seemed to demarcate the boundary between my solitary space and the distant shores where my friends and family resided. This effect reminded me of how, in the beginning, God used light to separate the darkness. The radiant boundary faded when a cloud scuttled across the moon, blending the spheres of light and darkness into unity. *One day I shall return home—this is not forever.* To leave an empty space in someone's life, made me feel guilty. *Only you, my nearest and dearest, could speak into my life the way you do. If we were still together, would I be happier, more content?*

Why is a shared moment richer than a solitary moment? When the moonlight had faded, I felt the immensity of the distance between myself and my loved ones, and I understood with a pang what "I miss you" and "I wish you were here" really meant. Sitting alone on a piece of driftwood, with only the gentle sound of waves lapping against the shore, I felt it: my fear of being alone had followed me to *Mexico.*

The next morning, an aloneness like the waiting in an empty house for my alcoholic mate to return, settled over me. In the face of my commitment to this shelter, the fact that I felt alone despite living with numerous women and children overwhelmed me. Did this sense of unease put into question my decision to come here—that decision I'd made believing God's hand had guided me, that decision that had taken me out of Canada, out of my routine, and out of my comfort zone? *How can I feel alone when I'm sure I am doing good for others?* After emailing several of my support people, and talking with my dad, I realized this could be the best place to position myself—desolate and raw before God. This realization restored my hope, and I vowed to keep going forward with a resolve to discover my identity apart from being daughter, sister, friend, and mom.

At our Thursday morning Bible study, Sue spoke with conviction, teaching lessons that I, as a Bible College grad, knew weren't theologically sound. I wanted to speak up, to challenge her, but since the other volunteers didn't seem concerned, I stayed silent, listening instead and pondering how wounded souls in recovery often engage in Christian ministry. In a regular job, people may be more whole, yet still in need of Jesus. This foundational reflection on my religious upbringing and my discomfort with divergent theological perspectives would later evolve as I'd cross paths with contrasting belief systems that would challenge my understanding of faith.

Dust. Chaos. As the days went by, darkness—an outpouring from the women's experiences—began extending its tentacles in my direction, dark feelers borne on the oft-repeated stories of mental abuse, neglect, physical violence. Any cheer I tried to bring to these women almost inevitably seeped right through them into the dust. In my dreams, my home that had once been the place I wanted to leave, tempted me to return to familiar faces, to lush green areas where I had space to walk and think, to drinkable tap water, to plenteous food. Women and crying babies admitted to the shelter in the middle of the night, woke me to feed them and direct them to a bed. *Will I ever sleep eight hours straight again?* Living in community is a worthy idea, but to live in endless chaos is a nightmare. *Does one become more spiritual when constraints prevent them from engaging in life-affirming activities?*

Clouds of dust that rose with every passing car made breathing—even though I used my inhaler daily—difficult. A rattling cough that hurt my chest settled deep in my lungs. My peace evaporated. A diet of watery beans and rice and not enough fresh water to drink gave me diarrhea, sending me dashing to the bathroom at all hours of the day and night. Cramps that torqued my legs into question marks drove me from bed to sob silently against the wall while stretching out my calves.

I want to help Sue and these women, but I also need to stay healthy. Is the value of my health less significant than doing God's will? God, where are you? Did I hear you correctly? What am I accomplishing here? Am I being productive? If I left, would I be taking the easy way out, or forging a new path?

The shelter had finished me. Feeling shackled wasn't the issue. Failing to discern God's will wasn't the issue. I simply had no physical strength left.

"Ding." The sound startled me, as we rarely had an internet signal.

Pulling my cell from my back pocket, I read the email my dear friend Esther had sent. "Thinking of you." The text included this quote, "Of any stopping place in life, it is good to ask whether it will be a good place from which to go on, or a good place to remain."

My eyes teared up, not because of the dust, but because I knew God had heard my lament and answered. Before my "should"—"I should have started with a short-term mission"—could rise like a spectre to guilt me, I made a conscious decision to leave this stopping place—I had learned at least to be a leave-taker. Leaving my alcoholic marriage had taken ten years, leaving the shelter took three and a half weeks.

After I finished my duties on Sunday, I sought again the beach where I'd learned that separation is only temporary. I saw the difference life-giving water made to the desert: closer to the wave-scrubbed shoreline waxy stubby plants thrived and the odd palm tree bent against the wind. Like me, the restless, fluid, ever seeking, ever searching waves are always confined within their bounds, not free to behave as they would. The waves are at the mercy of the moon's gravitational pull and the capricious wind. The power of the receding water tries to draw you, suck you back down to that place you used to be and make you start again, or never rise again. Instead of phoning to hear a familiar voice—dad, mom, sister, friend—I sat by the ocean in the urgent, demanding wind that set my emotions churning like the waves on the sand. The wind blew right into me, standing me to my feet. My hair whipped and stung my face. I yelled into the wind, "Yes! I can leave the shelter now!"

Farther down the beach I spotted a fluorescent green sign stapled to a tall pole stuck into the wasteland between the scrubby green plants, which became a Pilgrim's Progress-style signpost for me.

What is that sign doing out here in the middle of this nothingness?

"Wrong Way," the sign spelled in huge black block letters. In smaller letters at the bottom I read, "The *Baja* 1000 race."

Curious about the significance, I pondered the unexpected message. Then, staring at the "you are going the wrong way" sign, a flock of geese honked, flying noisily due south above my head. The understanding flooded into my spirit. *I need to keep going south.*

Early the next morning during our volunteer meeting in her living room, I asked to speak with Sue privately.

"Sue, I know it's only the sixteenth of November, but I can't stay here," I said in a hesitant, faint voice like Leah's—the sulphur butterfly who left no imprint on others' lives—a voice that I heard with the shame of knowing my efforts to do good fell short. *I hurt myself by avoiding hurting others.*

Sue inhaled her head backward, then put on her professional voice, "I understand, you are not suited for this climate, I see you struggling to breathe. Thank you for the time you have given us. We couldn't have gotten through these past weeks without your help. The donations your team brought us were a godsend. Thank you. You are free to leave anytime."

She gave me a dutiful hug and instructed me to catch a ride to the *Ensenada* bus depot with a fellow volunteer who would be coordinating a supply run the next day.

The following morning, exiting the shelter yard, I noticed our tracks that had briefly mingled in the dust, now separated; mine going south, while the others looped around and around in circles. A visual of my departure had imprinted itself on the dusty landscape—until the next windstorm.

Amidst the chattering, laughing Latino passengers on the rumbling, lurching bus, what enchanted me—inspiring the desire to shout "I'm leaving North America all alone" to my fellow seatmates—sprang from the taking of this first step toward Chile! *Ruth, the leave-taker, journeys solo toward La Paz, the nearest city with an airport, unable to express her jubilation in Spanish.*

Post-shelter euphoria struck, and I relived the emotions I had long buried, much like the liberation that followed after I had broken free from the alcoholic. Then, once the tightly coiled spring that had pinned my life to codependency had sprung, I had darted without restraint, in every direction. Now, bouncing toward my fears, I remembered I'd volunteered at the shelter due to my fear of solo travel. Misaligned motives, such as my desire to tour cheaply, reminded me that my first plan had been to fly directly to Chile; instead, I'd been with the guys or changing babies.

Instead of noting the endless sand dunes outside the bus window, I envisioned myself on the shore where the whale spewed out Jonah, watching him survey his new surroundings, checking over his shoulder to see if God lingered with his clipboard, pronouncing his dispensation again. *Had I done the easy thing? Had I shirked my duty any more successfully than Jonah had?* Our conscience, warning us that a judge is looking, can oppress both our heart and our voice. I'd left Canada believing the shelter might offer an anchor for me. But now that it hadn't, I felt more unmoored than ever. Yet, taking the first step toward being a leave-taker had given me the courage to depart for *Chile.* I hadn't wanted to travel alone, but what did I think would happen if I travelled alone? My only answer: not having companions to share experiences with, would diminish my joy.

After bouncing along for many dusty hours on the bus, I settled into my *La Paz* hostel and revelled in a refreshing swim in their small pool. Multitudes of birds sang as they flitted through the *moringa* and hibiscus trees. The *moringa* trees were heavy with stringy pods of edible seeds and the hibiscus tree branches hung low with ruby-hued blossoms scented with love. In the communal kitchen or *palapa,* a local woman walked by but stopped when she heard me hacking and wheezing.

"You have a terrible cough. Don't go anywhere, I'll be right back."

She returned with handfuls of red flowers and furry green balls the size of peas and dumped them into a pot of boiling water.

"What do you have there?" I asked, sitting at a stool beside the island near the stove.

"Flowers from the hibiscus tree and seeds from the *moringa* pods. God hides his secret healing powers in nature," she said, stirring the pot.

Observing the steam rise from the boiling concoction, I marvelled at its ability to soften the features of this kind-hearted stranger who cared enough to intervene in my life, making me hope that solo travel promised more spontaneous human connections.

She handed me the tea in a bright red-and-yellow ceramic cup.

"Thank you," I said, smiling and enjoying the fragrant, healing mixture.

The next morning, I embraced the new day listening to the melodies of birdsong instead of the rattling, harsh sound of my cough. Feeling grateful toward the woman, but not knowing I would never see her again, I pondered our unexpected, yet fleeting social ties. Retrieving my laptop from between multiple layers of clothes in my backpack, I noticed my little book, *Extreme Landscape,* fall to the ground, where it lay open to the much-read section on Mount Fitz Roy. The excitement of parting company with Sue had worn off, leaving me in a contemplative mood. Questioning whether I'd made the right choice to abandon the shelter prematurely, I spent my entire first day seeking validation for my decision by emailing friends and sifting through a potpourri of responses.

"No, I don't think you pulled a Jonah. Isn't *Mexico* on the way to South America?" replied a fellow Gospel Riders biker.

I felt better. The next email reply from a friend convicted me outright for having done the easy thing by walking away from a commitment and turning a mission trip into a holiday. I felt down and guilty.

My third email to my atheist, Canada-cycling Scotsman, now back home in Scotland, who delighted in his self-appointed role as my spiritual advisor, brought an irreverently humorous response.

"If you feel guilty, why don't you go do something worth feeling guilty for: after all, isn't Christianity about forgiveness?" he wrote.

Another Gospel Riders confidant emailed, "It is okay to change direction, the main thing is to start doing what we think is God's will. Once we are moving, it's easier to change direction."

A fellow volunteer at the shelter texted, "If you smile, with that million-megawatt smile of yours, everything will turn out fine." *Do I truly have a million-megawatt smile? It hasn't had much practice lately.*

Finally, my dear Doris wrote, "How can you hold a moonbeam in your hand? You are going to *Argentina*, right?"

Battling an uneasy, sick sensation in the pit of my stomach, I decided the encouragement and understanding from most of my friends overshadowed the lone negative—my fear of travelling solo. So, breathing in the sweet scent of magnolia and *moringa* blossoms wafting through the *palapa* windows, I perched on a stool, pulled my cell from my pocket, and called Flight Network.

"Hi, I want to book a ticket to *Chile* or *Argentina*. I am in *Mexico* now."

"*Si*, why do you want to go to South America?" *Is he a travel agent or a long-lost friend?*

"Well, I'm eager to climb Mount Fitz Roy. It's in *Argentina*, so I am not sure where I should fly to actually. I need to go to *Chile* later as well. What do you suggest?"

Engaged in a twenty-minute conversation, we delved into various routes and their corresponding price tags. The best routes and lowest fares always had an inverse relationship.

"Ma'am, considering your budget constraints, the most cost-effective option is the flight from *La Paz* to *Santiago, Chile*, with layovers in *Mexico City* and Atlanta. You can complete the payment over the phone and schedule your departure one week from today."

"I'm sorry, are you saying I also need the CVV number?" I inquired, having already given him my credit card number. *How did I memorize a sixteen-digit card number but overlook one with only three digits? I should have attended to these details before I left home.*

"Ma'am, you do have the option to book using your debit card."

"I tried that with other operators, but the connection kept dropping and it didn't go through," I explained. "But let's give it a go. I do know that CVV number, and departing in one week is fine."

Only one week? While I waited, praying for an uninterrupted transaction, a frazzled feeling rose from the pit of my stomach—an unsettling realization that soon I'd truly be on my own, grappling with sketchy language skills in a foreign land.

"All is booked and paid for now. I wish you the best in your travels. Thank you for choosing Flight Network."

The next morning, Bob entered my world while I devoured a fresh papaya at the hostel's breakfast bar, soaked in the tropical ambiance of the *palapa*. A retired American judge, he had dark penetrating eyes that made me grateful I had met him holidaying in *Mexico* and wasn't sitting between him and a jury. His *Mexican*-sewn clothing and bronzed complexion made him look like a local, not a tourist.

"I always endeavour to purchase indigenous apparel when I travel, to honour the people who live and work in that country," he explained, with an American accent that didn't match his sun-touched features.

He listened to me question the wisdom of having left the shelter earlier than originally intended, thus creating a huge chunk of time before my start date at The Lodge with nothing planned; he listened to me ponder the dilemma of when and how I could get to Fitz Roy. Then he said something I have never forgotten.

"Sounds to me like you are trying to find the place you fit. But, girl, the word *fit* only belongs with shoes. This quote from *Teilhard de Chardin* speaks to an attitude you might assume on your journey. *Teilhard* wrote, 'Accept the anxiety of feeling yourself in suspense and incomplete.' Think of this every time you take control of things that are not moving along according to your plan, any time you might want to 'push the river,' girl."

This profound concept would unfold into more wisdom during the brief period our paths intersected.

While I worked on accepting my anxiety, Judge Bob invited me to join him for a maritime adventure in his small sailboat. He had painted the word *Ethos* in a black Times New Roman font on the bow. Memories of winds filled my youth—Chinook winds blowing the yellowed poplar leaves ahead of its breath, summer winds overpowering my canoe and forcing me backward, and spring winds challenging me on my motorcycle, forcing me sideways. Back then, the wind seemed to be an adversary, but here on the sailboat, I would soon learn that those same opposing forces could propel me forward.

"Here. You try it. Put your hand on the tiller," Bob suggested.

"What exactly is a tiller and where is it?"

Releasing his grip from the elongated, polished wooden shaft approximating an axe handle, he directed his attention toward me, smiled quizzically, and gestured at it.

"This is called a tiller. Hold it lightly, like this. Feel the play of the wind. Listen to that crisp, staccato rhythm the wind creates with the sails."

"Sailing is like canoeing on steroids," I told him, laughing, as we skimmed across the *Sea of Cortez.*

The tiller moved like a willful, living creature in my right hand. Immersed in an ever-shifting aqueous world, the gurgling, splashing, and loud sloshing sounds made me feel unmoored, unstable. Nauseated.

"Ruth, heed this advice. Master the art of navigating opposing forces. By doing so, you'll propel yourself more swiftly against that resistance, instead of being swept in the direction the force dictates. Apply this principle to your life, and you'll thrive."

At that moment, Ethos became a bucking bronco, challenging the wind. Bob told me that I had angled the sails too sharply into the wind and unbalanced the forces, which made the boat shift sideways. He took the tiller from me and regained charge by skillfully moving it so that within seconds, the sails that had fluttered and collapsed under my attempted control billowed with air and snapped tightly open. I leaned over the rail and threw up. Once again, a gentle breeze flung salty spray on my face, stinging my lips. We sailed calmly and smoothly into the wind.

"Are you feeling okay now?"

"Yes, thanks," I said, my hands on my stomach. "This land-locked gal is astonished at how you can control your sailboat. I find it so strange to know we're sailing into the wind but we're not angling sideways or backward, we are going forward! And all you did was adjust the tiller which tilted the sails to catch the wind at the right angle. It's like magic."

Another magical water day had unfolded when my dad took me on my first canoe trip the summer that I turned eighteen, one month before I left for college in Edmonton. We had rented a canoe and paddled downstream along the Bow River to the Bearspaw Dam. When we had stopped for lunch, he pushed back his ball cap, settled in against a tree, and handed me one of the tuna and cheese sandwiches my mom had made for us.

Dad began one of his stories that I listened to with interest. I'd always loved a good "Dad story"; over the years they'd helped guide me through life's complexities, in many ways preparing me for my journey to *Patagonia.*

"See this water, Ruth, it's so clear and swift, pure, not like the Doghide River at Bucky Aldrege's place where we used to dive off a birch board he stuck into the bank. Me and Tubs Whitelaw had fun diving in, naked, of course, until he showed me three long bluish creatures stuck to his foot and stomach. I saw two on my leg and they looked just plain bad. Tubs took a willow stick and gave mine a good whack and blood flew all over my leg."

"I'm glad we don't have any bloodsuckers around here, Dad," I said, unconsciously feeling my ankles. Though his tales weren't always profound, I cherished how such times brought us closer.

He had kept talking; about anything, about everything, except about how my pending departure from home would tug at his heart.

When we put in again, we passed a couple of spandex-clad men in a canoe; the one in the back yelled "HUT," and they mechanically switched sides. Precision machines, their muscular arms pumped and pumped, propelling them past us with a speed comparable to a motorboat.

"Dad, see how painfully those guys are paddling. I'm sure glad we are just taking our time and having fun. That looks like work!"

"Yes, just taking our time and enjoying the scenery is best. It's really the best," Dad had said to me; then yelled to the seriously-focused canoeists, "How's the fishing, boys"?

On my present magical day, I observed Bob at the helm of his sailboat as I settled onto my rigid white plastic seat, and reminisced about a song Sue and the *Latina* women had sung back at the shelter: "I surrender, *Yo mi rindo*." In my imagination, I envisioned Jesus—not Bob—steering the sailboat, and Jesus smiled with an impish grin and said, "*Es mi barco* (this is my boat). Let go of your death grip on the tiller. Surrender to my plan."

What would happen if I did let go? Believing I can continue alone is different than doing it. I know I must do what scares me. But how do I break apart what I fear? How does steering my life while surrendering to God's plan look?

Bob craned his neck backward, "Where have you been?"

"Enjoying my sail in another's boat."

We docked at his private pier, and as he helped me step out of the wobbling craft, he proposed an idea.

"To facilitate a stress-free departure, I am offering my services to drive you to the airport on November 23. That leaves us sufficient time to appreciate a second sail, and to explore our environs. Starting with breakfast at Hotel California tomorrow morning."

"How can I ever thank you for all your kindness?"

"When you have the opportunity in the future, pay it forward," he said.

That isn't possible. I have nothing to give.

CHAPTER 5

Of Tangos and Rogue Waves: Santiago and Valparaiso

"Delta Airlines flight from *La Paz* to *Mexico City* now departing," the announcement, barely audible above the revving engines, heralded the next phase of my journey.

I buckled myself into row 8 seat F, unfolded the creased laminated "what to do if we crash," pamphlet and read each point while the stewardess demonstrated. *Nose mask will drop down above my seat, life jacket is under my seat, emergency exit is row 18—that's 10 rows ahead of me. Good to know.*

Wedged snugly into my space between the window and the young woman beside me, I felt like a caterpillar in a cocoon, entering a metamorphosis that would gain momentum after I exited the plane. Peering through the window, my thoughts took flight, weaving between the billowing clouds below and the reflections on the glass. *Clouds transform when viewed from above. Even the palm trees seem as tiny as the plastic palm trees in a Lego set from 30,000 feet above ground level. I can perceive what lies beyond all my duties.* The plane flew high enough to enable me to visualize my home in Maple Ridge—a rush of memories overwhelmed me. I heard Leah asking me that piercing question, "Why didn't you help me sooner?" Her inquiry had nearly ripped my heart out of my chest. I had told her about all the times we tried to visit, tried the legal system, tried the government agencies, tried to find her. For six long years, her mother had moved her frequently and secretly, left phone messages unanswered—we couldn't contact twelve-year-old Leah. During those years, her mother made their situation look normal to Social Services and had kept both Leah's father and our family from intervening successfully. Guilt and regret had washed over all of us after we had finally given up. We could only pray. When I examined my role as Leah's caregiver,

I thought I should have tried harder to find Leah and return her to a sane life. But I didn't. *That's the past, so all I can do now is to take my laser focus off those circumstances that mired me in the pain and look out at the immense beauty of the world. Now, maybe I can perceive the struggles I had with Leah from a new angle. Fears and anger are losing their power over me.* I could feel my spirit lifting far above the tangle of my flawed life. In the confined space of row 8, the slowly ticking seconds allowed for reflection; yet, as the plane descended into *Mexico City,* the pace quickened and became a race against time.

"Delta Airlines flight now landing in *Mexico City.* The temperature is eighty-nine degrees."

Every one of the 8.8 million people who live in heat-blasted *Mexico City* must have been in the airport that day. My lungs and calves ached as I hustled through crowds—fifteen minutes between flights didn't permit any ambling to my connecting flight to Atlanta. *Note to self: circuitous routes are an inevitable by-product of cheap fares, and making connections in life takes time too.*

"Delta Airlines now departing *Mexico City* for Atlanta, Georgia."

Before I'd finished reading five pages of my book, we touched down at the Hartsfield-Jackson International airport in Atlanta. *This is more like a cultural event than an airport.* Practising my new-found ability to see beyond the minutia of my life, I lifted my eyes from the crowd to the globular, iridescent beaded sculptures hanging from a network of steel super-trusses high above my head. Riding the Plane Train, the automated people mover, and figuring out how the passport scanning kiosks worked, as I raced toward my connecting flight to *Santiago,* made me feel as though I had entered a future world.

"Delta Airlines flight from Atlanta, Georgia, to *Santiago, Chile,* now departing."

The nine-and-a-half-hour flight from Atlanta to *Santiago* gave me pause to read and think. My creased map—flattened onto the food tray—showed me I would be landing one third of the way down the ribbon-like country of *Chile.* Reflecting on the journey from British Columbia to *Mexico* with Crawford and Stretch, which spanned over a week, I marvelled at how modern technology could whisk me from *Mexico* to South America in one single, long day. During our descent into *Santiago,* I noticed how the imposing *Andes* seemed to come alive. Delta Airlines had become Captain

Kirk's Teleporter, condensing all my dreams and plans, and rematerializing them into the craggy peaks I saw wrapping the city in a hazy blue grasp. On the flat pages of *Extreme Landscape,* they had seemed impressive, but now, in their awe-inspiring, three-dimensional reality, they brought me peace and joy. Stepping out of my teleporter into my altered reality incredibly early that morning, I felt proud I had turned my goal of experiencing Yvon and Doug's mountains into substance. *I did it! I did what scared me! I'm in Santiago, in Chile, alone. I'm alone! Solo! I've come so much farther than 11,000 kilometres!* Yet the unresolved tension surrounding travelling solo persisted, making me wonder—*Now what?* The anticipation of what lay ahead replaced the heaviness of my caregiver role. My feet touched down in the new realm that nourished both the lands and people, the same lands and people—yet unknown to me—who would nourish my soul and rekindle my joy.

Many years ago, when I first rode *Pegasus,* I had also felt the thrill of entering a new world. The days had ticked slowly by after deciding to purchase my first motorcycle but the prospect of riding with my red-headed friend Deb fuelled my search. When I finally bought my Honda Magna 750, one look at the raspberry-pudding red tank and the shiny silver-dollar chrome pipes and I knew I'd singlehandedly attempt to ride the monstrous beast home. During my motorcycle riding course, I'd ridden a much smaller Yamaha 250 and had gained the distinction of being the only person to ride across a field instead of stopping at the road's edge. Thank goodness my dad had taught me to drive a standard transmission as a teenager. Two women who had collided on the track the first day, never returned for the second day of lessons, and a woman who careened off the simulated hill into the fence didn't return for the last day. But I had persevered, passing both my drivers and my written test, thus marking the beginning of my motorcycling journey.

Lifting my leg over the seat of this 750 proved as difficult as backing out of the seller's driveway. As I rode along the gravel roads toward home—whenever I felt steady enough—I'd snatch a glance at the mountains in the distant west. The smell of the sloughs told me autumn approached. Impressed that I had paid attention during our "how to ride on gravel" lessons, I adeptly halted at a corner stop sign. A full stop. Jumping quickly out of the way as the bike fell, I had prevented it from crushing me. The weight of the motorcycle taxed every muscle in my legs and arms as I raised it from the dust where it lay. Back on the road, the wind in my face made me realize how fast we were travelling, like a flying horse. Like *Pegasus*. My uncoordinated hands struggled to open the throttle and use the clutch correctly, my feet often braking randomly, or kicking into first gear instead of third gear. *Look at me, everyone! I'm riding my own motorcycle. I hope I get home in one piece.* The new doors that motorcycling might unlock excited me—I felt giddy, as though I had ridden *Pegasus* into the gateway of a new realm.

In my new South American realm, masses of men, women, and children energetically waved, smiled, and yelled greetings to their loved ones from behind red velvet cordoned-off areas, propelling me outside the *Santiago* airport in a dizzying blur before I could devise a plan to reach my hostel. One airplane barely cleared the airspace above me when another one took its place. The scene before me swirled with activity: cabs, vans, and buses lined up, filled with passengers, and sped away. I caught the eye of a slender taxi driver, whose bright green, starched uniform set off his olive complexion, and headed toward him. As soon as he spoke, I knew I no longer resided in Canada.

"This is my one wife, and these are my three children," he said as he stepped out of his taxi.

He paused to reach into his back pocket, then carefully slid four well-worn colour photos from his wallet, holding them up for me to see.

Four smiling faces radiated happiness. Conversations in *Chile,* as I'd observed in *Mexico,* I believed began with stories of family because the people viewed family as the heart of their existence. This focus on family provided me with an insight into their culture, reminding me of our universal need to be loved. Once I'd settled into the back seat, I asked him about each child's health, their ages, if they had any hobbies, if they owned any pets, and his wife's profession and how long they'd been married.

The driver expertly wove through the bustling streets of *Santiago,* a city of five million souls, proudly pointing out the highlights of his city. Towering trees in full leaf, scented with flowers, filled the space between this capital city and the cloud-piercing *Andes*. Honking cars and zooming airplanes replaced the birdsong my ears used to love. Granite slab buildings and networks of asphalt roads and sidewalks replaced the empty expanses of water and landscape I'd left behind. A vibrant pulse swirled around intricate ancient architecture and massive religious stone sculptures that spoke of the conquering Spaniards who brought Catholicism to *Chile.*

Half an hour later, when my taxi-driver-cum-amiable-tour-guide stopped in front of the *Sol Hostel* and leaped from the front door to the trunk and popped it open for me in seconds, I wondered how all that luggage could possibly belong to me. Fellow travellers and my friends who faithfully read my blog referred to me as the globetrotting backpacker. Technically correct—I started my journey with one backpack. Between purchasing souvenirs and different clothing for the changing climes, I collected more than my pack could swallow. In *La Paz, Mexico,* I'd bargained for an already well-used wheeled suitcase that soon gained weight at an exponential rate. After I returned home, I didn't have the heart to part with my by-then tattered and worn suitcase, so I turned it into a decorative herb garden planter.

The taxi driver smiled at me and waved his brown hand back and forth, until I thought he'd forgotten he could control the gesture, then he pulled away, and left me smiling at the back of his taxi.

Staring at the doorway barely wide enough for thin people standing sideways, and the graffiti-marked paint, and crumbling brick, I sincerely hoped Gertrud from my Help Exchange Lodge had recommended *Sol Hostel* for a good reason. Once I'd banged my backpack and scraped my suitcase against the entrance walls, and shut the door behind me, the sensory onslaught of *Santiago*'s streets faded, replaced by soft music and conversations within a clean, tidy lobby.

His eyes are as black as outer space, as alluring as a mirage on the desert. His equally black hair is slicked back until each strand outlines the contour of his handsome, youthful face. He smiles invitingly at me, reaches out his hand to grasp mine, nods, and draws me toward the centre of the room.

"*Quieres tango?*" he says.

My raised eyebrows question the woman behind the lobby desk.

"He wants to dance with you," she says, grinning impishly.

"Oh. I couldn't possibly, in the last twenty-four hours I may have slept two. All I want to do is go to bed," I say.

His eyes meet mine with a mischievous spark. His smile persists.

"He doesn't speak English," shrugs the receptionist.

"I shall prove to be less than an ideal dance partner. And have you noticed I have a ninety-three-pound backpack on my back?" I say, swivelling my head to look back at her.

He reaches behind me, sliding my pack to the floor, as though freeing this little turtle from its cumbersome, heavy shell of defence. The process of shedding the weight of my "shoulds" and my failures has begun.

"I'm Canadian. This sort of thing doesn't happen in Canada." I try to communicate to him. We stand facing each other, my eyes level with the top of his head, my hand still in his.

"You're going to love this," says the receptionist, cranking up the stereo.

The lobby transforms into a dance floor; the air pulsates with the rhythm of Latino music—stilling the last argument preparing to leave my lips. Each joyful twirl pulls me from the shadows of exhaustion into a kaleidoscope of colour. He glides and pivots, he smiles, he sweeps me around and around the room until I laugh out loud. My feet have a life of their own, and the dynamic motion of the tango energizes me more than a full night's sleep. Each figure 8 is a skip toward freedom, a dance with the present that eclipses the fatigue of the journey, and a dance that unlocks a brighter future. My mood soars. The language barrier dissolves in the universal language of movement, and I feel connected with a stranger—our hands and feet speak where words stumbled.

Loving this country will be easy. My head is spinning, and my spirit is grinning by the time he releases me.

"Gracias, Señora," says my fellow dancing traveller.

"Thank you, *Amigo." Thank you for showing me that joy can surprise me in the most common of places.*

Bowing in front of me, he dances down the hall and flashes out of my sight.

The last syncopated notes of the tango faded and reality seeped in. My marathon twenty-two hours in transit had left me spent; nonetheless, *Santiago*'s charm and the thrill of the tango revived my spirit momentarily; but when the music stopped, and tango man left, the solitude brought back the crushing fatigue. My physical exhaustion became a gateway to an inner darkness, eroding my mental resilience, and dragging my spirits down into a melancholic abyss. As I dragged the dead weight of my pack to the woman's dorm, I felt the weight of one failure that had once haunted me—failing to be a good mother. Selecting a bunk to rest on fully clothed—too tired to sleep—my mind wandered back into dark territories. My ex-husband had lost his licence for driving while intoxicated when our first-born was four months old. Feeling relieved, I knew that, for at least half a year, he would not endanger others while driving home drunk.

"I have to stay home with our baby, so how are you going to get to work now?" I asked him. "You have to take me, or it will be your fault if I'm fired."

"But it's wintertime. I don't think I should pull her out of bed so early in the morning and put her in a cold car to drive you to work. Why don't you hop on a bus?"

"Your fault," he accused, stepping closer to me with a look on his dark face that sent chills down my spine.

Considering the situation, I suggested, "Here's an idea: I can leave her in her crib while I drive you; she probably won't wake up."

Living with an alcoholic had altered my brain, left me questioning where we'd find our next meals, made me wonder if I'd live to raise my children, and led to making illogical decisions.

My family admonished me, thinking I was a neglectful mother, and saying, "We will call Social Services and report your irresponsible behaviour. You should know better than that."

While I understood their well-intentioned love, how could they grasp the depths of my struggles? Feeling trapped, I had left our baby alone at home briefly every morning for six months.

When the mysterious, magnetic tango dancer had released my burdensome backpack, enabling me to focus my entire being on the dance, it reminded me that becoming a consistent, healthy, and loving mom in subsequent years had freed me from thinking of myself as a terrible mother. A terrible mom doesn't raise intelligent, productive members of society.

A good night's sleep banished the ghosts from my past, always exacerbated by fatigue and hunger. Deciding to explore *Santiago,* I rose early, eager to capture the essence of the city before the heat of the day set in. Yet, as I neared the downtown area, I shrank from the already-hot clamour of the street vendors beating out insistent rhythms on drum sets, playing haunting strains on pan flutes, strumming guitars that conjured up flamenco dancers in my mind, and motorcycles revving throttles, impatient drivers honking horns, and the metal-on-metal screech of faulty brakes. A dynamic and lively crowd shared the sidewalks with me and breathed in the blue haze of *Santiago*. Adrift on a sea swirling with colour and sound, I looked to the solid sandstone columns bracing the ancient architectural wonders that lined road and boulevards, and to the towering, broad-leafed trees that filled in the space between the city and the *Andes* to anchor myself. I couldn't understand why none of the men with man-buns and braids or women with ebony-black locks flowing down below their hips searched the skies for thermalling eagles or listened for the melody of a chickadee.

The sweltering noon sun drove me to seek refuge in a shady park. Wilting onto a cool bench to rest, I munched on a chicken *empanada*. A lithe, wiry man who stood well over six feet rolled his bicycle to a stop beside my bench and sat down. Our similar hair colour created an instant synergy, drawing us into conversation. Both his accent and mottled brown complexion reminded me of my Grandpa Charlie, who had emigrated to Canada from Holland at age nineteen.

"Are you Dutch?"

"Indeed I am. I've been cycling in *Argentina* and *Chile* for the past three months. It's been a carefree journey thus far."

"You're kidding! I admire, well, maybe even covet, your adventurous spirit," I said, determining at that moment to achieve all my personal goals.

Curiosity got the best of me, and I asked, "My Dutch grandfather, who once rescued a man from an industrial fire, always had pink and brown mottled skin. Did you also suffer through something similar?"

His response, free of hard feelings, led to an interesting conversation. "No, my mother is Filipino, and my dad is Dutch. My skin used to be all dark; but after I turned fifty, it turned whitish pink in blotchy patches," he said, pointing to the affected areas on his face and arms.

We sat together, sharing our lunches, and discussing my travel plans and his cycling adventures. We parted reluctantly; aware it might be our only encounter. Leaving the park bench and my cycling Dutchman behind, I ventured once more into *Santiago*'s streets.

The sun blazed across the sky, heading for the horizon. Over the din of the throngs, I thought I heard the mournful bellow of a cow lowing; I thought I'd heard a sound that would connect me to my world of nature and empty expanses of prairie. Following the sound, I discovered a not-so-unusual cart made with wooden poles strapped together with leather ties, precariously stacked with what appeared to be long, spindly, gold-green, wickless candlesticks, and yoked to something most unusual: a hulking ox with prehistoric-looking Texas Longhorn-style horns. A lively street scene unfolded before me. A vendor with a belly as round as his ox's stood beside the cart, peddling bags of his mysterious items. A woman in a vibrant dress of my favourite oranges and greens, her jet-black hair framing a friendly face, haggled with him—their Spanish too fluid for me to follow. This time contrasting hair colours would soon initiate a conversation. The sight of the ox reminded me of my Alberta roots. Drawn to the patient brute, I moved closer, caressing the stiff fur between its ears, and gazing into his mournful brown eyes. Suddenly, a familiar word emerged from their rapid exchange: "*Gringa.*" My head jerked around, responding instinctively to the non-derogatory term nationals commonly used to address me.

The woman, her voice filled with friendly curiosity, smiled at me and repeated her greeting, "*Gringa.*"

"*Hola, Señora,*" I said, pointing to the golden candlesticks spilling over the edge of the cart. "*Que es essa*?" (What is this?)

She reached into her bag and pulled out one of the long, golden-green objects, letting me smell the briny, pungent odour.

"This is seaweed. Boil this with cilantro. *Delicioso.*"

Her simple explanation impressed me; a street-corner culinary lesson from a stranger. Seaweed may be a wonderful delicacy in *Chile,* but not so for this gal raised on Alberta beef—my eye rested on the longhorn. In the span of one hour, I saw the marvel of solo travel: I'd met two individuals whose paths crossed mine solely because of the interplay of our differences and similarities—language and hair colour—creating connections that transcend cultural boundaries.

For the next hour, I wended my way through the colourful street vendor booths, taking care to avoid eye contact with the multitudes of clothing vendors who called out, "*Señora. Señora. Señora.*" While seaweed hadn't tempted me to part with my finite supply of *pesos,* their fanciful displays of fabric and colour promised something far more enticing. Then, in my peripheral vision, I glimpsed rows of hangers fluttering with neon-green shirts, electric yellow-and-purple jackets, and pairs of bright blue pants. No greys here. As a woman touched my arm and drew me deep into the depths of her bright, tempting wares, I realized the futility of resisting further.

Smiling at her, I stepped toward those pants; I brushed my fingers across the soft silk of the lacy, tropical-teal brocaded legs, loose and baggy until they narrowed to elastic-banded ankles. Supple leather ties around the wide stretchy waist band, weighted down with Fresno wooden beads and feathers and dangling to mid-thigh, demanded the purchase of a matching top in rich burgundy.

Only a genie would wear those pants. You'll look like a weirdo in them.

Not here!

The woman took my money, and I rolled up my new pants and top and placed them in my backpack, completely detached from the cautionary voices in my head. *The next time I stroll the streets no one shall peg me for a tourist.* Pleased to be honouring the locals, as Bob in *Mexico* had shown me to do, I stepped back out into the undulating sea of pedestrian traffic.

The longer I walked, the more the city pumped energy into my soul. The same natural high that I had felt when I had paddled briskly on frigid fall mornings spread through my body, energizing me, expanding me. Back then, my heart would pump deep in my core, and my blood would flow; hands that were numb and stiff would turn warm, and fingers would be able to bend around my paddles. So, too, the rhythmic pulse of the city seeped deep into my core until the line that divided my five senses blurred. Inhaling the savoury odours of the *empanadas* and fresh fish dishes wafting from the multitudes of restaurants; and admiring the gargoyles and cornices mounted on sandstone buildings darkened by smoke, time, and weather—I experienced both scents and sights intensified by the energy surrounding me.

Back home among the mountains and open spaces, I felt small. But in the capital of *Chile,* standing among the throngs of shoppers and businesspeople, I looked down from my 5′ 9″ height on a rippling mass of black heads. If I stretched higher, I knew I could look a larger-than-life statue of the Virgin Mary in the eye, as she peacefully guarded the entrance to a cathedral I planned to tour.

Perhaps I have grown.

After returning from my walk, I took my appetite to *Sol Hostel's* kitchen. At the beginning of my trip, communal kitchens intimidated me. Preparing meals, labelling food to keep in the fridge, doing dishes, and eating alongside a shifting variety of travellers, all speaking enthusiastically in foreign languages, seemed strange and awkward. Later I would come to love the shared cooking experience. An airy sunroom bordering the kitchen offered resident-travellers a quieter space to relax and eat at any one of the ten rickety green plastic dining sets. Choosing the only empty chair, I cautiously lowered myself and began scooping huge black seeds from an electric-orange papaya I'd bargained for at a main-street market.

"*Señora,* join us for *maté*?" asked a voice in heavily-accented, although impressive, English.

The invitation drifted through the hum of conversations in many foreign tongues as I sat in the hostel kitchen. I sensed, more than saw, the dark-eyed stare of a serene young woman with waist-length black hair and plum-coloured horn-rimmed glasses at the table next to me. Her face held a certain wisdom. She leaned against a youth whose intelligent brown eyes brightened with a radiant smile in response to her presence. Their linked fingers resting on the tablecloth and a tiny, shared cup hinted at a bond beyond companionship.

"My name is *Estefania,* and this is my boyfriend *Estevan.*" While introducing herself, she focused on him, and his smile expanded as he turned toward her.

"You travel solo?" he asked.

"I'm Ruth from Canada. Yes, I travel solo."

She is the love of his life. He is the love of her life. Soulmates.

Gathering my papaya and spoon, I left my table to sit with them.

"Thank you. I must confess that this Canadian knows nothing about *maté,* but I will try it."

Instead of pouring another cup for me, *Estefania* passed me the one they shared.

"You sip then pass it back to *Estevan.*"

Do they seriously mean I'm supposed to drink from their cup?

Estefania understood my confused look.

"*Si,* we drink everyone from the same *maté* cup," she said.

Making sure I didn't lose the metal straw, I accepted the gourd-like cup from her. When I noticed the mass of green herbs packed into the *maté* cup and caught a whiff of the pungent bitter odour rising with the steam, I asked, "Is this stuff legal?"

"*Maté* is made from a plant called *llex paraguariensis,* commonly known as *Yerba Maté,* which produces effects like caffeine," she read from the *maté* label with a twinkle in her eye. "Caffeine, not cannabis, *Amiga.*"

While I sipped through the hot straw, they chatted; *Estevan* twirling the tips of her long hair in his fingers. "We are journalism students from *Cordova,* in *Argentina.* In our spare time, we benefit stray dogs from the streets of *Cordova,* feed them, love them, and adopt them out into homes of love," she said.

"How kind of you," I said, holding back the gag the *maté* had induced.

"We go to *Valparaiso* tomorrow. Like to join us?"

Estefania's invitation for this stray Canadian to join them on their trip stirred deep emotional conflict in me. The wounds of my past failure to be a mother to Leah, and the haunting memories of my unsuccessful attempts to "do good" with the *Mexican* mothers, cast a shadow over this decision. The fear of history repeating itself clashed with a growing desire to break free from myself. I couldn't let them get too close to me.

"I'd love to but I'm still suffering from jet lag." I slid the gourd-shaped *maté* cup across the table to *Estefania,* hoping she wouldn't pass it back again.

She poured some more hot water from a thermos into the cup.

"Would not a trip to *Valparaiso* be a collective of forces to overcome this?"

I chuckled to myself. *Some expressions don't translate, I think, but I understand what she means. I should have taken my papaya to my bed, then I wouldn't have to deal with this. On the other hand, they don't look like joy-stealers to me, and they probably won't take no for an answer. Their invitation seems genuine. Their eyes tell me they aren't hoping I'll say no.*

"I'd love to go. What time do we leave?" I trust them, content that I've embraced the risk, and say "yes" to a new experience.

The next morning, we met in the lobby, me carrying my light daypack with some snacks, they carrying their full backpacks. On our way to the bus depot, we walked for six blocks down streets as wide as six canoes touching bow to stern. In the same block as the bus depot, I noticed the sidewalk vendors, who one minute ago had been calling out their wares, start shoving blankets, clothing, bracelets, hats, and toys into black plastic bags *mucho rapido* and saunter away like tourists.

"I've seen this before here in *Santiago.* What is going on?" I asked *Estefania.*

As we climbed into the bus, she explained, "See policeman? Sidewalk vendors not allowed in this area of *Santiago*."

"Ah, okay," I said, sliding into the seat directly behind them.

For the next hour, we chugged to the northeast. I studied the navigation screen on my phone. Yes, the blue GPS dot indeed moved north, yet the bus travelled toward the sun.

Maybe I have my phone upside-down? No...what a weird curiosity. Oh, right. I'm now in South America, where the early afternoon sun shines in the north, not the south. I'm not in the Northern Hemisphere anymore.

The noise of the bus prevented conversation, so I gazed out the window. Over the shudders and roars of the bus, I absorbed the fantastic beauty of the *Andes* and watched the California-like grape and olive groves scrolling past my window, palm trees dancing in the breeze, and coniferous treetops reaching skyward like explorers in search of new lands. In the distance, I saw the antiquated bright blue, yellow, red, and green houses of *Valparaiso, Chile.*

"Wow, what a view!" I shouted to *Estefania* and *Estevan,* thumping on the back of their bus seat to get their attention. They nodded, beaming.

In breathless wonder I contemplated the frolic and pursuit of the performing waves as they smashed into the rocky shoreline, sending foaming spray spiralling mesmerizingly high into the air. Tightly packed dwellings perched like barn swallows' nests on the cliffs framing the ocean. *How could they build houses on rock?* Each narrow cobblestone road ran either straight up and down or disappeared around twisty corners. Intricate and colourful murals, boldly painted on buildings, and fences, flashed past my view, adding to the whimsical charm of *Valparaiso.* This quaint port city contained a captivating blend of nature and artistry.

As it stopped, the wheezing and shuddering of the bus reverberated in the covered bus depot. Leaving the depot, we noticed the crowds gradually thinning.

"We have surprise for you. We are taking you to beach," said *Estefania.*

"Yes!" The thought of being near those dancing waves excited me.

Este and *Este*—my trail names for my new companions—seemed to enjoy my company, asking question after question about my life in Canada. Following a four-block stroll on city sidewalks, we crossed the road and climbed onto a seawall that provided a 360-degree view of the distant ocean arc. Negotiating wide cracks, we stepped up, down, and around angled chunks of concrete.

Este and *Este* stopped at an information sign. Unlike Canadian tourist signs in both English and French, this sign contained only Spanish.

"Translation, please. What happened here?" I asked them.

They explained that in 2014, a tsunami had destroyed most of this once-level seawall. The 8.2-magnitude earthquake that struck off the coast of northern *Chile* had generated waves with enough force to buckle the concrete.

I couldn't imagine how difficult repairing such destruction would be, but I thought this most unusual sea walk added to the character of *Valparaiso*. Nor could I imagine such waves. We paused at the top of concrete stairs attached to the seawall. Far below us, throngs of brown bodies in bright bathing suits mingled. Scattered across the huge expanse of beige sand, some lay under neon-yellow and-red umbrellas, some swam, some surfed, while here and there various groups of young men played beach soccer. About twenty people lounged in the shade of the concrete seawall near the stairs. The shore seemed alive with colour and activity against the blues of the water and sky. The waves here on the calm *azul* blue Pacific Ocean were rhythmic and restful, compared to the waves I'd seen from the bus window along the rocky cliffs.

"These are the only stairs going down to the beach. Let's go!" said *Estefania*.

Later, I would remember how fast things happened after our seawall walk.

Estefania, Estevan, and I walked side by side down the nine steep concrete steps attached to the seawall, my right hand braced on the wall, *Estevan*'s left hand on the railing. We dropped our packs onto an open space on the hot, dry sand about three metres above the wet-sand-line and about five metres from the seawall stairs. *Este* and *Este* took off their shoes, stripped down to their bathing suits, and ran hand in hand across the hot sand. They leaped into the waves; diving and splashing each other as they resurfaced, shaking water out of their hair.

I should have brought my bathing suit. I need to remember one can swim the last week in November in Chile.

Rolling up my shorts and taking off my runners, I followed them into the warm water, enjoying the feel of the waves as they gently rose and fell, caressing my knees.

After about half an hour of swimming and wading, we walked back up the beach. *Estevan* pulled two fluffy yellow beach towels from their packs and lay them end to end on the sand.

"Please to sit," said *Estevan*.

Working my heels into the scalding sand until they touched the cool sand beneath, I lowered myself to sit, one *Este* on either side of me. Between questions about each other's lives and loves, we watched the lazy waves lap against the shore far down the sand. Watching the beachgoers who were playing nearer the shoreline, I wondered why some mothers began to collect toys and youngsters, even though the sun still shone from high in the sky. Being unfamiliar with oceans, I also wondered why the waves sounded so much louder than the once-playful shrieks of the children, even from such a distance. Before I could ask *Estefania,* she shouted at me.

"Look! The tide never comes in so fast." *Estefania* suddenly appeared perplexed. She pointed at our feet.

Sea water soaked into the light-beige sand stopping mere centimetres from us, staining the sand a mocha brown as the level receded.

"No the tide. Rogue wave!" yelled *Estevan* in his broken English, standing up and pointing toward the shoreline.

My eyes follow his finger. A wave twenty metres high and several hundred metres wide is thundering toward the shore.

We snatch up water bottles, energy bars, and towels, and thrust them into our backpacks.

Leaping to my feet, I breathe in and forget to breathe out—panic has tightened my throat. My entire body freezes as if from an electric shock at the sight of the unexpected wave. Instead of my survival instincts kicking in, my eyes look oceanward in hypnotic fascination. *Estevan* shoves my arm hard enough to unlock my limbs and free my stare.

"No stand there. RUN!" he shouts.

Within minutes, all three of us join the throng fleeing in panic toward the stairs, our world spinning in disarray. We run on a wet, sandy beach littered with forgotten beach balls, shovels, pails, towels, thermoses. Slow motion. The wave crests and whooshes up and out over the dry sand. Before we have sprinted a dozen steps, warm briny water sloshes up over our ankles, then recedes.

A dad with two children bouncing up and down on each hip, their bright pink-and-blue bathing suits silhouetted against his dark muscled arms, bumps into my arm as he dashes past me. People scream. People scramble away from the wall. Rushing and racing along the beach, we all funnel toward the stairs—our only route to escape to higher ground.

Checking over her shoulder, *Estefania* spots *Estevan* and me.

"*Estefania*!" I yell. "You're so tiny, if a wave hits you, you will be slammed into the sea wall. Keep going. I'm right behind you."

Estevan takes a final look back at me to ensure I'm following him. He gallops up behind *Estefania*. Maintaining his stride, he grasps her hand and pulls her along in his wake. In a single motion—with a strength amplified by love—he hoists her onto the stairs and follows closely behind her. The backs of their heads blur into the crowd climbing the stairs. In seconds, *Estefania* and *Estevan* are lost in the hordes of curious vacationers in dry clothing, standing, watching from above, along the seawall. *Thank goodness my new friends are safe now.* The stairs create a clogged bottleneck of almond-skinned bathers, forcing those of us farther behind to slow to a shuffle. Walking on sand cooled by the recent wave is easier than running on hot, parched sand. The steps appear so close, I let myself believe safety is within reach, and my pulse settles into a steadier rhythm. Scores of groping hands conceal the railing. *Please God, let us all get to safety in time. Yes! The stairs are close enough for me to reach in the next few minutes.*

Craning my neck, I snatch a glance at the ocean. A second monstrous wave crests and catapults water toward us. More screams and shouts—some distant, some right in my ears. The force of the now chest-deep water sweeps me off my feet. I'm no longer in the middle of a wide wall of people. The water scatters us like a bowling ball scatters pins. Water swirls over my head for one long second. Saltwater stings my nostrils. My eyes are tightly closed against the salty water, so I only feel limbs colliding with mine. *Which way is up?* The stairs and the seawall rush toward me. I try to brace my feet in the sand. Staggering, I manage to stand, raising my arms high, above the water. I spit out a mouthful of seawater. Only a metre away from the stairs, the strength of the receding wave slams me down again. I can keep my head above water this time.

The ocean is sucking me back into her lair. She has us in her clutches. When will she rest? I see a blur of thrashing bronze limbs. Disconnected voices call out names in Spanish. *Davidito*! *Bruno*! The swarm of rag-doll people is being swept back to the place where our dry towels once lay.

Before I can orient myself, another wave gathers strength and height, cascading back up the beach for the third time and heaving us as one mass several metres closer to the seawall. The aquatic assault blasts grains of sand against my body, stinging my skin. Once upright, I notice that the water is now waist deep. My wet clothes and daypack feel so, so heavy. The weight unbalances me.

I falter and crash into the water as the current rushes back toward the former shoreline. Submerged once more, I hear an underwater chorus—the muted, gurgling, bubbling sound of many mouths and nostrils exhaling. My head bobs above the surface. A dizziness that mingles with panic seems to turn my feet to lead. The sight of the railing moving past me, but within reach, gives me hope and strengthens me enough to gain a footing that doesn't dissolve under my feet. I stand up. *I've grabbed the railing!* Thankfully, I now see more sunbathers and swimmers above me on dry land than I see in the water. I drag myself up the stairs with the crowd. One step. Two. My drenched clothes cling to every contour of my frame, adding an oppressive weight. On step number 3, I look ahead to the bodies above me. A man is forcing his way down the stairs through the upward rush of humanity. His outstretched hand is reaching—reaching—toward—me. His dark eyes fill my entire field of vision; all the other sights and sounds vanish.

Estevan!

Keeping one hand on the railing, I stretch an arm toward him. Skin touches skin. His dry grasp feels warm, safe. He clutches my hand tightly, muscling us up the stairs, past wet bodies, connecting us until we reach the seawall, where he finally lets go. Behind me I can hear the roar of the receding rogue wave above the yells and commotion of the swarms of people.

But where is Estefania? Oh, I see her! She's watching us. She's smiling.

"*Estefania*!" The crowds of jabbering bathers bump and jostle us unnoticed. The beach, now deserted, appears calm, each wave rolling in more gently than the last. All three of us hug and smile in relief.

"Thanks be to God for everyone is safe." *Estefania* said, with relief and gratitude in her voice. "We have never see such fast or such big waves. In fifteen minutes, all these peoples is up on top of the seawall."

Her words resonated with me. In the time that had seemed like an eternity to me, I witnessed the resilience of the human spirit to adapt and overcome.

Estevan stepped back in mock horror, looking down at my drenched clothing.

"*Señora,* you steal South American ocean water."

His comment broke the tension. *Feels good to laugh again.*

"Not to worry, *sol* will dry you," said *Estefania,* pointing at the blazing sun. "I think you must be over jet lag now!"

"Yes, indeed," I laughed.

The sound of our laughter faded until I saw only the sunlight glinting off *Estefania*'s glasses. I saw their lips moving; but instead of trying to understand them, I breathed a prayer of thanks.

By late afternoon—with the rogue wave's disruption still vivid in our minds—we'd reached the bus depot, where I discovered how not understanding their personal conversations in Spanish back at the hostel had excluded me from their plans.

"*Root,* we go back to *Argentina* from here. You find your way back to *Santiago* alone?" asked *Estefania.*

This news took me by surprise. The reality of the situation landed hard, as I faced the new challenge of finding my way back to *Santiago* by myself. The unfamiliar surroundings heightened my anxiety—so different from the camaraderie on the beach.

"Oh. Oh, yes. Sure, I will. *Estevan,* I want to thank you for thinking of me when your life could have been in danger. And thank you both so much for a wonderful visit. A most exciting visit. I will never forget *Valparaiso*! Or you two!"

I will never forget your goodbye hugs and South American style kisses either. Reaching up as I stooped down, they each kissed me—a firm smooch first on one cheek, then the other—then they embraced me trustingly, warmly.

Estefania and *Estevan* waved at me from their bus. Swinging my daypack into my arms to let the sun dry the back of my top and shorts, sticky with seawater, I noticed that the lineups for a dozen buses looked like a wriggling mass of earthworms. The challenge of finding the right bus to downtown *Santiago* felt overwhelming, yet oddly exhilarating.

A sinewy young man with rare cranberry-blonde hair who towered above the sea of black heads, nodded at me, a delighted smile softening his angular features.

"Excuse me, which lineup should I stand in to get to downtown *Santiago*?" I yelled in English above the voices of the other travellers. Unlike with *Estefania*, this time I took the initiative to engage. Initially, I had sought solitude to protect myself; now I chose to be more aware of those around me—appreciating the interchange of help and ideas.

"That's where I'm going. Come with me. My name is *Seoras*, and you?" Thankfully, he responded in English, carrying a Spanish accent infused with a Scottish burr.

"Ruth from Canada."

My eyes never left the back of his head until we were seated together on the jam-packed bus. The slight breeze no longer chilled me—my clothes had air-dried in twenty minutes. The sun now skimmed the tips of the colourful buildings in *Valparaiso*, creating a Legoland-like appearance that intensified the farther south the bus rolled. Before *Seoras* told me he made a living with his art nouveau, his long, fine fingers and his metaphysical, metaphorical language had made me guess his profession.

"Pleased to meet you. I was born and raised in *Santiago*, but my grandmother came from Scotland," he said, craning his neck to converse with me.

"My grandmother was born in Scotland, too." *That explains our matching hair colour, and why I feel so comfortable with you.*

Pulling his cell phone from his shirt pocket, he guided me through his online portfolio while the bus bounced down the highway, then ground to a halt in thick traffic, and slowly accelerated numerous times.

"Spirit moved me to paint this one," he pointed. "My purpose on *Gaia* is to express in art form what I see in nature. Every day I set my intentions to further my innovative endeavours. I create when I'm in a cosmic dream. This painting is a tree experiencing angst."

No matter how hard I tried, I couldn't locate a tree among the splashes of free-form colours. We discussed his loose attachment to earthly possessions, the economy in *Chile*, the wonder of Scottish haggis, and his love of language studies. Time sped by at a steadier rate than the bus travelled.

"Oh, the bus hasn't moved for ages," I said, finally noticing that we'd halted.

Seoras chuckled and said, "We've arrived at the *Santiago* station. But it closed at eleven o'clock, so your connector train is not running."

"Can I walk from here?" Peering into the dark streets punctuated with criss-crossing patterns of vehicle headlights, I didn't relish the thought; but with enough directions from him, I vowed to manage.

"No, it is much too far. We will take a bus. I insist. And I will accompany you directly to your hostel."

"Oh! You don't need to, I'm sure you have a home to go to," I said, giving myself more time to determine that I could trust him, and his motives. *He could be taking me anywhere.*

He pulled coins from his pocket to pay our fare. The more we talked while waiting for public transport, the more I wondered if he operated under a personal obligation to protect one of "his people" —a vulnerable *gringa* walking alone late at night. *But if I walk with him, I won't be alone. Seoras* would prove to be my vigilant protector as we strolled through the dark streets together.

Stepping off the bus—the last of its passengers—we faced a scene near the depot that spoke of hardship and stirred conflicting emotions. Tattered tents, tarps flapping in the breeze, shopping carts filled to bursting with belongings, and clothing were scattered across the sidewalks like discarded dreams. The realization dawned that the hostel's affordability likely stemmed from its location in a sketchy part of town. When *Estefania* and *Estevan* and I had walked here, the light of day had concealed the existence of this counter-culture mini-city. But that night, the shadows projected by the streetlights morphed this disorder into monstrous dragons, casting eerie silhouettes on the faces of the street people huddling in the dark entrances of their makeshift homes. These were humans with stories and struggles, each face nameless, each life voiceless. Gazing into one woman's hollow eyes, a deep sadness welled within, and I wished for the language skills to convey, "I understand your humiliation, your pain, and your hunger," and for the ability to offer comfort and hope, and to ask her name. But I felt helpless, my desire to comfort her thwarted by the barrier of words. Instead,

I stumbled over one of the countless stray dogs in this section of *Santiago,* and unconsciously moved closer to *Seoras,* bypassing the opportunity to connect. Feeling the sting of my inability to help, my heart ached as *Seoras* and I kept walking.

"I will walk you right to your hostel door. After all, the hour is late, already after midnight," said *Seoras.*

"Thank you so much for watching out for me. Sorry I took you so far out of your way."

"Don't worry, I have all the time in the world."

Once we'd arrived at my hostel, the idea of crawling into my bunk appealed to my physical senses; I found watching *Seoras* more interesting. The brightly lit interior of the hostel accentuated the darkness swallowing *Seoras* after we'd said our farewells. My shoulder leaned on the door frame and my eyes followed his back until—like the shorebirds back home camouflaging themselves against the rocks—*Seoras* became one with the graphite-black night.

Unable to unwind, I lay on my thin mattress staring into the absolute blackness of the dorm. *Whoa! You would never see a rogue wave in landlocked Alberta! The ocean seemed bent on scouring her shores of us humans to restore herself to her primordial perfection. Why had I shied away from letting Estefania and Estevan into my life? What if I had rejected their invitation?* Punching my lumpy pillow, I rolled to my left side, trying to trace my finger around the name of the quality *Estevan* had perceived in me. What made him turn back from safety toward danger for me—a stranger—a person he'd never known existed before? *Would he have rescued anyone? Did I remind him of his mother? Does a person need to have value to deserve help?* I rolled onto my right side. Once again, I saw my struggles with Leah from a new perspective. *I hadn't planned to bring her with me, but here she is tugging at my pajama sleeve. I saw filial compassion in Estevan and received it from him. I saw and received compassion from Seoras, too.* I sat up, my thin sheets falling in tangles around me. *That's it! I did have compassion for Leah, even though she couldn't receive it because she thought of me as the substitute mother she wished she never had.* Sliding onto my stomach, I drifted into sleep, grinning.

Six days after my adventures in *Valparaiso,* the onset of December settled over *Santiago.* Each of those days, I'd explored the city, and that particular afternoon I wearily returned to *Sol Hostel.* The promise of a quiet night cocooned beneath the covers—earplugs positioned—beckoned.

Upon entering my room, I noticed a navy canvas overnight rucksack stuffed to the hilt, a flaming red cosmetic bag with silver corners, and a truckload of fluffy pink sweaters piled on MY bunk. Noticing Natalie reminded me of skipping smooth flat stones across the river while canoeing back home. Our lives would touch down and intersect in four places throughout my journey. At first glance, her appearance seemed that of a fellow tourist, with her big blonde—instead of black—hair and fire-engine-red lipstick, making her transparent skin glow even whiter as she sat on her mattress pulling lacy underwear out of her pack. Ultimately, she would inadvertently help me reclaim my voice.

"Excuse me, but this is my bunk; my stuff is here. I've been sleeping in this exact spot for the past week," I told her.

"Look, Doll, this is my bunk. I'm a tour guide and whenever I work in *Santiago,* this is where I sleep. *Sol Hostel,* Room 1, Bunk 12."

My eyes scanned the room. Several unclaimed bunks without bedding indicated their availability.

"Well, sure, no problem." I moved my backpack and suitcase onto the bunk above hers.

"Name's Natalie, and you?" she said, extending her dimpled hand as a peace offering. "I can tell by your accent we're both Canadian. I used to live in Vancouver, that is until I met this handsome *Chileno* man at an international food festival. That was sixteen years and two children ago."

For the next half-hour, we sat on the edge of her bunk while she told me more about herself than I'd wanted to know. Feeling like a leaf caught in her gust, I watched Whirlwind Natalie's animated expressions with a mixture of admiration and wariness in my heart.

When she finally stopped talking about herself, she asked, "Are you ready to go, Doll?"

"Go?"

"Let's take ourselves out for a meal. I have a favourite restaurant that makes *chupe* that is to die for. You aren't allergic to shellfish, are you?" she said and then described the dish made with shellfish and cheese in such detail I began to anticipate eating during normal sleeping hours.

"Sounds like fun, but I've had a long day of sightseeing and I'm ready for bed," I yawned. "No one, and I mean no one, goes to bed at nine o'clock in *Santiago*."

My feet ached and my head throbbed after bargaining with multiple street vendors that afternoon for just the right souvenirs to take home. But since she insisted, I decided to accept.

"Uh...well, sure, why not? Eating during normal sleeping hours... sounds interesting," I agreed.

This will give me the chance to talk to another woman travelling solo about my impressions of Chile so far. Plus, I could use a confident and assertive friend who knows how to have fun. Especially one who is fluent in Spanish.

Our quest for *chupe* led us to hail a taxi, driven by a man whose flirtatious nature became quickly evident. Natalie later relayed the sensual drift of their conversations. His reluctance to part with us added a humorous twist to an adventure that would not have happened in a Canadian taxi. He eventually dropped us off at an enormous open-air, mall-like complex—a vibrant space crammed with restaurants, craft stores, and pubs. Our surroundings echoed with the sounds of forks clinking against plates, chair legs scraping wooden floors—sounds tiny and lost in the clamour. Enthusiastic, animated people wearing vivid clothing ate dishes I struggled to recognize, passed *maté* back and forth, all the while hollering and gesturing with their hands. Plumes of cigarette smoke rose and vanished into the darkness, leaving behind their noxious smell. I felt as if I were the only person who noticed how the black sky around us muted the flamboyant colours splashed on buildings, walls, doors, windowsills—the others remained blind to nature's quiet transformation. The energy in that space rebooted my downward spiralling stamina. The scents of perfumes, liquors, temptingly delicious food, and fresh-cut flowers wafted through the air.

Natalie gestured toward vacant chairs in a section serviced by a waitress who reminded me of a zombie in her black-and-white formal attire—I made a mental note to tip her generously.

"I'll have the *chupe* and the *prietas*," said Natalie. "And, Doll, by the look on your face I can tell you don't know what *prietas* are. The most delicious *Chilean* blood sausage. Shall I order two?"

I hesitated, torn between politeness and my aversion to trying unfamiliar foods. Natalie's amused gaze hinted at a challenge, an unspoken dare to step out of my comfort zone. Ordering the same dish felt like surrendering, yet refusing might strain our blossoming friendship.

"I'll have the *chupe* and the chicken *empanada,* please," I said, smiling up at the waitress.

After an hour of sharing our stories and discovering how delicious the *chupe* and the delicate pastry turnover filled with spiced chicken known as an *empanada* could be, Natalie told me about *Stella*.

"I met this woman *Stella* at a concert four years ago. She invited me to her home in *Pichilemu*. Get this, *Stella* died during a heart by-pass operation! But she came back to life, yet she still felt sick. That is, until she had reiki treatments. I totally believe in reiki. Because this reiki master, *Aziz,* he healed her. She's 100% now!"

"That's interesting. Someone I met in *Mexico* practised reiki. But most Christians in my circles believe it's of the devil. I shouldn't explore reiki; it could be dangerous for me."

"Listen up, Doll. Back in Canada, we separate ourselves from the land all winter long, so faith takes on a different shape. You don't see trees the size of these there. Freezing weather limits the growth of plants in the same way a cold place limits belief in other forms of spiritual healing. We become as harsh and unforgiving, or close-minded, if you will, as winter. Here in *Chile* people are enriched spiritually in surroundings that provide food and beauty all year around. Why don't you look at this from the perspective a different landscape gives you?"

"I get what you're saying," I said. "It makes sense that different environments shape different faiths."

"Good. I'll arrange for you to meet *Aziz*. He teaches classes for free on the condition that once he has trained you, you also have to practise reiki for free. He lives in *Pichilemu,* too. It's on the coast south of *Santiago*. I'll ask him if he can teach you."

"I'm not so sure about that." *If God wants me to pursue reiki training, then he'll have to put it together. She'll forget all about it, as we'll likely never see each other again.*

"Oh, I'll contact him, and you can become his pupil," Natalie promised.

"Natalie, thanks so much for taking me out to experience the night life this evening. I really appreciate it, but I'm so tired. I hear my bunk calling."

Natalie nodded and we settled into the back of a taxi at 2 a.m. Before I retreated into the comfort of closing my eyes, I said, "You know, tonight's been a revelation. I dashed two of my Canadian paradigms. First, I vow never again to paint my walls taupe. All these vibrant colours splashed on the buildings, the bold hues in the clothing, and the rich tones of the landscape inspire me more than I expected. And second, bedtime can be much later than nine o'clock."

Late the next morning, I wandered into the hostel kitchen. Above the gas stove, a wooden window framed the scarlet-pink light spreading across grey stone buildings down the street. The beams streamed into the room, making the sky-blue walls that reminded me of a winter's day in Alberta, look even brighter. I placed a pot of cold water on a burner. The matchbox in the drawer beside the stove contained five wooden matchsticks. Lighting one match after another, I bent over the range trying to ignite the burner. *Nothing happens.* The flame scorched my fingers as I flung the last one under the metal grate, where it sputtered and smoked into nothingness among four other splintered matches. The smell of gas and sulphur spread through the hostel kitchen, stinging my nostrils. No flames appeared beneath the grate. No more matches.

Why on earth can't I light a simple gas stove? I have one like this at home. I should be able to do this. Now I won't be having boiled eggs for breakfast.

Picking up the aluminum pot, I prepared to abandon my culinary aspirations and fetch a granola bar from my room. A sudden voice filled the kitchen's quiet, offering unexpected help.

"Do you require some assistance?" A young man with tightly wound ebony curls and braces on his teeth waved the unfavourable smells away from his nose with his left hand, smiling.

"No thanks, this stove is broken," I said.

"This is my pleasure." He took a lighter from his shorts pocket, adjusted three dials, and motioned for me to put the pot back on the grate. A burst of blue flame danced to life, illuminating the room, and dispelling my frustration.

By placing the empty match box into my pocket, I would remind myself of what could happen when I stop avoiding situations that don't work out smoothly, face them head-on, and accept some loving kindness along the way.

"Thank you! How did you do that? I'm Ruth from Canada."

"A pleasure. Hi, I am *Leandro*. I am a fellow traveller. I live in *Sao Paulo*," he said, his metallic smile unwavering.

When he noticed my raised eyebrows, he continued with a precise and polite diction not common in Canadian youth, "*Sao Paulo* is the capital of *Brazil*. Please pardon my English, as my native tongue is Portuguese."

Natalie entered the kitchen at that moment and said, "Ah, Doll, I see you have met my *Brazilian* 'son.' *Leandro*, meet your second Canadian 'Mom,' 'Ruth.'"

His eyes crinkled up and his mouth widened into another huge metallic smile. Flashing a smile back at him, I shook his hand, secretly wrapped my left pinky around the match box in my pocket, and said, "Pleased to meet you, 'Son.' Can you join us for breakfast and tell us your story?"

CHAPTER 6

Riding the Trail of Faith: Temuco Calls

A WEEK LATER, NEAR THE HEART OF *SANTIAGO*, IN *SOL HOSTEL'S* KITCHEN, the acrid aroma of *maté* mingled with the clatter of dishes and chatter of tourists preparing for the day. Natalie, with a cherry-red grin on her face, plunked her plate of toast smeared with mashed avocados down at my table—her presence adding a touch of intrigue to my bland morning. Scooping yolk and white from the eggshell with my oversized spoon, I said with mock sarcasm, "Natalie, would you like to join me for breakfast?"

We laughed.

"Don't plan anything for this afternoon, Doll. I'm not working, and we're taking a bus to a restaurant called *La Vaquita Echa* for supper."

"Oh, Natalie, that sounds tantalizing, musical, and alluring. What does it mean in English?"

"Amusingly, *La Vaquita Echa* translates to..." Natalie paused. "The Thrown Down Small Cow," she finished, enjoying her theatrical reveal.

We laughed again.

"I'd love to," I said, accepting her invitation instantly and enthusiastically this time. While washing our dishes, we planned to meet again at 4:00 to begin our culinary evening.

At 4:05 we were strolling to the bus stop, linked arm in arm, in true *Chilena* fashion. After we'd ridden a short distance, our bus slowed, and we noticed a stretch of road swarming with racing cyclists in bright yellow-and-black matching spandex outfits. Our bus driver detoured around them, making our route longer, presenting me with the perfect opportunity to enjoy some different scenery. Natalie, however, fumed.

"Oh, no! Can you believe we left the hostel sixty-five minutes ago and this bus is already forty minutes behind schedule? And look at those obnoxiously yellow-and-black get-ups they're wearing. There always seems to be something in this city intent on ruining my plans. I always eat supper at 5:30," Natalie said, tapping the glass face of her watch with a long red fingernail.

Instead of replying, I stared through the grimy-steam-streaked bus window, pretending to study a giant blue, pink, and yellow butterfly painted on the corner of a white building. Natalie's brain appeared to whirl with alternate scenarios.

"If the bus had been on time, my plan would have succeeded. Now we might miss our next connection. Not to mention supper," Natalie exclaimed, hyperventilating.

Her turmoil felt like a thick blanket threatening to smother my present joy. Natalie lived in *Chile* and worked in *Chile*; she probably found herself at the mercy of schedules and business decisions. She'd once told me that being a tour guide wasn't as easy as it looked; that researching the history and highlights of a neighbourhood required hours of studying. *She's letting the unexpected time delays spoil her afternoon right in front of my eyes. She's not going to spoil mine.*

Just then, at one of the many stops, a portly *Chileno* dressed in white jumped onto the bus—his appearance as surprising as the colourful butterfly on the building we'd just passed. He deftly lifted his trolley of baked goods into the bus without losing a single one, providing the perfect way to divert my attention from Natalie. The bus chugged on, yet the travelling Baker—wearing a blue apron and showcasing a beaming smile beneath his black-and-white checkered chef's hat—somehow managed to keep his balance.

"Look at that! Now this is something you don't see in Canada," I smiled at Natalie.

Natalie's angst calmed when she spotted the man pushing his trolley loaded with muffins, cakes, pastries, meat pies, and *empanadas* down the aisle. She caught his eye and held up a handful of coins. The vendor grabbed an *empanada* with his fingers, took her payment, then bowed and vanished—trolley and goodies and every trace of him—out the back-exit door several stops later.

Natalie smiled with every bite of her *empanada's* crunchy deliciousness. Eating food that had previously sat near the dusty highway in the hot sun didn't appeal to my Canadian sensibilities; watching the roving chef, dedicated to his honourable profession, certainly dissolved the tension Natalie's actions had threatened to embed in my spirit.

In the overheated, confined space of our third public transit bus, I thought about how we had somehow managed to make our connections despite her fretting. After jostling along shoulder to shoulder with Natalie for another fifteen minutes, she nudged me out of the seat and pointed to our stop. We descended the rubber-matted steps—with stiff legs protesting—arriving at *La Vaquita Echa* well before 5:30.

Oh, how I miss my car.

"This is it, Doll," Natalie said after we had walked several metres.

"Where?" I asked, thinking that Natalie had pointed to a farmer's home.

A life-size black-and-white plaster cow with blue eyes too big for her face and legs too short for her body gazed at us.

"Meet *La Vaquita Echa's* bovine guardian," laughed Natalie.

Beyond the cow's vacant stare, tables covered with jaunty red-and-white checkered tablecloths, umbrellas, and bright red flowers in vases competed for space among scattered straw bales. Waiters and waitresses wearing cowboy hats and red-and-white checkered shirts hustled around tables packed with boisterous diners.

I glanced around, breathing in the whimsical charm of this haven of peace within the bustling city, and said, "Oh, how quaint! That aroma! An outdoor restaurant!" *A breath of fresh air after the bus kerfuffle.*

"I knew you'd love it, hey, Doll." Natalie jabbed me in the ribs with her pillowy elbow.

Several of the dozen or so tables were vacant, so we seated ourselves. Within seconds, a waitress appeared from a brick building near the sunny dining area.

As she placed dishes heaped with vegetables and a cheesy tomato sauce resembling pizza without the crust, the aroma of the meal filled our nostrils. Natalie's earlier stress seemed to melt with each bite, and I took time to think.

"You know, Natalie, I'd like your opinion on something. I feel like that cow's empty eyes are trying to tell me something. Maybe I'm missing the bigger picture of my journey. I'm restless. Or I've reached a saturation point. I've been on the road eight weeks now, the longest I've ever been away from home. Sometimes, I feel like abandoning the rest of my journey."

Dropping her fork to use both hands, Natalie snapped a greasy string of melted cheese still attached to the serving dish and sucked it into her mouth. "A wise guru once said that we should ride the waves of our feelings instead of letting them submerge us. Speaking of submerged, I have an idea for you. Why don't you come with me and work as a tour guide on the cruise ship? It's a wine tasting cruise that goes from *Santiago* down the coast of *Chile* and back to *Santiago*. That's where I'm heading next month."

"That's an interesting offer. Tempting. Maybe if I give enough notice, The Lodge could find someone else to replace me and I could go with you," I said.

The purple plastic grapes on the table suddenly looked fascinating—I reached over and fiddled with the smooth, uncomplicated globes and said, "I'm thrilled with all that I've done, all the people I've met and helped, and maybe I've already seen what I wanted to see. Maybe I couldn't bear to experience more."

But is this detour what I want? I do tend to go around the hard things, like loneliness, when what I need to do is go through. Would I be taking an easier path or betraying my journey for comfort's sake? Reneging on my commitment to The Lodge would make me feel guilty. My path must lead to The Lodge.

"Actually, thanks, but no thanks," I said before she could speak.

Natalie's brows furrowed in thought, the sun highlighting wrinkles where none existed seconds earlier. She stared into my eyes and said, "Now you listen to me. It's interesting, isn't it? You started this trip with the romantic idea that you could go into the disturbed world of abused women and change it. That romance died quickly. It did for me too. Ten years ago, when my son and daughter were four and six, my husband and I split up—he took them back to Vancouver, I stayed here, and I haven't seen them since."

Diverted briefly from her lecture, she blinked back her tears, sipped her water, and continued.

"Now, you've come to *Chile* for a dreamy horseback ride in a foreign land. Yet, you're willing to let that dream wane in the face of reality. Have you figured out yet what you're really seeking, Doll? From what you've told me, none of your planned goals on this trip has held your interest once they stopped being dreams and started becoming fact. It makes me wonder whether you're running to something or running from something."

Kicking off my sandals, I curled my toes around the green grass under the table so I could pull little tufts from the lawn; so I could ground myself; prepare myself to receive the words Natalie spoke. Next to us, a couple engaged in a noisy standoff—I caught glimpses of their strained expressions as they continued to disagree with each other. Before I'd left home, others had asked me similar, uncomfortable questions. Natalie's probing words made me long for the self-awareness to navigate these turbulent internal waters. I didn't want her to be right; I needed to find a way to make sure she wasn't right. *I wish I hadn't told her so much about myself during our late-night bunk chats. This woman has no trouble looking into my soul or calling it how she sees it. I must keep going somehow.*

"So, Natalie, you're saying that I can't see my way forward?" I asked, feeling defensive, and at the same time defenceless.

Reflecting on Natalie's words, a ripple of memory carried me back to Maple Ridge, to the serenity of paddling my canoe through dark waters. Late at night, under millions of sparkling stars dancing with the full moon, I'd had a profound spiritual experience. Those spectacular stars made me believe I could reach out and touch God; I sang out, "Praise him, you Sun, Moon, and Stars"! A beaver smacked his tail on the surface; a loud cracking sound that suddenly broke the stillness yet didn't frighten me. Slowly, quietly paddling downstream, I saw what seemed to be an impenetrable black wall of trees looming before me on the water. Yet, as I continued, the illusion—merely shadows cast by trees lining the shore—dissolved. Only by moving forward, paddle stroke by paddle stroke, did the way through open, revealing itself in the moonlit ripples. My lesson in faith—the way forward often appears as we dare to move ahead into the darkness.

This memory guided me back to the present, looking across the table at Natalie.

"Natalie, thanks so much for giving me your frankly brutal opinion. You've made me realize that I need to keep my commitment to the two anchors of my trip: working at The Lodge in January and climbing Fitz Roy. Only when you press on does the path reveal itself. That's what I must do now. God will lead me through. And I'll pay the bill," I told her, feeling a renewed sense of purpose and direction.

"Thank you. So that's your plan? To have no plans except to have some great adventures on Fitz Roy and end up at some Lodge by January?" Natalie seemed pleased that her counsel had benefitted me.

"Yes, I have my heart set on trekking Mount Fitz Roy. And that's my plan—more or less," I chuckled.

The waitress flashed the bill back and forth between Natalie and me. Grabbing the thin paper with a pink streak across the top, I counted out my *pesos*, with Natalie's help.

Leaving the sanctuary of *La Vaquita Echa*, we boarded the tightly packed bus, the rhythmic hum of the engine providing a backdrop to the thoughts rumbling around in my mind.

"When you mentioned horseback riding at the restaurant, I recalled that when I was in La Paz, in Mexico, I met Amos, the director of a Christian camp, through the owners of the hostel where I stayed," I began, craning my neck to look at Natalie. "When Amos found out how much I love horses, he took me for an amazing ride through the dusty *arroyos* near his camp. After a long gallop, we cooled down under a lone tree, and he gave me some advice that stuck with me. He said, 'When you get to Chile, go to Temuco. It's a small city, but they have a strong Christian community there.' Right now, that memory is giving me a definite sense of certainty. I've just figured out where I will go next! To Temuco!"

"I thought you liked it here in Santiago."

"I do. I love the energy of this city, but I'm a small-town girl. Plus, I feel more comfortable around Christians. You know, my tribe, we all have the same speak," I said.

"So, you're hoping your Christian tribe will have all the answers? Maybe a prophetic word or two to guide your way?" Natalie's tone wavered between jest and curiosity.

"That would be a bonus." I laughed. "Christians will accept me instantly; I'd be safe. It's a fantastic way to make new friends. I hope I'll find some ministry to get involved in; something that would shape my life's work and give me some direction."

"Following another dream, are we?" Natalie said, as she directed me off the second bus, and hailed a taxi.

"Yes. I've decided to go to *Temuco* tomorrow."

After our two-hour bus and taxi journey mercifully ended, our steps led us straight to the hostel's communal bathroom.

"Natalie, how can I ever thank you for all the help you've given me here in your adopted home?" I asked over the sound of splashing showers.

"Don't worry about it, Doll, happy to help a fellow Canadian. The night bus leaves in one hour. Be on it. You'll be in *Temuco* by seven in the morning. My eighty-eight-year-old priest friend lives there. He can give you a place to stay. Maybe he'll be your guru. I'll email you from *Sol Hostel* at 8:30 tomorrow morning with his contact information."

After disentangling myself from her engulfing, rib-crushing hug, and her double-cheek kisses, I regained my balance.

"Thanks, so much, Natalie. That would be great; I appreciate that you would do that. Really, I can never pay you back for all you have done for me, but I promise to find a way to pay it forward."

"Sorry, Hatchi, you're more comfortable than this cold glass," I said, wedging his soft, cuddly body against the windowpane in the bus en route to *Temuco*. He complied; but before I could tell him how much I yearned for the comfort of spending our first night with a friend of Natalie's, he nodded off. Leaning against him, my nerves coiled with uncertainty. Dealing with the challenges of finding hostels in unfamiliar towns and grappling with language barriers made me wonder how and where I'd find kindly guidance.

As my mobile bus-bed bounced, swung, and lurched through the next interminable eight hours, I found myself alone with my thoughts—the discomfort of the journey a backdrop to a deeper unease. Memories of when my discomfort had been more than physical—when the emotional turbulence of helping Leah had gripped me—surfaced. *After all this time, I still don't know if I'm capable of handling the unpredictability of solo travel. What am I searching for? Am I still evading, as Natalie had hinted?*

The night stretched on for an eternity. I teetered between moments of stifling heat and chilly anguish, constantly contorting my arms and legs to find a comfier position. Twice, I stumbled down the dark aisle to the bathroom, yearning for the relief of morning. *Never again. No more night buses for me.*

Then, with the mastodonic deciduous trees whirling past the bus window like a great wagon wheel, blinding shafts of intense mid-December light from the rising sun pierced through every gap in the drapes. The landscape outside, ever-changing, mirrored my journey—beautiful but disorientingly different from home, thrilling yet daunting. Sliding the blue curtains open, I saw rolling hills covered with a gradient of rich greens dancing with happy-faced flowers, both reaching out to touch distant snow-capped volcanoes. The tranquility and small-town charm of *Temuco* relaxed my sleep-deprived brain. Tucking Hatchi into my pack, I left my seat, stretched out my stiff limbs, pulled a hat over my matted hair, and swished warm water from my water bottle around in my mouth to get rid of the stale taste.

I have no idea where to go from here. Next time, I'll plan this more carefully.

Unsure whether my 7:00 a.m. arrival, its location on the outskirts of the city, or the smaller size of the city made the bus depot so silent, so lonely, so eerily vacant; I slid my backpack off, and sat on a bench between two long lines of tour-bus kiosks; all advertising various bus tours, all still shuttered. I munched on flattened grapes—a sweet yet bitter sensation on my tongue—and did some *Tai Chi* stretches. The clicking sound of a woman's high heels on tile floors echoed in the empty space, breaking the quiet of the few voices speaking in hushed tones.

A man juggling a briefcase, clinking a bulky ring of keys, and with a windbreaker draped over his arm, caught my eye as he approached one of the kiosks. His gentle, sad smile, that couldn't have disturbed any heart, made my wary heart decide to trust him with my vulnerability.

I wonder if he could help solve a couple of my problems. But he looks busy and overworked, and he hasn't even started his day yet. Will he be able to understand my Spanish?

Seeking help clashed with my desire for independence. Yet, sitting here, lost in an unfamiliar city, I recognized the limits of self-reliance. Gathering my gear, I got up and approached him.

"Do you work at this kiosk?" I asked in Spanish, my voice wavering. "My phone is dead. Could I please use your outlet to charge it?" I chided myself for not bringing an external or solar cell phone battery charger. *I have yet to perfect the timing between plug-ins.*

"Come into my office," he answered in an unaccented English, likely honed by talking with English-speaking travellers all day. Leaving his shutter down, he gestured for me to sit on the only other chair in the cramped room, across from where he sat on the opposite side of his paper-strewn desk. "My name is *Gabriel*. And whom do I have the pleasure of having in my office at this early hour?"

While my phone charged, he told me about his wife's job, the economy in *Chile*, the social problems their children faced in school, and his despair over the disparity between the lives of the rich and the poor in *Chile.* He delved into *Chile's* troubling neo-Nazi issues with an intensity that made me uneasy. Despite my discomfort, the bond we formed in that tiny kiosk began to erode the barriers I'd built around relying on others.

"*Gracias,* you have been too kind. Can you recommend a hostel? And can you tell me how to get there, please?" I asked, noting that my cell phone had reached one-hundred-percent charge.

"Go to the tourist bureau. They will point you in the right direction. I will take you to the *collectivo* stand," he said, and taking my arm and my suitcase, he guided me into the corridor.

Gabriel perused the lounging *collectivo* drivers smoking near their vehicles. "See that one, he is too old. He will drive too slowly and charge you more. And him? He is nosy, he wants to know where you are going and if it's too close, he refuses the job. And that one? His car is too old—no air conditioning."

Gabriel guided me to a young female *collectivo* driver with the perfect 2012 Ford Focus, helped load my gear into her trunk, and kissed me goodbye on both cheeks.

"I feel touched by an angel, *Gabriel.*"

"Trust me, I am no angel," he said, waving and walking back into the depot.

Sitting alone in the back of the young woman's empty car, I reflected on God's hand on my journey and at how soon its forward momentum had set me sailing into the wind—yes, the wind truly can seep into the human soul. Stretching out my legs, I leaned against the passenger-side door and pondered the curious word *Gabriel* had used for taxi: *collectivo. I wonder why they are called collectivos.* From my window, I saw a shopper standing on the edge of the street, balancing grocery bags on her hip, and appearing to flag us down with her free hand. *Surely, she can see this vehicle already has a passenger. Me!* The driver slowed and pulled up to the curb. The door I had been leaning against moments earlier flew open. I scooted into the middle seat and re-buckled myself. The woman's perfume wafted into the car ahead of the tall brown paper shopping bag with carrot greens dangling over the top. Using me as her personal side table, she placed the bulging bag on my lap. She looked at me with a warm silent smile, likely sensing my foreigner status. She settled herself into the space that seconds ago had been mine and patted my leg and smiled again. I smiled into her black eyes, trying not to inhale the fragrance-scented air between us. As we were about to resume speed, the door on my left opened and another woman slid into place beside me. Her feathery light sweater billowed up into my face, now so close to hers that I had to lean back to focus on her. We smiled at each other instead of attempting conversation. *What on earth is going on here?* A phrase I had used with my gliding instructor Tom popped into my head. *Help Tom, I do not have control. I could almost see him grin and hear him say, "Then let go of the controls, let me fly the plane, and you enjoy the ride."*

Collectivo... collect, I think I've guessed the difference between collectivo and taxi now. I need to get out of here and find a taxi!

My widened eyes focused on the driver's eyes in the rear-view mirror. She smiled at me. *She's not understanding me.* My Spanish didn't include "please let me out here" yet. *Yes, she's stopping.* Before I could shift to the left to follow the sweatered woman out of the car, a heavyset man took her place, as though they had choreographed the movement, and the driver accelerated back into the flow of traffic.

"You get off at my stop. We will take *maté* together," my new seat mate said to me.

"No entiendo," I said, pretending not to understand him.

Every time the vehicle turned a corner at warp speed, he smiled as our shoulders and thighs touched—a smile gleaming with the vitality of a much younger and leaner man.

No personal space in this car. Tensing my muscles against the g-forces, I tried to hide behind the carrot tops that were wilting with every passing second.

But I could understand the sign *información turística* I spotted across the road. The driver caught my eye and pulled over to the curb. My new suitor heaved his body through the door, reached his hand in to lift me out, snatched my luggage from the trunk, then fell back in his seat. He waved and beamed at me from his rolled-down window. Shaking my head, I had to smile as I watched the odd collection of travellers drive off.

This bone-weary Canadian who rides her motorcycle alone, who lives alone, who paddles her canoe alone, and who flies to South America alone paradoxically craves the chosen peace and introspection of solitude, yet grapples with the imposed isolation and despair when solitude crosses the line into loneliness. An irony as striking as the contrast between the prairies and the Andes. I suppose, if I had joined a tour group, I might not have let nationals into my life nor gotten joy from a distinctive style of doing life. Perhaps Canadians miss out on a robust socializing experience in our collectivo-absent country.

Stepping into the *Temuco* tourist information centre, I entertained the idea of updating my glasses to match the sass and vibrancy of the attendant's stylish glasses. They complemented her modern, boldly coloured attire; a stark contrast even to the bright blue "genie" pants and orange, flowered cotton "babydoll" top I wore.

"My name is *Carlita*. May I help you?" she asked, first in Spanish then seamlessly switched to English when I gave her a bewildered look and replied in English.

My elbows rested on the counter between us, and my backpack and suitcase rested against my legs.

"I'm waiting for a friend to email information about a place to spend the night. Could you please direct me to an internet café?"

"No need." She lifted a stack of papers and a coffee mug from her desk, motioned for me to bring my luggage into her office, and told me to sit at her computer.

"You're letting me use your desk? Wow, so kind of you, thanks." *Carlita and Gabriel. Two strangers, two beautiful people.*

Once I had plugged in my laptop, unread emails from back home filled my inbox but I couldn't see the one email I wanted. *I'm depending on Natalie to get me in touch with her priest friend to connect me to my tribe. Could she have forgotten, or does she figure her obligation to help me has ended?*

"May I suggest you wait for your email in the public market square across the street? Your laptop will be safe here." *Carlita* smiled, seeming to understand that observing the activity outdoors could make the time pass more pleasantly.

After thanking her, I settled onto a bench in the square to wait for something to develop—the skill I'd perfected in *Mexico*. I hadn't sat among the cool, shady, tree-lined walkways long before faint strains of pan flutes and guitars drew me from my bench in a Pied Piper-like reverie, past men, women, and children dressed in colourful clothes, most with extravagant hairdos, all squinting in the radiant sun. Two musicians in jujube-green cotton pants, with dark skin, and jet-black shoulder-length hair, played their instruments on a corner in the open air.

Drawn to the guitarist's magnetic pull, my eyes focused on his fingers as they flew with precision over the strings, crafting melodies that intertwined with the pulse of the bustling street.

Initially, my attention fixated on his peculiar instrument, a guitar-banjo hybrid. Then I felt the *Chilean* minstrel's eyes searching for mine, staring inquiringly, welcoming me. He barely skipped a chord as he pointed a long thin finger at a bench. Obediently, I slid down with my back against a cool cement wall, wedged between two couples. My body and feet ached to dance; they unconsciously absorbed the haunting pan-flute tones of the lively street musicians, as well as the activity of the crowds ebbing and flowing past my seat. A whole hour passed in what seemed like seconds.

When they paused for a break, I approached the guitar player; I wanted to see those talented fingers up close.

"Please may I buy a CD?" I asked in English, pointing to a white metal rack of CDs near the microphone. "Do you have one with that song that you played earlier? Unchained Melody?"

"*Si, Señora. Te gusta*?" the guitarist asked.

He must be the one who understands English.

I wonder if he means: do I like their playing, or their music, or perhaps that song? Figuring out the nuances of communication in a foreign land intrigued, yet perplexed, me.

"Oh, yes, I love your music. I've never heard such a beautiful a version of that song where I live in Canada."

Anticipating listening to their music later on my laptop, I stowed the CD in my computer case in the middle of my daypack. The sun arced slowly across the sky, her destination the western horizon far beyond where pedestrians and cars teemed around the park. *Have I been soaking in the exuberant level of energy and activity in this park the entire afternoon? Before night falls, I'd better get back to Carlita.*

Still no email from Natalie.

"*Señora*, may I help you to find a hostel perhaps?"

Carlita drew red lines on a colourful city map to indicate routes to the nearest hostels. She called each until she found a vacancy. Travellers streamed through the information centre, yet I'd not seen another *gringo* with whom I could converse in English.

Carlita folded and creased the map. "*Señora,* I do so greatly appreciate you think my English is good. I am planning to get a new job. Those who are bilingual can find better jobs."

"No worries, your English is nearly unaccented and super easy to understand. As we Canadians say, you went 'the extra mile' for me today. I'm sure you will find an awesome job."

"Good luck in finding your hostel," she said, glancing at her *Canadian Idioms* cheat sheet.

"Thank you."

My encounter with that young tourist agent spoke volumes about how our presence in this world counts. Little did she know how much her assistance had uplifted me. *No, I didn't waste today, not one bit.*

Possibly seven days blurred into a whirl while I explored the rural feel of *Temuco*—a welcome respite from the frenzy of *Santiago.* In the early morning quiet of the hostel's kitchen, I opened my laptop, and Natalie's latest digital thoughts greeted me.

She wrote, "Are you still in *Temuco*? If you are, don't leave. I have an important task I want you to do for me."

She didn't mention her elderly priest friend, and I wondered if I should ask about him. *Am I searching for a connection to my tribe or am I looking for an easy accommodation solution, a free night or two, or free transportation?* I decided that she must have forgotten, and so I didn't ask.

Instead, I replied, "I haven't found any Christian community around here; I'm planning to go to *Villarrica* next. The woman at the tourist bureau highly recommends it. The logistics don't make sense for me to meet you here, Natalie. I'm in still in *Temuco,* but you live way up north in *Santiago.*"

One minute after I hit "send," her reply arrived.

"I will take the bus down to *Temuco* for the weekend while we work on it. I haven't been in touch with *Alfereza* for four years, but I've already arranged for us to spend a couple of nights with her. You and me, Doll. Meet me at the depot tomorrow at 4:00."

"Wait. Natalie. Couldn't we both stay at my hostel?" I hoped my reply didn't convey the apprehension I felt about lodging with her old friend purely for reasons of our convenience. From my perspective, the hard dividing line between using someone and true friendship looked clear-cut, but from Natalie's perspective it must have looked a bit blurry.

"It's all arranged, Doll. See you tomorrow. Don't be late."

"Okay, I'll be there." I hit "reply," then "send," thinking that staying with *Alfereza* seemed wrong; yet a voice within urged me to accept this unforeseen twist.

My fingers slid up and down the smooth black cord attaching my laptop to an adapter plugged into the wall near my table. Natalie's words, her tone, streak back across my memory-scape, the familiar impact of their oppressiveness reminding me of my ex-husband's words, his tone, his coldness. He had created situations that forced me to keep my thoughts silent, to freeze my voice so it wouldn't escape and cause fights. His voice began to replay in my mind, as vividly as the day he had spoken to me.

"We're going to the bank this morning. I found out I can get a loan if you co-sign for me," my ex had said, his expression void of warmth, in contrast to our kitchen heated by the sun.

"Why do you need one?" I asked, feeling the weight of his expectation.

"So that I can pay off my truck faster."

Knowing full well that he was unemployed more often than he worked, I had asked, "What if you can't make a payment?" carefully wording my question to avoid triggering a drinking binge. Yet, beneath my cautious exterior, I held a genuine concern and empathy for him, particularly when witnessing his earnest attempts at sobriety.

"You never were good with money. Leave the details to me. C'mon, get the kids in the car and let's go."

"What can we use for collateral?" I asked. Surely, he wouldn't want me to put my car on the line. My grandmother had willed her little Gold Rambler to me. She and I had spent happy months driving and laughing together in it, and now I depended on it to buy groceries and to attend church, to visit my family—so many essentials.

"Your car, of course. Now hurry up, we'll be late."

Nine weeks afterward, he had defaulted on his payments. The day the bank manager came to take my car away, I cried my eyes out. And yet, I had never said a word about it to my ex-husband.

The echo of his verbal daggers faded, pulling me back to the present.

Glancing around, I noticed how the hostel kitchen had filled with hungry travellers. I unplugged my laptop. *I cannot allow Natalie, or anyone, to silence my voice, ever again. But perhaps I can reframe this. Perhaps this can be my ministry—helping with Natalie's project, whatever it is, and inspiring her by showing her kindness.*

Arriving at the bus depot on Friday night, right on time at 4:00, Natalie greeted me *Chilena* style, then hailed a taxi. During the ride to *Alfereza*'s house, she revealed the details of her "important task."

"I've got a big-picture idea for a business venture related to the cruise ship job, but I need someone who can write. I know you keep a journal, so that's you, Doll. Then I need you to upload my profile and a promotional video onto the internet. That's also you, Doll."

Natalie's proposal made me feel torn between anchoring my journey to her vision and my desire for independence. *She must have remembered when I told her about my drafting career at DC Holdings and she's concluded I can handle the detail-oriented computer work required.*

"Let's do it!" I agreed.

As we entered *Alfereza*'s row housing complex, the globular red South American fuchsias lining the walkway caught my attention. Unlike the meek and mild Canadian fuchsias confined to tiny pots indoors, these reminded me of a scene from *The Day of the Triffids*—they seemed eager to swallow me whole. The wrought-iron gate creaked on its hinges, and *Alfereza* welcomed us as she stood in the open doorway of her humble condominium, a broad smile lighting her face.

"Come in, come in out of this heat. I have been waiting for you. Supper is ready," she said, her English flavoured with a thick accent that hinted at her preference for Spanish.

At first glance, I knew *Alfereza*—with her serene grace and simple attire—wouldn't get mad or reprimand us. The holes in her ears where earrings once dangled, the streaks of grey in her hair, and her loose, comfortable cream-and-white sweater revealed a woman touched gently by time; she exuded a calm and welcoming presence that reassured me despite Natalie's impromptu self-invitation.

Alfereza's quiet wisdom seemed a world apart from Natalie's vibrant presence. The differences between them stirred my curiosity about their unlikely friendship. Their bond must have flourished on mutual support and understanding. *Alfereza*, I surmised, provided a grounding balance to Natalie's effervescent energy.

Glancing around the living room, I noticed a 9″ × 12″ framed photograph on a wooden table near an overstuffed floral-patterned chair, highlighting the striking difference between the gentle-spirited woman before me and the ecstatic young lady in the picture.

"Is this you?" I asked, pointing to the photo.

The young girl looked radiant in her large, hooped gold earrings, a diamond tiara in her flowing black hair, red lipstick, and magenta-red crinoline dress. Seated high on the rear of a shiny red convertible, she energetically waved with both hands at the clusters of people gathered along the street.

"*Si*, that was for my *quinceañera*. When every young lady in *Chile* turns fifteen years old, she has a special party. We take many photographs. We dance. We eat. I will never forget that day when I became a woman."

"You looked so happy."

"*Si*, and I am still happy."

She sat us at her compact kitchen table covered with a plastic tablecloth decorated with diamonds containing roly-poly chefs displaying their wares—cupcakes, pies, cheese rolls, layer cakes, spaghetti and meatballs—all of it in shades spanning the entire chromatic spectrum, alternating with diamonds of green and white.

Alfereza's home—with its wood-panelled walls, counters cluttered with ornaments and baking supplies, and couches draped with crocheted blankets—reflected her intentional creation of a comfortable place to live. After a delicious meal, she graciously allowed Natalie and me the time to work on our project, leaving us alone after leading us to a large second-floor room. Many hours later, after interviewing and videoing Natalie, I uploaded all the information I'd written, and we watched her presentation on YouTube. Clapping her hands, she ran toward me and gave me another rib-crushing Natalie hug.

"Finally, I feel like I have paid you back." I coiled up my cord, strapping it with the narrow black Velcro strips, shut my laptop, wrapped it in a sweater, and returned it to my pack.

"Yes, thank you, Doll. I am delighted."

Natalie's big-picture personality clashed with my detail-oriented nature;

yet, at the time, we collaborated harmoniously. Little did I know that the dynamics would shift in our next encounter.

"I'm exhausted," she said, "I'll see you in the morning."

I'm tired too. I worked hard. Once again, Natalie had kept me up far past my Canadian bedtime.

Due to rainy weather the next day, we decided to put the finishing touches on her presentation after lunch. Her presentation complete and polished, we walked together down the stairs, Natalie gripping the handrail. In the living room she sprawled on the couch, put her arm over her eyes, and left me alone in a stranger's home. *I think I'll go upstairs to nap too.* My hand froze in indecision while reaching toward the railing. *My journey is more than just a physical traverse across continents. I'm gaining a deeper understanding of my strengths and weaknesses. I need to show my appreciation for our supportive hostess.*

The hiss and crackle of hot oil plus the mouthwatering aroma of freshly cooked pastry helped me locate *Alfereza* in the kitchen. She hummed a lively tune. Beneath the steaming bronze vat, *Alfereza*'s woodstove—with its ebony doors and silver knobs—radiated a heat that made her brow glisten with sweat. She dropped a dripping dollop of dough into the pot with a wooden spoon, its handle scarred by a sooty, burned streak.

"I am making *sopaipillas* for you. I make them when it is raining," she said, noticing me standing in the doorway.

The warmth from both her simple statement and the flickering flames drew me into her kitchen.

"Do you only make them when it's raining?" I asked, attempting to correlate the two events.

The smoky odour of the wood fire and the heavenly fragrance of the *sopaipillas* mingled with the steam, creating an aroma far superior to anything that wafted out of a hostel kitchen.

"I feel good having the woodstove on when it's damp and chilly outside," *Alfereza* said. "*Sopaipillas* remind me of my mother. She taught me how to make these. When the rain pounded on our roof, we would make them together. We loved to sit here by the stove, eat them fresh, and talk about our good life in *Chile*."

"Is your mother still alive?" I asked. Leaning forward on a chair, I propped my elbows on the table, delighted to be chatting as she baked.

"No, she died in 2002. We lived here together until then."

"You must miss her."

Alfereza lowered her eyes, pausing before scooping more fat-saturated pastry into a metal bowl on the counter, and said, "Yes, *mucho*."

"Did you ever marry?"

"No, I never found the man who is wonderful," she replied without any regret it seemed—this woman actively nurturing her sense of contentment.

"Do you have *sopaipillas* in Canada?"

"We have something similar, I think. They're called doughnuts," I said.

Then, with the bowl of steaming hot *sopaipillas* placed in front of me on the table, and *Alfereza* still humming, that strange feeling came over me. Sadness seasoned the sweetness of the present moment. After three months of living in hostels, *Alfereza*'s welcome highlighted the importance of making houses into homes, leaving me to question whether I had ever made Leah feel at home.

"Do I smell fresh *sopaipillas?*" Natalie's entry into the kitchen reined in my thoughts.

"These are *deliciosa, Alfereza,*" I said to our beaming hostess, who seemed noticeably pleased that her treat delighted us. "You'd better get yours now before I eat them all, Natalie."

My second *sopaipilla* vanished quickly. The clip-clopping of a horse's shod hooves drifted through the wide-open kitchen window—an out-of-place sound in our modern world. Yet *Alfereza,* with a twinkling smile, turned off the flame, took my hand, and whisked us outside. The sun now cast its warm glow on the damp streets. In front of the house, an elderly dark-skinned woman with a baseball cap, long black pigtails, a pink skirt, a blue-and-white checked apron adorned with frilly, creamy lace around the pockets, and a green cable-knit sweater, sat on a flimsy-looking seat, casually holding the reins of her chestnut mare's bridle. From beneath her blue cap, her eyes sparkled with curiosity, focusing on me from her world of vibrant colours and vegetables. My grey cotton tank top and matching shorts made me feel like the misplaced character. Heavy oak poles attached to a network of mismatched belts and straps connected the horse to a tiny wooden cart overflowing with shucked peas, beets, carrots, lettuce, and piles of other unidentifiable vegetal mysteries.

"*Root*, meet *Anacita*, our vegetable lady," *Alfereza* explained when she noticed my wide eyes and gaping mouth. "We will buy fresh for supper."

While she bargained with *Anacita* for a bag of thick, straight carrots, I snapped photographs, soon to be posted on my website with the subject line, "things you don't see in Canada."

The next morning, when the sun shone into our upstairs bedroom, I could hear *Alfereza* puttering in the kitchen, and Natalie softly snoring in the bed beside mine. This gave me a chunk of time to luxuriate in the quiet; time to think before I had to get up. *This Alfereza—a woman discovering joy in baking on rainy days and buying veggies from a horse-drawn cart—and I seem worlds apart; we're so not of the same tribe.*

The warmth of *Alfereza*'s home reminded me of another warmth I once knew. When I had left home after high school to attend college, I had looked for my tribe—fellow Christians. Finding none, I had located another group I came to love. Joining the college women's canoe team had thrust me into a world where Carolin, my stern paddler, guided our synchronized paddling by yelling "HUT" at me, her bow paddler. Tireless evening practices, whether under raindrops or sunshine, had fine-tuned our paddling changes. Through our capsizing drills—followed by our swim to shore towing our canoe—our friendship had flourished. This bond culminated in our first-place finish in our division at the final competition. Our victory was about our collective effort and belonging to a team, more than about individual strength.

The memory faded as I stretched out on my bed, yet the warmth lingered. *Alfereza's world seems so grounded—unlike mine. Although Alfereza and I have nothing in common, if I had limited my visits to Christians—my tribe who would instantly welcome me—I would have missed this unexpected blessing. Establishing friendships with people like Natalie and Alfereza is a good thing.*

To show our appreciation for making us *sopaipillas*, Natalie and I prepared *Alfereza* a Canadian-style breakfast of French toast with strawberries and whipped cream. She watched in wide-eyed wonder as we prepared a dish entirely new to her. Following a delightful day of exploring *Temuco* together, the three of us gathered around her kitchen table, accompanied by the ever-present noise of her television. Even during our evening meal, the blue glare accompanied us. In the background, we heard through a torrent of incomprehensible programming—as though delivered by an angelic messenger—an announcement for the *Metodista Pentecostal de Temuco* choir's Christmas concert on December 22.

"Whoa, did you hear that?" said Natalie. "December 22 is tomorrow! My heart skipped a beat, I love Christmas carols. We should go."

That would mean we'd have to spend an extra night in Alfereza's hospitality, but the thought doesn't seem to occur to Natalie.

"Perhaps *Alfereza* has other plans," I said, glancing at both Natalie and *Alfereza*.

"This is fine. You are both welcome to stay in my home as long as you like."

"Thank you kindly. Will you join us at the concert, *Alfereza*?" I asked, touching her shoulder.

"Oh, no, I am Catholic," *Alfereza* said, pulling her silver crucifix out from under her sweater. "I would not enjoy this type of singing."

On the evening of the concert, seated in the front row of the church, Natalie and I entered a celestial realm, ushered in by an electrifying drum solo. A conductor in a powder-blue uniform directed two groups of singers surrounding a soloist. In each ensemble, twenty women, in long metallic teal gowns, and men, dressed in sleek black suits paired with white shirts, expressed their tunes with their entire bodies. Dresses swirled, hips swayed, raised hands clapped to the beat of a hidden live orchestra. Lyrics in Spanish flashed on the full wall behind them, red and green lights strobed, images of time-lapse clouds streaked across the words. Every performer's face glowed with bliss, illuminated by the divine love of God. Their enthusiasm carried me to the throne room of grace and swept me into a place of worship. Surrounding me, the crowd—a singular organism pulsing with joy—cheered and applauded in total un-Canadian style. *Alfereza* would have preferred an orderly Canadian rendering of Christmas music, but I preferred this exultant celebration of Christ's birth. We had unintentionally found one of the many groups within Temuco's Christian community—just as Amos in *Mexico* had mentioned during my horseback ride with him in the *arroyos*.

After the service, the woman beside Natalie leaned across and whispered to me, "God has something very special planned for you."

"Oh, thank you," I said. Natalie and I looked at each other; she spoke not a word for once.

The woman reached across Natalie to put her hand on my knee. "You have been through a rough place, but God will restore you and bring something good to you shortly. And you were a *refugio* for the young woman." Then she slipped out of her seat into the aisle and disappeared in the crowd.

"I think someone from your tribe just prophesied to you. I'm mystified." Natalie's face glistened in the glaring lights.

"Now I'm genuinely prepared to move forward. I've found the purpose behind my journey to *Temuco,*" I said, thankful for the woman's encouraging, prophetic words—words that stirred my spirit. I got it.

Natalie handed me a tissue, and together, we wiped away our tears.

Our time at *Alfereza*'s home had ended. The morning after the concert, I embraced our gracious hostess warmly and thanked her for her hospitality, promising to visit her if I returned to *Chile.* At the bus depot, I hugged Natalie tightly, our parting filled with shared successes and gratitude. After a final wave, I bought a ticket for *Villarrica,* stepping into the next chapter of my journey.

CHAPTER 7

Rosa: Drawn to Villarrica

LURED BY THE AFFORDABILITY OF THE NIGHT BUS, I CHUCKLED TO myself, thinking about how I had once again traded comfort for cost. While the bus swayed and rattled through the darkness, I sifted through the memories of my travels thus far, and focused on the fact that my struggles were lightening.

Stepping off the bus into the dark streets of *Villarrica,* I felt confident in my usual "commit first and figure out later" approach. But within half an hour of walking the streets, the rain had drenched me to the bone; and uncertainty about where I would sleep crept in, making me question my next move. *I should have gotten a data plan for my phone so I can book hostels while I'm en route. If I walk far enough, I'm bound to see one. However, stumbling upon an open internet café would greatly lift the strain from my tired body.*

The idea had appealed to me when *Carlita,* my stylish tourist attendant in *Temuco,* had described the town as a quaint village surrounded by lakes and trees and volcanoes. Raindrops, falling in saturating sheets, glistened in the glow of the streetlights—I might have admired each drop's delicate beauty had the bus-induced fatigue not clouded my brain.

I should have asked Carlita if Villarrica often had monsoons. Splashing through unavoidable puddles on the deserted sidewalks, I repeatedly doused my suitcase with muddy sludge. Trudging toward I knew not where—with water seeping into my runners, squishing between my toes and creating rhythmical squeaking sounds—my uneasiness grew. My spirits felt as heavy as the wet jeans clinging to my skin.

I can't see those lakes Carlita had described; for that matter, I can't see anything.

Two long blocks of dark storefronts later, I noticed a halo of light shimmering onto the street. The moment I leaned into the door, wedging my suitcase and backpack through the narrow doorway, dry, coffee-scented warmth rushed into my nostrils and wrapped me in a soothing, welcoming embrace.

A sleepy barista carrying a clanking tray of mugs on his hip regarded me with surprise.

"*Los sientos, Señora,* but we are closing at 10:00. In five minutes. *Adios,*" he said, holding up five fingers and nudging me out the door with his shoulder.

"I understand. It's late and I can see you are footsore," I said, intending to depart.

Farther down the block, not a single ray of light from a single shop window illumined the sidewalk. I swung back toward the coffee shop.

"Could I please use your internet? I'm relieved to find a dry place where I can search for a hostel. You're the only shop open at this hour, and since it's wet weather out here..." My voice trailed off, desperation creeping in.

"*Señora,* if you are quick, you can stay."

While he hustled around the tiny space, I pulled out my laptop, making sure to keep the water droplets from my jacket from short-circuiting my only connection to the outside world; asked him for their Wi-Fi password; and located a hostel five blocks away with a romantic name: *Don Juan*. Perhaps not the best selection criteria, but at that hour it made perfect sense.

"Thank you so much for letting me come in," I said, my voice high-pitched with weary gratitude. The steady beating of rain on pavement soon drowned out the sounds of the clinking of my few coins in the barista's tips mug.

Following the *Don Juan* attendant, the clunking of my luggage broke the silence in the narrow stairwell leading up to my room. Behind me, I left a trail of water-soaked imprints on the wooden treads and the memory of a tedious bus-confined evening. *If only the silence had lasted throughout the night.* Arriving at that late hour, I hadn't known that the hostel overflowed with energetic young trekkers. Every night for the next two nights, reliably, the moment I dozed off, boisterous laughter, strumming guitars, and clinking glasses jolted me awake. In the room above mine, raucous revelry replaced the silence. Tossing and turning, I seethed inwardly and buried my head under the pillow, wishing for morning.

Despite the sleepless night, I rose early, impelled by the promise of a new day, and stumbled into the *cocina* (kitchen) for my first breakfast at *Don Juan,* with the noise of the partiers still ringing in my ears. There, the comforting aroma of coffee and a delightfully international couple, Chantal and Richard, greeted me, making the weariness of the previous night fade to black.

"So, how did you two meet?" I asked them, after Chantal told me she grew up in France, whereas Richard told me he hailed from *Chile.*

"In *Bolivia,*" they both said in unison, beginning the story of their serendipitous meeting with a poetic synchronicity.

"Of course, I should have known," I laughed, warming my hands around my porridge bowl.

"We both trekked in *Bolivia* for a couple of months. We've lived in France for the past seven years but returned to visit Richard's family," said Chantal. "Do you have a handle on the Spanish language yet?"

"Well, this should answer your question," I told them, "The gal I stayed with in *Temuco* told me she was going shopping on *Lunes* (Monday). I recognized lune as the French word for the moon, so I had said to her, "What? You are going to the moon?"

Richard slapped his thigh, laughing himself so far back on his chair I feared he'd tip over backward. Chantal laughed and said, "Don't you just love Canadians?"

"That reminds me. In the *Atacama Desert,* the moon appears larger than anywhere else in the world. Did you know a *Chileno* once owned the moon?" Richard asked.

"Oh, really?" I said, raising one eyebrow and thinking that he sprinkled as many untruths into his story as sugar on his porridge.

"*Mais oui,* it's true. Back in 1954 this guy named *Jenaro Gajardo* wanted to belong to the *Talca Social Club.* To be a member you had to own property. So, he bought the moon!"

"I wonder how much he paid for it. I hope he got a good deal," I said, still not buying into his tale.

"I don't know, but get this, before Aldrin could land on the moon in '69, the U.S. President had to call *Jenaro* to get his permission."

Later, I googled Richard's fantastic story, discovering it to be true, and that when *Jenaro* died, he said, "I leave my people the moon, full of love for his pains."

Breathlessly, Richard launched into a volley of random facts. Between his French-tinged Spanish accent and his rapid-fire speech, I caught, "The climate in *Chile*... Humboldt Current... creation of the desert. Minimal life... extreme arid clime..."

"Which direction you headed, girl?" Chantal asked, cutting short his enthusiastic monologue and reminding me of the journey ahead.

"I want to explore *Villarrica* today," I said.

"Make sure you watch the *Villarrica Volcano* at night; you'll see it glowing," said Chantal, pointing in the direction of the peak.

Our breakfast bowls all sat empty, yet we chatted on. Waddling along, carrying imaginary bags full of groceries, Richard said, "*Chilean* society is strongly matriarchal. Next time you go shopping, watch to see who carries all the stuff. It is always the man, because he is the donkey."

The image of a man as a donkey—braying complaints, with its long ears flopping and its back swaying under its burdens—struck me as hilarious, and before I could control my laughter, he had me in stitches again with his next story.

"You know why I married a woman from France?" he asked, pointing at Chantal. "Because she doesn't force me to cut my hair." He patted his man-bun affectionately. "She doesn't mind if I stop for a few beers with the boys on my way home from work. She doesn't stop me from drumming or stop me from dancing. I tell you, all my friends here in *Chile* may as well be in prison. They had to stop doing all these things as soon as they said, 'I do.'"

Chantal took Richard by the arm and said, "Time to get ready for our hike, *mi amor*."

Later, as I roamed the bustling streets, I scanned the crowds for couples shopping together. The men, carrying bags and belongings, resembled the donkeys Richard had described. Everywhere I travelled, I saw the subtle influence of this matriarchal society.

Richard and Chantal disappeared with a wave, their laughter trailing behind. Inspired by their lively energy, I ventured out of the hostel to explore *Villarrica* with a new-found curiosity. The warmth and vibrancy of the town reflected the *esprit de corps* connections I'd just experienced. The morning sunshine bathed the town in a golden hue, revealing *Villarrica*'s true nature. Transient wisps of vapour etched intricate designs against the azure heavens above the snow-capped crater of *Volcan Villarrica*, yet much later that night, those wisps would glow with a red haze that held this prairie girl spellbound. The density of the trees and shrubs, nourished by the expansive lake, made me wonder if overzealous tree planters with an extremely generous budget had planted them. Surely an artist with a palette containing only the richest tones of blues and greens had painted this scene. Brightly coloured modest brick-and-wood homes with peaked roofs all competed for desirable lakeside locations. Distant hazy mountains constrained the waters, as if beckoning—enticing—those exuberant tree planters. Peace flooded my soul as I walked *Villarrica*'s sunlit streets.

Villarrica favoured an out-of-the-way setting on the southwestern tip of a serene lake, where birdsong and the sound of lapping water replaced the sounds of traffic. For reasons unclear to me, another village a short bus trip away on the southeastern corner of the same lake bustled with tourists. Extreme trekkers flocked to *Pucon* to experience volcano climbing adventures or white-water kayaking expeditions. *Carlita* had read me well when she recommended that I travel to *Villarrica,* as the expat-free town offering peaceful walks along the shore conformed more to my style.

A patch of leprechaun-green grass welcomed me to pause along the winding lake path. Eagerly, I accepted the invitation, settling onto the cool surface—my daypack serving as a makeshift pillow—and surrendered to the hush of nature that surrounded me. Enveloped by the towering vegetation that stretched into the distance, I breathed in the living, moisture-saturated air—each inhalation a balm to my spirit. The steady rumbling of water as it tumbled into the mystic depths of the lake below heralded a nearby waterfall, providing a soothing backdrop to my moment of repose. The Lakes District locals ambled past me at a leisurely pace, exuding calmness, exchanging smiles, or meeting my gaze—unlike the bustling crowds of *Santiago.* Here I wandered through fewer billowing clouds of cigarette smoke along the sidewalks. Here arms, legs, and faces free of tattoos and piercings absorbed the sunshine; plaids or denim and hair pulled back into functional ponytails replaced the bright cotton business attire and fancy hairdos of the city. Here a peaceful, countrified culture replaced the frenetic culture of the city.

Jerky, unsteady movements of miniature dimpled feet in the grass caught my eye. The sight of a one-year-old princess in a frilly pink sun dress gladdened my heart. A man, his black curls captured in a bun, walked beside her. He obviously adored his little daughter, holding her tiny hand in his massive paw, while she, with one fragile arm outstretched for balance, brushed her soft, black locks against hairy calves as round as her body. She took six hesitant steps to each of his. He looked down at her, brimming with paternal pride.

Whether he sensed me beaming at the little girl, or whether he wanted the entire known universe to share his joy, I couldn't be sure; but when his eyes met mine, I rose, and said, "Such a beautiful little girl."

"*Gracias.* My daughter. She can walk and she can smile. I love her," he proudly stated in English.

Scooping her up, the father tossed her giggling form high into the air. When she landed safely in his arms, I reached out a forefinger to her. Chubby cinnamon-brown fingers squeezed mine. Her toothless grin and laughter took me back in time.

A pang of nostalgia hit me. This father-daughter bond—so pure and joyful—reminded me of my children's early relationship with their father. I could still see him sitting on a couch with baby Ben lying on his thighs. Annie stood beside him, dipping a comb in a plastic glass of water, and with each stroke through his hair, droplets streamed down his neck. She giggled with approval as we admired his new hairstyle. Ben's legs kicked; arms whirled. When my ex-husband gazed into his children's faces, I knew he loved them; but before they had started school, he left, forever. Love and loss intertwined.

I yearned to tell this *Chilean* father four things. *Always be faithful to your wife, always be kind to your daughter, always be there for her, always love them both.* The most frustrating part of my limited Spanish involved not being able to share wisdom—the thought of using sign language passed quickly.

"*Adios,*" I said to them.

She released her grip on my finger and grasped the few locks of hair escaping from her daddy's man-bun. This daddy's goodbye smile for me showed me that his daughter would be loved well her entire life. He gently placed her back on the grass, and for the next few moments the kiss she blew me made the sun reflecting on the lake shine brighter.

Because long, unplanned hours stretched before me, I lowered myself back onto my pack, my fingers futilely attempting to wrestle my rebellious bangs into submission behind my ears. At that moment fate intervened, in the form of a passing stranger wearing a red headband, her locks neatly held captive away from her eyes. Suddenly inspiration struck. *That's it. I found the solution to my hair dilemma.*

A little-known travelling fun-fact is that one's hair continues to grow when one can't access one's favourite hairdresser; therefore, one learns to adapt, to evolve with the circumstances. Grabbing my pack, I set out on a quest. Amidst the bustling energy of the outdoor market, I bartered and bargained until, at last, I became the owner of an outrageously orange-and-green cheesecloth square *cum* headband. Day and night that headband stylishly kept my curls under control. Its frequent appearances in my blog posts earned me the endearing title of *Bohemian Hippie,* courtesy of my sister's quirky teasing.

My growling stomach drove me to seek sustenance, steering me toward a quaint eatery tucked away on the market's edge. The owner—standing in the doorway—hailed me in perfect English. Recognizing my accent, he told me he'd been born and raised in Toronto; and like a fly caught in a web, I found myself ushered to a scenic spot—surrounded with red hibiscus trees and green shrubs—on the patio with a sweeping view of *Villarrica* Lake. Rewarding myself for my negotiating prowess, I decided to treat myself to an authentic *Chilean* lunch.

"You want a milkshake? Lady, we don't do milkshakes in *Chile,*" laughed the metrosexual owner, shaking his black *Chileno*-style ponytail. "I'll bring you the next closest thing to it, though."

My nostrils inhaled the sweet perfumes of the flowers and the divine scent of pine needles. Leaning back on a wicker chair, I stretched out my sandaled feet and stuck a metal straw into the glass containing my blueberry "milkshake." The watery blue substance resembled dishwater more than a Canadian milkshake but tasted healthy. Melancholy thoughts—fed by something undefinable—crept into my mind.

For two days I'd felt the unfamiliar elements: purchasing meat from two well-aged men in red-and-white checkered aprons in a tiny butcher shop; purchasing dried fruit, herbs, almonds, dates, and coconuts from an ancient woman with a frosty grey bun, pearly blouse, and pleated plaid skirt; purchasing fruit and vegetables from a bald gentleman who held my arm while walking me around his store, filling my bags with produce. Even watching bright rainbows flicker in the spray churned up by plunging waterfalls, hiking along rose-scented trails, listening to the water splash against the lake shore, and soaking in the baby-powder-soft humid air or gaping at a wispy white vapour rise above the *Volcan Villarrica*'s peak felt out-of-place in this unfamiliar December. December in Canada meant flowing rivers' songs icily silenced in blue-white mounds, and snowshoeing on snow-packed tracks one metre above the trails. The sheer magic of my warm breath transforming into billowy clouds of supercooled ice crystals, dancing before my nose, had always captivated my senses.

My fingers absent-mindedly lifted and dropped the straw in my milkshake glass. I entered a space deep within myself. *I can't be getting lonely again. Every day I chat with folks—at hostels, in buses, on the street.* Every morning, I would strategically plunk my porridge bowl on a table where the new arrivals vacationing from international countries sat and glean locations to visit on my next trip; each place described as the best in the world. *But these days fewer guests are arriving. C'mon, how can I feel gloomy in such a beautiful place? What is that annoying noise?*

Touching down in the moment, I realized that my straw clinking on my glass created the noise. I dropped it on the red tablecloth. *I fear that Judge Bob from Mexico may have been correct when he told me to accept the anxiety of finding myself in suspense and incomplete. Instead, by "pushing the river," I'm teetering on the brink of depression. I've traversed this trail before, and I know from my experience with Leah that depression leads nowhere.*

Had *Don Juan* not been packed with youthfully exuberant trekkers—whose party time coincided with my bedtime—I may never have crossed paths with *Rosa*—an encounter that would add a touch of serenity to my journey.

The owner returned to my table. His onyx locks—now styled in *Chileno* fashion—had transformed his appearance and spoke of how he had distanced himself from his Torontonian origins.

"Is there anything else I can get you?"

"Yes, a quiet place to sleep tonight. I've been staying at the *Don Juan*, and..."

"Say no more. I'd recommend *Azul Hostel*. *Rosa* and *Fernando* will make you feel homely. They will provide you with both comfort and nocturnal silence."

"Thank you," I said, chuckling at his misuse of the word homey.

"Check it out, you will love *Rosa* and *Fernando*," he said, kissing me on both cheeks.

Placing my empty milkshake glass in a plastic tub near the kitchen, I wandered into the streets. As I strolled past a clothing store, a figure that seemed plucked from a *Salvador Dalí* painting caught my eye and halted me in mid-stride. Red shorts bagged around wiry black legs, and a white-trimmed red jacket enveloped dark hands. Above this curious ensemble sat a face obscured by a fuzzy, faux white beard. The sweltering *Chilean* heat made this Santa Claus seem like an illusion. The man smiled charmingly and waved at me, sitting there in his oversized chair, looking like a king on his throne, and I chuckled to myself, waving back. *Santa Claus! Today is December 24! This will be my first Christmas away from family!* Memories of white Christmases past with my grandparents, parents, cousins, siblings, and children contrasted with my current surroundings, making me feel nostalgic.

Time becomes a foreign concept when you travel—only the present moment exists. Every birthday in my family had come and gone without so much as a happy birthday email from me. Weekdays packed with new experiences passed as pleasantly as weekends had when I worked. Yet this timelessness held a healing quality.

Leaving *Don Juan's* plain brown-and-tan buildings behind, I walked the four blocks to the *Azul* in about half an hour. I pressed the buzzer beside a locked metal gate surrounding a two-storey cedar building hidden behind a brick wall lined with heavenly scented, dusty-pink roses. In the reception area, I felt a peace as deep and pure as an Albertan snowdrift in winter. Shifting his enormous weight from side to side, a man lumbered into position at the desk. Normally, a smile lights up a person's face; in poor *Jairo's* case, his smile brought a scattered assortment of blackened teeth and raw gums abruptly into view. But his imperfect smile heralded a perfect welcome. *Jairo* handed me the keys to my room and pointed upstairs.

"Welcome to *Azul Hostel, Root*. Soon you shall meet the owners, *Rosa*, and *Fernando*."

By the time I'd reached *Azul*, I had decided nothing. *Moving on will be the best way to keep my mind off spending Christmas alone. But where to?* During the years I worked, my project managers drove my daily routine. *Now, without schedules and deadlines, I have freedom: too much. Too much freedom makes me feel unnerved.* The dizzying array of choices overwhelmed me.

Searching for supper among the leftovers in the vacant hostel kitchen felt like a relaxed, almost meditative process, completely opposite to my frantic end-of-day routine back home in B.C. There, I would rush through project after project, only to abandon them after I quit my job. Collapsing onto a chaise lounge in the foyer to eat my meal, I pondered the contrasts between my former life and my current nomadic existence.

Suddenly I knew what to do. *Fitz Roy! I'll pack tomorrow, go to the bus depot in Pucon, buy my ticket, and climb Fitz Roy with plenty of time left to arrive at The Lodge in January.*

On the coffee table—along with an empty paper plate—my laptop sat idle, left there after I'd posted photos and happy tales on my blog. A "bing" notified me of a new email.

"Whatcha doin' for Christmas, Doll?" Natalie wrote. "Thought you'd be lonely. I'm taking the bus down from *Santiago* to share a Christmas meal with you in *Villarrica*. I'll arrive Christmas Day. We will cook a turkey and all the fixings."

Conflicted, I snapped my laptop shut. *Is she stalking me? I'll have to think about my reply first. I'm excited about finally going to Fitz Roy. Still, I would love company for Christmas.* Slowly I opened my laptop and typed, "I appreciate the suggestion Natalie, but I'm just planning to pack and to leave for *Argentina*, to climb Fitz Roy."

Natalie's determination to create a joint festive meal made me wonder if she sought my companionship because she also faced a solitary Christmas. Seconds later, my laptop binged.

"You can go to Fitz Roy after The Lodge. We only have Christmas once a year, Doll. Besides, I will fix us a turkey dinner you will never forget. I'll arrive on the Christmas morning bus. I'll see you at the depot."

Here she comes encroaching on my right to decide where and when I want to go. What to say? Like all introverts, being followers, I felt irritated. *I don't intend to be redirected. But hadn't Natalie befriended me in Santiago? Fitz Roy has waited this long. Sometimes the familiar warmth of friendship trumps the lure of solitary adventures.*

"Okay. Sounds good. See you then," I wrote.

Later that evening I meandered through the halls of the hostel, driven by my love of linguistic curiosities. The humorously translated signs offered a diversion from updating my blog. In the kitchen I read, "While you're cooking, please open the window. The fire alarm is very sensible" and "Keep calm and do your dishes." My least favourite theologian, John Calvin, who advanced the doctrine of predestination, would have approved of this one: "Garbage: For organic waste we have a compost, please deposit your garbage in the trash destined for them." Posted beside the trash sign, I read the "hause rules for the hostel. Please be quit at night. Please close your room, we are not for los or missing responsible. Please do not handle the current conductor for their own safety."

In the reception area I read this warning, "Most people in *Chile* are good people but specially in bus terminals there are people expert in stealing tourists and never leave your staff alone in your room." Each notice, steeped in lost-in-translation humour, reminded me of how communication can both divide and connect us.

The sound of soft-soled sandals padding across the hardwood dining room floor alerted me to someone's presence.

"Welcome to *Azul Hostel*. I am *Rosa*. This is my husband, *Fernando*. Your laughter is like music in our hostel. I am pleased to see that our signs entertain you," she said, giving me a gentle hug.

A burgundy covering wound snugly around her head exposed her high forehead; wisps of auburn hair that matched the colour of her freckles snuck out from the scarf near her ears. Anchored at an improbable angle, *Fernando's* embroidered cap defied gravity, clinging inexplicably to the back of his head. Their distinctly different clothing led me to wonder if they belonged to another faith tradition. *Rosa's* warm handshake conveyed the heartfelt welcome she extended to me.

Here is the source of the peace I feel in this place.

Wide eyes peeked at me from behind *Rosa's* leg.

"And this is our two-year-old daughter, *Glenda*."

Glenda vanished into the cottony fluffiness of *Rosa's* skirt the instant I knelt, smiling and reaching my hand toward her.

"We are planning to have a meal in this dining room on the 25th. Please, *Root*, you will join us?" asked *Rosa*.

The way she looked—as eager and as sincere as if she were extending her offer to a family member and not this stranger, this new client of hers—touched me. Their warmth and sincerity were undeniable, yet it seemed unlikely they would be celebrating Christmas. And should I be involved in their celebration? Yet, that face—anticipating my "yes"!

"Thank you kindly, I accept. I had planned to move on, but a friend is coming to spend Christmas with me. Would she be welcome as well? We will bring a Canadian-style turkey, stuffing, potatoes, and vegetables."

"Of course. I will make some special *Chilean* dishes. We will see you both tomorrow," said *Rosa*.

Once settled into my upper-floor, slant-roofed room with two beds and zeros roommates, I stood on my tiptoes to peer out through the skylight. Gazing over clay-shingled rooftops, the unusual trees with bare trunks topped with an intricate network of branches masking the setting sun, caught my attention. Across the lake loomed the rocky, barren, and snow-capped *Volcan Villarrica*, so different from my immovable Canadian Rockies. Unlike the solid, reassuring permanence of those mountains, this volcano gave me the uneasy sensation that at any moment molten lava could smother me.

Tiptoeing so that I could see out through the skylight, I recalled the passage in *Extreme Landscape* that spoke of embracing the raw wildness of *Argentina*. Though I'd not yet reached Fitz Roy, this idea resonated deeply inside me. The relationship I had endured with Leah, much like this mountainous landscape, had been filled with tumultuous energy. In the same way that its fierce charm shaped *Villarrica*, my experiences with Leah had shaped me. Acknowledging the dark aspects of my nature, I realized that the volcano—threatening yet majestic—reminded me that even in the most extreme landscapes—whether outside or within—beauty, joy, and strength can thrive.

Every feral dog in town whined and barked their misery over being alone and hungry. When I had first arrived in both *Mexico* and *Chile*, the number of strays wandering freely made me want to adopt them all to bring home, and I'd lost many a night's sleep disturbed by their constant howling. To the locals, they were invisible. The mystery of why multitudes of them roamed the streets, or, at the other extreme, ate in restaurants with humans baffled me. Gradually, I'd adapted, and their sounds eventually became as common as the chirping of sparrows. Rolling into my bed, I drifted into a peaceful slumber.

On the morning of my first Christmas away from family, the dawn broke with radiant sunshine, sweltering heat, and an unclouded sky. I took some peaceful moments to Skype with them back home. As their familiar faces popped up on the screen, and their familiar voices reached my ears, I felt a closeness and a quiet strength that only my solitude could have amplified. Next, I savoured the many Christmas emails from friends to the north, thankful that our bonds spanned continents.

On my way to the street markets, cheery birdsong issuing from within lush, green, colourful bushes replaced the silence of the white snowscape that marked Canadian Christmases. Wearing just a light hoodie and shorts, I felt the liberating absence of the down-filled ski jacket, boots, mitts, toque, ski pants, and scarf I would have been wearing back in Canada at Christmastime. Each vendor's stall I passed, each grocery store—displaying unusual produce—underscored the vast difference between our cultures. By mid-morning, I'd lugged a fresh turkey, potatoes, vegetables, and fixings for the dressing back to the hostel, where I came face-to-face with the challenge of preparing the Christmas feast in a foreign kitchen.

Natalie's third phone call, her voice high-pitched with urgency, snapped me back to the task at hand.

"Hello, Ruth, I'm almost there. Talk to me about the cranberry sauce. Did you find the sauce?"

"No, not one vendor understood the word 'cranberry.'"

After Natalie's insistent call—which once would have grated on me—I took a deep, cleansing breath and calmly dialled *Ricardo,* a fellow Gospel Rider from B.C. and a native of *Paraguay.*

"Hi, *Ricardo.* Yes, I'm still in *Chile.* Wonderful. I believe you can help me. I want to make cranberry sauce for a Christmas dinner. We absolutely cannot have turkey without it. But no one in the markets or stores understands the word 'cranberry.'"

"*Si,* that's easy. Ask for *grosella.* Back home we used the *grosella* berry. Make your sauce with them and you'll never eat another cranberry," *Ricardo* said.

"Thanks, *Ricardo,* you're a Christmas-dinner hero. Merry Christmas." I hung up, feeling as if I'd accomplished what I'd set out to do, and feeling ready to face Natalie's expectations with my brilliant solution.

All morning, I prepared the vegetables and placed the stuffed turkey into the oven, so when I returned to the market for *grosellas,* I stooped to inhale the sun-warmed scent of the pink roses in *Azul's* garden first. At last, a vendor, grinning widely, presented me with a basket of plump, juicy gooseberries, and said, "*Grosella.*"

Success! Thank you, Ricardo!

Back at the hostel, my WhatsApp jingled again. Natalie rang for the umpteenth time.

"I'm about three quarters of the way to *Villarrica*... yes, I'm still on the bus... what? Do you think I would walk? Did you put the turkey in the oven at 350 yet? Make sure you use the potato water to make the gravy," she commandeered from the confines of the bus travelling on the *Chilean* highways connecting us.

"Don't worry, I'm on it, Natalie. I even bought some *grosellas.*"

"Those *grosellas* better be good, that's all I can say. And for the stuffing, make sure you use both breadcrumbs and sausages with the rice. And don't forget to use lots of poultry seasoning."

Do you think I have never cooked a turkey dinner before? Albeit not once have I ever prepared one on a stovetop that is level with my kneecaps, in a hostel kitchen, in South America before.

"And I bought a bottle of *Chilean* wine," I said, hoping to raise her spirits.

I'd discovered a few evenings ago while making cucumber and mango salad in *Azul's* kitchen, that *Chileans* produce delicious wine. Cooking in unfamiliar kitchens and trying new things, like this wine, seemed to be a recurring theme on this journey. Historically, I'd only tasted wine at Sunday morning Communion, where a few ritualistic drops punctuate a spiritual observance. The half-empty bottle sitting in the hostel's Free Box might have gone unnoticed in a different life; here, I hesitated, debating whether to stick to the familiar or to lean into the freedom that comes with being in a place where no one knew me. I had poured a small glass, fully expecting the usual bitterness. Instead, a sweet, velvety warmth that tasted like a hot fudge sundae spread across my tongue. As I took another sip, I thought about how little acts like this might be what opens me up to the bigger changes I've been seeking. Maybe this is less about breaking the "thou shalt nots" and more about redefining the rules that no longer serve me. Maybe stepping outside the lines is the point. I finished the glass with my meal.

Feeling a sense of quiet resolve, I left the kitchen and went downstairs to *Rosa's* kitchen to further coordinate our meal planning. Her gentle presence felt comforting. *Rosa* glanced up from her preparations of *Chilean* applesauce, green salad, and onion bread.

"What time do you want to eat, *Rosa*? My friend Natalie should be here around six o'clock, so we could be ready by 7:00."

"Soon, I think. You may help set the table in the dining room later," said *Rosa.*

However, we later realized our dinner plans were out of sync with the *Chilean* timetable.

At 5:50, Natalie walked in the hostel door, dumped her luggage in my room, and without a greeting or a hug, took full control of our preparations.

"Okay, Doll, get the turkey drippings into the biggest pot you can find. Time to make the gravy," said Natalie, her voice echoing off the walls in the tiny kitchen.

I relinquished the job of making the *grosella* sauce and the gravy to her. The fragrance of the roasting turkey wafted through the hostel, catching the attention of *Joras* and *Fleur,* a tall, young Dutch couple, as they stepped inside, weary from their long bus journey.

"This is for real?!? You are cooking a turkey meal tonight?!?" *Joras* and *Fleur* both asked with eyes beaming with anticipation.

"Yes, for real, and you are invited to join us. *Rosa* and *Fernando* want us to eat with them downstairs in the dining hall!" I said, excited at the prospect of sharing our feast with new friends.

Joras and *Fleur,* relieved at the thought of avoiding a Christmas dinner of dry noodles, changed their clothes, and returned to the kitchen, eager to join in the flurry of activity.

"We will help you make the filling," *Joras* said.

"The what?" I asked.

"The breadcrumb mixture you make to eat with the turkey," he said.

"Oh, you mean stuffing! We make it first, so it's already cooking inside the turkey. But thanks for offering," I laughed, thinking that such fun can be had when different languages and cultures collide.

"Stuffing? Inside the turkey?" *Joras's* eyes widened, then sparkled with amusement as he joined in my laughter.

After *Fleur* and *Joras* arrived, Natalie softened, and soon the kitchen hummed with the sounds of clanking utensils, sizzling turkey grease, and laughter. The four of us steered our way through our distinct culinary traditions with good-will.

"Back home, everyone would be eating by now," I said to Natalie, when I felt my stomach growling, and noticed that the clock had ticked past 7:00 p.m.

"Don't worry, Doll. I ate before I came. Remember, I live here. Why don't you have a rest like those Dutch kids are doing?"

Embracing a new rhythm, I climbed the stairs to my room, where I reviewed the once-anxiety-inducing moments of my day with acceptance in the welcomed silence.

At 11:00 p.m.—after we were well past starved—*Rosa* invited us all downstairs, beckoning us to the long-awaited feast. Natalie's creative culinary skills created a Christmassy atmosphere even without snow and jingle bells. Natalie had arrayed the dining room table with festive décor: holly branches cut from the trees in the *Azul's* garden; white napkins folded into the shape of lilies; touches of fresh parsley on each dish. The hostel's dining room—once a plain space—now glowed with the warmth and love reminiscent of my grandparents' homes during family Christmas gatherings. *Glenda,* perched in her highchair between *Rosa* and *Fernando,* radiated innocent joy. The Dutch couple sat close together between Natalie and me. We formed a tapestry of cultures, our hands entwined, heads bowed in reverence as we listened to *Rosa's* heartfelt words of gratitude.

"Thank you, God, for bringing Jesus to the earth to be a good prophet. Thank you, God, for friends, food, and family."

When *Fernando* noticed my questioning expression, he explained, "We belong to the *Naqshbandi* order of *Sufi,* the mystical section of Muslim. We are like monks are to Catholics."

"Now you say a Christian blessing, *Root,*" said *Rosa.*

"May the peace of Christ rule in all your hearts on this special day," I prayed. *Sharing Christmas with a family of Sufis has taught me how to see Jesus from their perspective.*

The turkey—reheated to a moist, golden perfection—and the *grosella* sauce—with its tangy sweetness—both tasted delectable. The savoury aroma of *Rosa's* onion bread infused the room, tempting my taste buds with every irresistible whiff. Each dish burst with flavours, making our Christmas feast a lovely experience. When *Joras* and *Fleur* asked for the "filling," everyone laughed, highlighting the delightful outcome of colliding cultures. Our universal conversations led us from religion to home births. *This Christmas stands apart in its unparalleled uniqueness.*

As I glanced around—from *Rosa* and *Fernando* with little *Glenda,* to Natalie, then to *Fleur* and *Joras*—I saw how this fusion of *Chilean* and Canadian traditions, the shared effort, and the new-found bonds captured the essence of my journey.

Late Boxing Day morning I awoke before Natalie stirred, and quietly penned in my journal an entry about her influence on my "spreadsheet mentality." "Christmas with Natalie effects a transformation of my small, organized two-bed hostel room into a space that looks like the aftermath of a cyclone. Every available inch of floor, shelf, bed, and wall hook has disappeared under lipstick tubes, lotion bottles, powder puffs, eye shadows, Q-tips, panties, bras, hairbands, nail polish, air fresheners, toothpaste, and shoes for every conceivable type of terrain." Her habits, so different from my entrenched habits, spoke to me of the varied paths we walk. *This journey will do me good.*

Over our mid-morning breakfast of microwaved oatmeal, Natalie and I plotted our adventure for the day.

"I want to take you to *Huilo Huilo Huereque* Park," said Natalie.

"Oh, I've already been there. What a spectacular waterfall!"

"All right, then," she said, swaying over to a brochure rack. She pulled one out and handed it to me. "Have you been to *Termas de Peumallen* yet?"

"Sounds like an intriguing way to spend Boxing Day. Does *termas* mean hot?" I asked.

"Close, *termas* means hot springs. Get your daypack and let's go."

Our bus windows offered unobstructed views of radiant, life-giving scenery—towering trees shading lush greenery—with volcanoes in the distance. An hour after we left the hostel, the bus dropped us off on a gravel road near a highway sign that read, "*Termas de Peumallen.*" Recalling how its name had shifted between *Peumallen* and *Peumayen*—depending on which sign I'd seen—I surmised that *Chileans* must respect linguistic preferences.

"I distinctly recall seeing pictures of beautiful cedar buildings and two outdoor springs in the brochure. Are you sure the bus dropped us off at the right place?" I asked Natalie.

"You are absolutely right," said Natalie. "And I remember seeing a row of heavenly log *cabañas* tucked away in the trees. So don't tell me we've walked all this way for nothing."

My aching legs told me we had been trudging up a steep, dusty path toward our unseen and obscure destination for a stiffeningly long time. Natalie preferred taking taxis to using the more taxing form of transportation—unknown to her but known to me as walking—but as we didn't see any, we'd begun to walk. She linked her arm through mine so I could steady her heavy frame. I tired more rapidly than her mouth.

"We're following the bus driver's directions… For heaven's sake simmer down…Have you always been so high voltage? ... What if we are lost in the wilderness? ... You are NOT taking one more picture… Calm down… Carry my bag, it's too heavy for me… Oh, look at that beautiful butterfly," she went on and on.

Natalie's blethering grated against my desire to soak in the peace of the surroundings—lost or not—underscoring our contrasting approaches to travel and life. *I'm feeling tense, not the usual camaraderie one feels when walking with one's friend. Do I exist purely to have the honour of co-existing with her? I must consider the pain she surely carries because of how her husband ripped her children away from her.*

After walking another twenty minutes, I thought we'd stumbled upon a mirage. A cedar gift shop, a large indoor spa, and a restaurant suddenly materialized through the thick canopy of green leaves that had obscured our view of the road ahead.

"YES!" Natalie and I exchanged victory signs.

In the spa's humid change room, Natalie and I donned our bathing suits and slipped into the indoor pool. Refreshed, we then followed a path—surrounded by stunningly gorgeous natural beauty—to the hot springs which took us along a ground-level boardwalk, from where we glimpsed the verandas of the *cabañas*. Far beneath them, a steep ravine yawned, its leafy canopy sheltering a narrow creek that wound its way through the dense trees. *The brochure for these cabañas should have said, "Not a place to bring small children or pets unless the pet is a flying squirrel."*

From the boardwalk, we descended a steep, crooked cedar-plank staircase with a rusty rebar railing to two inviting hot pools sculpted from natural river rock. Natalie gravitated toward the larger pool, where a lively family splashed and laughed, while I sought the peace of the smaller, more secluded one. Faint strains of unintelligible conversations mingled with the babble of the crystalline water cascading along the riverbed below. Leaning against the rough rim of the pool, I inhaled slowly, filling my lungs with the sweet essence of the flowers, and allowed the comfort of the expansive blue *Chilean* heavens, and the soothing motion of the warm water to lull me into a blissful sleep.

As if all the cells in my body were spontaneously combusting, I jolted awake, disoriented by how the shadows cast by the ginormous trees surrounding the pool had shifted. *How long had I slept?* Struggling to rise onto the sun-heated stones, I dragged my molten self to the adjacent pool—my limbs heavy and sluggish—where I heard Natalie presiding over the conversations with the family.

"You look like a boiled lobster. You could join the ranks of the local delicacies. C'mon in, Doll," Natalie said. "This is the cool spring. And by the way, how DO you stay so slim?"

As I submerged in the refreshingly cool pool—without responding to her—Natalie introduced me to three generations of a spirited Latino group from *Buenos Aires.* Those were the last words I deciphered of their rapid-fire Spanish. The animated chatter between Natalie and the family members spoke to me of the enduring power of familial love. My gaze lingered on the grandmother, her laughter like music as the grandchildren splashed her or the daughters hugged her. I envied her.

"Our new friends invited us to visit their homes in *Buenos Aires,*" said Natalie.

Though I responded with a nod and a smile, a twinge of regret pressed on me when I realized we had no phones, no pens, no paper to exchange contact information, and that these would just be fleeting associations lost to the passing breeze. No detour to *Buenos Aires* for me.

After our rejuvenating soaks in the indoor pool, the hot spring, and the cool spring, we went for supper in the log-cabin-style restaurant, where we both ordered the blueberry vinaigrette drizzled elk medallions and asparagus. We thoroughly enjoyed our delectably unique meal, then Natalie abruptly ended our relaxing day.

She tossed her crumpled napkin onto the table, stood up, caught the waitress's attention, and told me, "Time to head back to *Villarrica,* Doll. I have to be on the first bus to *Santiago* tomorrow morning, so I'll arrive for work on time."

I'm so glad she's only staying one more night with me. I find it so annoying that she's not open to my ideas. It's as though mine don't count; she doesn't even listen to what I say. Everything is on her timeline.

"Okay, no problem," I said.

"That elk was delicious, thank you so much," I told the waitress, pushing my blue-stained plate toward her.

The downhill slope of the road leading away from the *Termas de Peumallen* helped somewhat to lessen the strain of carrying both my bag and Natalie's, each weighed down with our soaked bathing suits. Yet the slog to the main road still seemed to drag interminably. The bus ride back to *Azul Hostel* stretched deep into the night, offering us a peaceful interlude. We wearily sank into the time-worn seats, the monotonous rumble of the engine soothing us after our eventful *termas* Boxing Day.

The next morning, upon leaping from bed, Natalie slung her overnight pack over my shoulder, wordlessly conveying that my breakfast would have to wait. We lumbered down the hostel steps as the eastern horizon glowed *grosella-sauce* red; then our pace quickened, fuelled by the need to ensure she caught her bus.

"This is goodbye once again, Doll," Natalie said, giving me another rib-crushing hug. "I still haven't heard from *Aziz* in *Pichilemu* about your reiki course but don't worry; I will let you know when I hear from him."

Oh, I won't be holding my breath on that one. I haven't forgotten that you forgot to connect me with your priest friend, so I think the probability of you following through on this is zero percent.

"Yes, another goodbye. Thanks, we'll keep in touch. Christmas has dimmed to a wonderful, heartwarming memory—thanks to you," I said, and meant it.

She grabbed the bus step railing to steady her frame as she shuffled inside without my support. The astute driver relieved me of her luggage. Draping the faded fabric curtain across her face like a sultan's wife, I saw only her eyes twinkling as she waved regally to me.

"Time for you to go to Fitz Roy," she yelled from the open window.

"Yes!" I waved back.

The mere sight of the bus taking Natalie around the corner, taking her away, exhilarated me—prompting my feet to tap a joyful jig, my hips to swivel, and my hands to trace arcs of happiness through the air. The building tension between Natalie's and my contrasting approaches to life made me question the wisdom of continuing our journey together.

Fantasizing about a breakfast of warm porridge smothered in cream and brown sugar, I returned to the *Azul Hostel* and pressed in the code for the metal gate. She could have chosen the small square of green grass or the edges of the scented flower beds; instead, little *Glenda* crouched on the hard, hot concrete sidewalk. Her bare knees were drawn up on either side of smooth butterscotch cheeks. Not spotting *Rosa* or *Fernando* near her, I assumed they were busy with clients indoors. *Glenda* sat alone, but not alone. Using her left hand, she walked a black, curly-headed doll back and forth in front of her, and with her right hand she walked a stuffed parrot. She didn't raise her head when the gate clicked shut. *Will she make strange again? I should go to the front door, so she won't be frightened.* Then she looked up. My right foot stopped in mid-stride—I expected her to run into the hostel; but she lifted her doll toward me, inviting me to sit with her. The sidewalk scorched my legs at first, yet once I found a comfortable position beside her, I entered her imaginary world—and the hot sidewalk and the sounds of cars and motorcycles speeding past, people talking, vendors yelling beyond the gates of the yard, all faded. She placed her doll in my palm. Her doll felt like peace. We smiled at each other; she laughing and chattering in simple Spanish, I speaking to her in simple English. The best of friends. *She's perfectly engaged in mothering her baby, anchored in this present moment. So happy. So calm.*

"*Glenda*!" *Rosa* flung the screen door wide. *Glenda* scooped up her doll and parrot, dashing eagerly to her mother's side. "Oh, *Root*! Good. I would like to ask you to join us for our *Dikr* this afternoon. You can wear one of my headscarves."

"What is a *Dikr*?" I hesitated to ask.

"It is our meditation ceremony when we say prayers of thanksgiving and remembrance. The prayers will connect your soul to your heart. You will feel the presence of God," she said in her delightfully accented English.

"Thank you, *Rosa*, I would love to come. I'm heading up to my room, now, but knock on my door when you are ready. I'll be waiting," I said, skipping up the stairs two at a time.

My head leaned against the wall behind my bed, my fingers typing a new entry in my digital journal. "I see this is my ministry. When I asked why Sufis wear headscarves and caps, *Rosa* told me the coverings keep out all non-God-like energy. She invited me to attend their ladies' meditation. So today, I'll have a chance to witness to her. To tell her about the one true God."

Rosa knocked on my door about two o'clock. She draped a silky burgundy shawl around my head and led me downstairs to a small room behind the kitchen, shutting the door on the sounds of the hostel. Red cotton fabric hung on the walls, covered with rows of large green-and-mauve circles surrounding yellow, six-petalled flowers. Five cushions with geometric patterns were scattered on the floor; their design made me think this religion originated in the Middle East.

Of the three women *Rosa* introduced me to, I only remembered *Amina's* name.

Their hair bound up in head scarves, their pastel blouses, and their skirts flowing to mid-calf—looking like a group of pioneers—these barefooted believers were concealed much like female mallard ducks. They all lived on a commune outside town, and I admired their dedication to raising their children with distinct values; yet I wondered if they would carry on these traditions in adulthood. The women smiled, I smiled; but as only *Amina* and *Rosa* spoke English, we silently communicated with sparks of life dancing back and forth between our eyes. When *Rosa* first placed the shawl over my head, I had felt out-of-place, strange; yet here, seated with these women, the same shawl drew us together in a sisterhood of belonging. *I should tell them about Christ now, and that the narrow way alone is the way that leads to eternal life.*

Just then, *Rosa* said, "Please to sit everyone."

Carefully observing how these women sat cross-legged on a cushion, I attempted to twist myself into a comfortable position.

"We will begin by thanking Muhammad, Jesus and Mary, David, Moses, and Abraham, our six top messengers of God."

After this short prayer, *Amina* reverently took from her purse a small, thick book with a hard cover in a rich burgundy, embossed in gold with the words *The Book of Remembering.* Many pages had sticky notes on them, many pages had turned down corners.

I hope and pray that I don't pick up some wrong spirit from them.

"Thank you," I said, holding hands with the woman on either side of me, to represent linking soul and heart.

"As we sing our chants, we breathe in deeply. Each time, we breathe in deeper than before," said *Amina*, "As we breathe, we open our hearts to God."

Amina's sweet face glowed with a radiant, joyful peace as she read two mantras from her book. After every chant—sung in Arabic—she slid a bead along a counter that looked like a cross between an abacus and a rosary.

During the prayers, when we all had our eyes closed, I sensed a powerful presence of God. My hands tingled. My breathing came in rapid, shallow pants. I felt Him lay His hand on my heart. When I peeked through one eye, I noticed each woman had her head bowed, her hands on her heart.

In closing, *Amina* prayed. Between her lilting Spanish words, she repeated my name several times. *She's praying for me.* She looked at me and said, "May you find the existence your heart seeks. May you find peace. You have a beautiful heart and open spirit."

Tears tasting like wonder and serenity flowed down my face. *How could she see into my heart?* These tender-hearted women barely knew me, yet they loved me well. Suddenly I had no advice or answers for them, only questions. *How can I presume to judge how they interpret holy scripture?* They met their interpretation of God; I met mine. I can only trust that God will be just with all his children.

"I had to come to *Chile* to have this touch from God," I said.

Amina said, "I had to go to Cyprus to find the proper form of spirituality for me."

Attempting to rise, I discovered my legs wouldn't respond. The women immediately leaped to my aid, offering their support, and gently lifted me. Enfolded in their *Chilena* style embraces and double-cheek kisses, my mind clouded with a tranquil haze, overcome by the urge to rest for days right there in that room brimming with love, sweet stillness, and joy. After the three friends left for their homes, *Rosa* took me to the kitchen and set a plate of papaya in front of me.

"Now you will sleep," she said, and taking my elbow, she walked me to my room.

Minutes later, I fell into a deep sleep. After I'd slept for three hours, I woke to a knock at my door.

"Oh, *Rosa*. Come in. I slept so blissfully, in perfect peace." *My spirit feels so calm. I know God is in control of my journey. Letting go of the need to control and plan, frees me to another level of development.*

As the night deepened, we ventured into the yard, merging with the infinite expanse above—a black satin dome sprinkled with stars that shimmered in a celestial theatre.

Rosa pointed her finger upward and said, "Look! The Southern Cross!"

In the Southern Hemisphere, the constellations presented themselves with wholly unfamiliar patterns.

I gazed heavenward, "Where?"

"See those four stars that look like a diamond on its side? Now draw a line between the horizontal stars and the vertical ones in your mind. Is this not a Cross?" said *Rosa,* tracing the Cross ever so patiently. "If you see the Cross, you are blessed."

"I see it! And we are both blessed, *Rosa,* so very blessed."

"Come sit on this bench, and we will talk," *Rosa* said.

The lights of the town sparkled in competition with the heavenly lights.

"See the lights of our home? *Villarrica is* a very spiritual area of *Chile.* That is what drew you here," said *Rosa* as we sat close together, her hand resting on mine, tears rolling down our cheeks.

Rosa's words, inspired by her beliefs, offered me a window into her world.

"*Root,* always remember to be in the present, be happy, be relaxed. The paths leading to God are as many as human breath. Let go and let your heart lead."

"Thank you so much for making my second-last day in *Villarrica* so special," I said. She gathered me in her maternal arms and kissed me on both cheeks.

Later, lying in bed, I thought of how different cultures and landscapes informed a community's spirituality. I thought of Doris, my friend in Maple Ridge, the woman who opens her heart as wide as the Rocky Mountains and whose smile can thaw a snowbank in January. She touched so many lives purely by loving on people. She had told me that we don't need a focused mission; but we need to focus on living our best lives; and that true ministry unfolds in our ordinary moments, as we share God's love with those around us, changing hearts one by one. She reminded me of St. Iraneus' words, "Don't ask yourself what the world needs. Ask yourself what makes you come alive, then go do that. Because what the world needs are people who have come alive." The more I travelled, the more I felt myself coming alive. In that instant, I made a vow: Never again will I fill in another missions' agency application form! Real mission work is not so much about going "over there" as it is seeing others' needs here. Doris was correct; I must do what makes my spirit flourish and seek out that abiding place where my affections live. The lives I've already touched have been enriched for our having sojourned together.

As I observed the *Naqshbandi* women living out their beliefs with genuine devotion that afternoon, the depth of their profound faith struck me. Developing an appreciation for how different cultures and landscapes informed a community's spirituality fascinated me. I believe God sees how they live and love, and I believe he approves. My job isn't to decide their spiritual fate; that's God's job. No longer do I view them as a people group who missed the Messiah. Now I admire how our unique spiritualities contribute to the beautiful harmony of existence, much like different instruments enrich a musical composition in a symphony.

The next day, I dubbed my "sit on a bench to watch *Villarrica* do life around me" day. I sat in the shade near the *Mapuche* Indian museum where I'd marvelled at the similarity between their intricate beadwork and our natives' handiwork. Shortly, an ample, plainly-dressed Chileana with work-scarred hands, and her husband, wearing overalls and cowboy boots, sat down next to me. They told me that they lived across the lake in the countryside. I easily envisioned her pulling weeds in her garden and him milking cows in the barn.

"*Solo*?" she asked me.

"*Si*, I am travelling alone," I replied in Spanish.

"*Estas casado*?"

"No, I am not married."

Her eyebrows lifted in surprise, and then she nodded thoughtfully, saying, "*Valiente.*"

The woman's calling me brave struck me deeply, as I hadn't considered myself brave. But as we chatted and shared my almonds, her perspective sank in. Their encouragement left me feeling seen and affirmed. *Yes, I am brave. Valiente!* Their expressions lit up when they heard me speak Spanish—augmented with sign language—clearly valuing my attempts to communicate, while I soaked up their compliments about my Spanish-speaking abilities. As they left, the woman gave my thigh a friendly pat; we parted as new friends.

At the hostel the next morning, my suitcase and backpack leaned against the reception desk while I ate a quick breakfast. Somehow *Glenda* figured out that her tall, pale playmate—the *Gringa* who spoke the funny language—would be going away.

She lifted her tiny arms toward me and said, *"Besos."*

Bending down, I scooped her up to meet my gaze, kissing each delicate cheek, fulfilling her touching request.

My heartstrings stretched to breaking point as I studied her trusting eyes. Another leave-taking. Soon, the current moment—when I'm experiencing the warmth of flourishing in this place—will pass, overshadowed by the feeling of impending loss. *Would living in a state of perpetual leave-taking be a healthy lifestyle? How would it look to always be suspended between love and longing?* Only a traveller who says "farewell" daily can understand how leave-taking stirs up complex feelings of the grief of separation mixed with the anticipation of future adventures.

"Where will you go now?" *Rosa* asked, taking *Glenda* from my arms.

The saw-toothed, cloud-enshrouded mountain range, vividly depicted in Yvon and Doug's essay in *Extreme Landscape,* resurfaced in my mind.

"Thanks for asking, *Rosa.* I want to climb a mountain called Fitz Roy. I read about it in a book. To do that, I need to travel to *El Chaltén* in *Argentina* where the trailheads are, and to do that I have to start from the bus depot in *Pucon,"* I said, naively assuming that crossing the border would be as easy as substituting *grosellas* for cranberries.

"Oh. *Inga*! *Pius*!" *Rosa* summoned a young couple. "You told me you are driving to *Pucon* today, could you give *Root* a ride, please?"

Rosa turned to me, "This way you can get to *Pucon* in fifteen minutes. The bus will take *mucho* longer."

Waving our goodbyes to *Rosa, Inga* and *Pius* and I departed together. A silent thankfulness enveloped me; their compliance with *Rosa's* request had granted me a reprieve from the rigidity of bus schedules.

Leaving the corner where *Inga* and *Pius* dropped me off, I merged into the flow of the bustling streets—the atmosphere buzzing with energy—toward the bus depot, counting eight groups of joggers, seven families lounging on the beach, and fourteen cyclists whose colour coordinated spandex outfits seemed painted onto their bodies—all expats. Two categories of people congregated in *Pucon*—the super fit and the super fat. In *Pucon*—a melting pot of expats and tourists—adventurers gathered, all drawn to the adrenaline-fuelled action of climbing volcanoes, white-water rafting, cave trekking, and vibrant nightlife in the bars. Here I blended in with the crowd. In *Villarrica,* being the only *gringa* and a tall one at that—the unusual one—I often had the opportunity to engage in intriguing conversations centred around vivid descriptions of my homeland, Canada, with locals. The tranquil ambiance of expat-free *Villarrica,* particularly during my peaceful walks along the grassy lake trails, held more appeal to me than the paved streets of commercialized *Pucon.*

Attempting to select the correct lineup at the depot, I dropped my heavy pack onto the floor beside my suitcase, and resumed my people watching, nudging my gear inch by inch toward the ticket booth with my foot.

Half an hour later, I slid my passport across the counter toward an attendant and said, "A ticket to *El Chaltén, Argentina,* please."

The employee lowered her eyes, flipping open all its pages.

"This is the first passport from Canada I have seen this week. But I'm so sorry. Canadians, Americans, and Australians must pay a CAD 100 reciprocity fee on top of the ticket price," said the woman in thickly accented English. A stream of sweat trickled down her forehead into her black eyebrows.

"Why?" *Is she sweating because of the heat or because of the unfamiliar situation she has found herself in?*

"It is because these countries charge Argentinians to visit them," she said.

That's not very nice of us nice Canadians.

"Sounds reasonable enough. Can I pay the fee right here, right now?"

"No." Her accented voice, already hard to understand, blended in with the cacophony of trekkers shouting and talking around me.

"Did you say no?!"

"*Si,* first you have to fill in this form online, print it, and bring it back here," she said. She wrote the government website address on a sticky piece of scrap paper and slid it across the counter to me.

"Couldn't you print out the form for me here?" I asked.

In answer, she raised her eyebrows and pointed to the lines of adventurers standing, walking, directing, laughing throughout the entire small depot.

Perhaps an aide at the Tourist Information Centre can assist me. Hefting my pack onto my back, I pulled my suitcase to the Centre.

"We do not allow trekkers to use our printers. I'm sorry but this would take too much time, and we are too busy. May I help the next person please?" the young man behind the counter told me.

Seated on a bench outside the Centre, I connected my phone to the Wi-Fi and reached into my pocket to pull out the note the woman at the bus depot had given me. Squinting at the tiny screen, I struggled to enlarge the form fields, determined to complete the task on my device. But upon reaching the payment section and finding only "credit card" as an option, I hit a roadblock. Selecting it would be impossible without my CVV number. Remembering past challenges in *Mexico,* I decided to call my Canadian bank for assistance. Not wanting to risk rejection from the Centre again, I lugged my gear to the nearest hostel, joining the queue behind two athletic teenage girls.

"Do you have an international phone I could use for a few minutes?" I asked the harried-looking hostel clerk.

"I am sorry, we don't have one," she said. She veered to the next person in line.

Is this merely an unfortunate turn of events, or something more? Ever since I landed in Santiago, I've slowly been wandering south, toward fulfilling my dream of climbing Fitz Roy. I must find a way. Travelling to El Chaltén should have been simple. What can I do if I can't get into Argentina?

"May I please leave my gear behind the counter for a couple of hours?" I asked the clerk. "Thanks."

In that pivotal moment, reality crashed in on me: no random guesses could correctly combine the elusive three digits for my CVV number; no crumpled reciprocity fee form a frustrated trekker had discarded would show up in a garbage can. My dream of conquering Fitz Roy—nurtured for so long—shattered.

Freed from the weight of my gear, I walked away from the source of my frustration, moving my feet with no destination in mind, only the desire to find a place to think. Angling across roads between traffic, I strolled up a tree-lined lane where I spotted a sign. *Santa Clara Convent. The perfect place to meditate.* The path leading to the convent—with its uneven stairs and overarching leafy boughs—took me farther from the city's bustle, closer to a sanctuary of serenity where I could unravel my thoughts. The top stair brought me face-to-face with two massive marble feet. Raising my gaze, I encountered a magnificently larger-than-life white marble statue of Mother Mary, gracefully poised, with her arms resting at her sides. From her pedestal in front of a modest, stormy-grey building crowned with a tin cross, her holy face surveyed the *Pucon River.* The open door of the chapel beckoned, tempting me to step inside, where I slipped into a seat in hushed anticipation, careful not to disrupt the sacred stillness of the empty house of worship. However, the unattainable prospect of venturing into *Argentina* felt like a firmly shut door.

My finger traced along the grain of the teakwood pew. The smell and feel of the wood reminded me of a similar church pew, and a little girl with auburn ringlets bouncing beneath a pink-ribboned hat. A tall man clad in a flowing, white robe—he resembled the Jesus I'd seen in my picture Bible—stood at the front of the church repeating words I knew well, but whose meaning I couldn't grasp. "It is meet and right and our abounden duty. Be sure your sins will find you out. Thou shalt. Thou shalt not." Those words had stayed with me; those words defined my intense sense of Christian duty; those words shaped the way I expressed my faith. My Bible taught me to be good-natured, let others win, be patient, be agreeable, to live well so God would love me: this is the honourable style of the Christian. Yet, when I had left home at seventeen, I left the church and my Bible far behind for four years.

Maybe I'm an idealistic, save-the-world, pie-in-the-sky visionary who thought she could rescue Leah yet didn't deserve to see that goal come true. Does God still have an obligation to help me pay my reciprocity fee? I don't think so, no matter my elevated level of guilt over my past sins of walking away from him for four years. Is God punishing me by blocking me from fulfilling my dream to get to Fitz Roy? If I haven't done what God expects of me, why should God do what I expect him to do? A sick feeling churned in my stomach. My sins had found me out. *God, why are you treating me like the Israelites in the desert?* When they had misbehaved, the God of retributive justice struck with a heavy hand.

My fingers rested on the smooth teakwood. Gradually I became aware of someone watching me. A cautious glance to my left revealed a smaller statuette, depicting Mother Mary cradling the infant Jesus—their creamy-alabaster features glowing with a divine quiescence, their cheeks touching, the folds of Mary's robe swathing their bodies.

"Can both of you please forgive me? And I have a question. How can I pay this reciprocity fee?" I whispered to her.

"Let it go." The phrase surfaced in my consciousness—as though God had spoken to my spirit—giving me the answer I sought.

Let it go? But now is when I still have time before my tenure at The Lodge begins. Now is the time for Fitz Roy. Or never.

In the silence of the chapel, the words of a fellow traveller in *Villarrica* whispered to me. "*Puerto Montt.*" She had told me *Puerto Montt* was en route to *Puerto Natales,* the place where athletes congregate to trek in the *Torres del Paine* mountains of southern *Chile*—less romantically known in English as the Towers of Blue. At that moment, with the strains of *Feeling Groovy* playing in my head, I decided that trekking the *Torres* would embody my personal transformation. The promise of a brighter future—as sure as the sunshine after the rain—beckoned me forward. To the *Torres* then!

Kissing both Mary and Jesus on the cheek, I thanked them, then skipped out of the chapel, jumped down the stone steps two at a time, collected my gear from the hostel, and ran to the bus depot.

"A one-way ticket to *Puerto Montt* please," I said to the clerk.

"No more *Argentina*?"

"You're right, this gal can't travel to *Argentina* now. But she can travel in *Chile,*" I said, waving my ticket at her as I trotted toward the bus lineup.

CHAPTER 8

"W" for Adventure: Puerto Natales and beyond

THE BUS RUMBLED ALONG, TRANSPORTING ME FROM *PUCON* IN THE *Lakelands* of *Chile* to *Puerto Montt* in the belly button of *Chile*. Vast rows of freshly harvested bales of hay in the rolling pastureland transitioned to screaming seagulls pirouetting above the blue expanse of the South Pacific Ocean. Lively waves crashed into cliffs topped with green trees. Within five hours, fish-flavoured salty air had replaced the "duck hunting season is pending" smell in *Pucon*'s air.

In late December, the Northern Hemisphere has yet to awaken. Wildflowers have yet to pop up through the cold earth, grass hasn't taken on the colour of life, and birds haven't returned to nest. Existing in the upside-down seasons of the Southern Hemisphere made me feel like the kid who used to hang upside-down on the monkey bars my dad built. During my lengthy journey, my mind took a sombre turn, spiralling into depths of contemplation. *Was chasing the Torres, based on a stranger's words, unrealistic? Will I achieve this goal in a place where everything is new daily?* Such questions once tethered me to fear; but now I needed to see them as opportunities, leading me away from a life once ruled by uncertainty. Each passing kilometre distanced me from my old patterns and marked my entrance into a world erupting with unexplored possibilities.

Stepping off the bus onto the teeming streets of *Puerto Montt*, I stepped away from my reverie. While walking toward the Information Centre, I gazed upward at a giant plaster-cast man and woman, sitting hand in hand on a larger-than-life bench mounted on a six-foot-high concrete platform, grinning as though they had just finished dancing a tango. For a moment, their motionless eyes caused me to yearn for that special man to hold my hand, or at least carry my luggage. Hundreds of families meandered along the width of the sea wall, while their hyperactive children raced around each other. The eternal dialogue between waves and cliffs provided a rhythmic backdrop. Behind me bumped my tightly packed suitcase with the worn-down, rapidly disappearing wheels. My equally bulging backpack felt heavier with every step I took.

"*Señora*, getting to *Torres del Paine*—it is very complicated," the young, long-haired, English-speaking *Chilena* at the Centre explained. Placing her map of *Chile* on the counter—carefully smoothing its folds—she marked potential routes with a red highlighter, each line representing a different outcome.

"First you must take the ferry to *Puerto Chacabuco*. Then you take the bus to *Puerto Natales*. Or you can fly from here."

I hesitated, my thoughts tangling. *Should I choose the faster flight or the slower-paced, scenic bus-and-ferry route? I imagined my suitcase and pack, weighing more than my canoe, causing the small Cessna I might board to nosedive into the ocean. Opting for the land-and-water combination would align more with my desire for grand adventures and personal growth—as well as result in sleep deprivation.*

"The ferry sounds good to me," I said to the attendant, making a decision that would lead to an encounter that would prove pivotal to my travel plans.

She pointed me toward the ferry office, her well-wishes carrying the warmth of the *Chilean* hospitality I'd come to cherish. Backtracking along the sea wall, I located the office. The door clanged shut behind me. A female clerk and a couple standing at her desk talked and gestured loudly. As I studied the ferry routes poster, I noticed that the woman occupying the other desk seemed oblivious to my presence. As I waited, uncertainty crept in. *Is choosing the longer route foolish?* I approached her desk. The graceful, delicate-featured attendant folded a fluorescent pink sheet of thin cardstock into an equally delicate paper crane and reached for a peppermint green sheet, a look of intense concentration on her face.

No, I must have left it at home, I thought, checking to see if I'd put on my cloak of invisibility.

Stacks of cranes in multitudes of bright colours covered her entire desk! *I am learning to appreciate the slower pace of life that Chilenos embrace,* I repeated several times. My impatience with Leah had long since melted into nothingness. *In my new life, I look for the joy instead of getting frustrated. I can wait. The adventure is already beginning.* The clerk's dedication to folding cranes intrigued me. Her focused, methodical creasing and bending took me back to the days when my children made paper cranes for school projects, which had taught us all patience and persistence. Scanning the other prospective ferry takers, I noted that several couples lounged in chairs and two families with adult daughters stood near the window, engrossed in conversations. *They don't mind waiting either.*

I cleared my throat. The clerk noticed my interest in her task, and she said, "I must make 1000 cranes because I make a mistake with someone I love. If I make all these cranes, he will forgive me and come back to me."

Maybe that's true in the Southern Hemisphere. Still forgiveness is a worthy goal.

"Could you please remind me how to make one?" I asked. "My kids used to make these origami cranes in school."

Others in the office asked technical questions about the ferry and our destination, but I pulled up a chair and sat in front of the spurned lover. She demonstrated, I folded, and before long I held a miniature ocean blue paper crane up for her approval.

"Beautiful, you are a natural," she said. "Please keep it."

"Thank you. I admire your dedication," I said, flattening my crane, and carefully placing it in my wallet.

"Oh, and by the way, I would like to buy a ticket for the overnight ferry to *Puerto Chacabuco,* please."

By the time the clerk found her ticket forms under her mound of cranes, and processed my payment, I could honestly say I appreciated the *Chilenos* slower pace of life.

She handed me my ticket, waved goodbye, and said, "Now I only have 934 cranes left to make!"

Over the next twenty-four hours, I concluded that ferry travel is far superior to flying. The huge white ferry swallowed up hundreds of ethnically and economically diverse people and turned its levels into a floating micro-city, gifting me plenty of time to chat with many fellow travellers. Gazing at the fjords from the upper deck, I marvelled at how the steep valleys once filled with glacial ice now trapped blue-green water between tree-crowned cliffs. They reminded me so much of the Stave Estuary near my home. I pictured myself gliding through these waters in the S. S. Stallard, enveloped in a seascape shaped by God's hand.

Leaving the ferry's transient community, I boarded the bus to *Puerto Natales,* and in an isolated seat began a journey marked by deep sleeps and fleeting glimpses of oceanscapes. Many hours later, with rain streaking down the bus windows, I squinted my eyes to peer through the tiny hole I'd wiped in the condensation. I couldn't decide whether the first snows of early winter had salted the mountain tips or whether the white patches belonged to the mass of sodden clouds hanging depressingly over the peaks surrounding *Puerto Natales,* a port town cradled near a network of fjords watered by the South Pacific Ocean. Three short steps down took me from the muggy warmth of the bus into bone-chilling rain falling in sheets. The breeze from the ocean fjord that defined half the boundary of the town tossed crispy brown leaves through the air, rippled across flat grasslands, and made me shiver as I realized that any season here could bring chilly weather. *If I believe that all travellers can control how long frigid autumn weather should last, that means I can escape from the chilly south to the warmer northern climes anytime I want.*

Relying on the recommendation of *Milovan*—a fellow traveller I'd met on the bus—I scoured the area in pursuit of the hostel with an urgency I wouldn't have if I'd arrived near the 52nd parallel south of the equator in the morning, instead of at sundown. *I am incredibly close to the southernmost tip of Chile!*

"What were you thinking, *Milovan*?" I questioned aloud, dropping my luggage with a thud while I surveyed my hostel room.

Each of the four narrow beds crammed into the dingy, gloomy, and dirty space looked equally unappealing. Avoiding the kitchen, where stacks of unwashed dishes and a collection of mismatched, unwashed tables stood, I stepped through the common area, searching for the receptionist. In the hall, I passed a seedy-looking smoker, his stooped silhouette blurred in the noxious blue clouds he exhaled. Communicating with the attendant—her form slumped in a dark nook—proved as futile as conversing with a Martian. Resigned to the room's dust and despair, and focused on both the hostel's and the town's shortcomings, and bone weary, I fell asleep atop the bedspread, planning my escape to somewhere better with the first light of day.

At dawn, I left. Just beyond the bay, I encountered a figure from a bygone era—a statue of a *Mylodon*. This prehistoric giant, rearing startlingly at the town's entrance, seemed to say, "Welcome to *Puerto Natales*." Later, in a local museum, I would find an exhibit on the *Mylodon Darwini*. I learned this herbivore, a curious blend of long fur and armadillo-like scales, had once roamed through *Patagonia* during the Pleistocene age. The display described it as a "robust sloth," but I would have described it as an enormous grizzly bear crossed with a tortoise.

Rounding a corner two blocks from *Mylodon*, I spotted a small house redesigned as a hostel, with a large sign hanging above the door—*Casa Lili. Will this place be any better?* When I stepped inside, a rush of bright, warm, aromatic air enveloped me. The contrast to the cold damp morning spoke to me that I'd stumbled upon my new temporary home base. I'd just begun to unload the contents of my suitcase onto my bunk, when the captivating rhythm of a Spanish guitar lured me into the sunny communal space. A *Chileno* pulled his harmonica from his shirt pocket, his music blending with a *Brazilian's* guitar samba—they crafted a cultural symphony that threaded through the room.

"Take a seat and let our *música* revive you," said the guitarist, in accented words as rhythmic as the movement of his fingers, drawing me closer into their group. He pointed to the couch with his chin.

My knees buckled into the warmth and softness of the couch. At first, the surge of energetic tunes seemed too intense for my travel-worn spirit; but, gradually, the notes filled my exhausted void with vibrant energy and a sense of belonging. The harmonious sounds brought back exhilarating memories of the Latino music that accompanied my first and only tango upon my arrival in *Santiago*. A ponytailed woman danced a tango with a ponytailed man, striding sinuously between coffee tables and couches. The entrancing beat wrapped around me, energizing me, compelling my still-frozen hands to clap, my hips to sway, and my aching feet to tap with the rhythm. Each accented voice, including mine, blended with the musical melodies—our stories and laughter intertwined, speaking to me of how shared human experience transcends language and culture. Their international jam session elevated my impression of this deep southern coastal town. An hour—or could it have been two hours?—later, I sought my bunk—Hatchi's reassuring softness warming my cheek on my pillow—and my mind drifted downward through the blur of the last few days; I closed my eyes, and slept.

On my second day waking in the picturesque little coastal town of *Puerto Natales,* while eating my morning porridge, I enjoyed watching three trekking enthusiasts—all young enough to be my children—engaged in an energetic discussion in front of a topographical map covering the entire kitchen wall. The warmth of the room, filled with excited voices—loud, and in numerous dialects—plus the odours of sweat mingled with bacon, created an atmosphere rich with life.

After my last swallow, I peered through the maze of bodies, trying to study the map from my rickety chair at the hefty, square oak table. Four long narrow lakes in light blue formed the base of the map: the three lakes on the east side lay east-west; the lake on the west lay north-south. The dark-blue background showed a trekking route in a yellow, dashed line to the north of the lakes, following the contour of a mountain range. Studying all the waterways reminded me of my solitary times on the reversing tidal Stave River, where observing nature's resilience had always inspired me.

Maybe these kids can help me choose a mountain to climb.

Deciding to seek the young trekkers' guidance, I pushed back my chair, left my bowl next to my laptop on the table, approached the group—where multiple fingers danced across the map, pointing at assorted destinations—and introduced myself.

"Ah, *Chica,* good morning," said *Amelia,* "Tomorrow is New Year's Day. A good resolution is to trek the 'W' at *Torres del Paine.* Is beautiful."

Tall and freckled, with a thick Ukrainian accent, *Amelia* stood out in the group. Her long, auburn braids hung below a woollen toque, while her eclectic multi-coloured sweater exuded a charm that reminded me of my fellow draftsmen's quirky traditions at DC Holdings, bringing back memories of our "ugly sweater days." The way she'd already picked up the local slang for "sweetheart"—*Chica*—spoke to me of her easygoing nature.

Tomorrow is New Year's Day? This is the last day of 2015? Unbelievable! Although New Year's Day does usually follow close on the heels of Christmas!

"What does 'W' stand for?" I asked.

"Let me explain," said *Lucas,* stray black hairs from his man-bun springing out in all directions, his large, navy rectangular glasses reflecting light from the kitchen window. "See this dot?"

He pointed to a yellow circle on the east side of the map, north of a lake with an exceptionally long name.

"You start the trek here at the *Torres Norte* base, then hike west along the lake, take the trail north up the French Valley, then back down along the southern edge of the mountain range to *Paine Grande,* then north to *Grey Glacier,*" he said, tracing the "W" shaped route with his forefinger.

"Can you complete that in one day? Do you think I could I really do this?" I asked. A surge of daring washed over me as the thrill of the challenge ignited my passion.

All three of them laughed at me.

"Oh, no," said a woman named *Miko. Miko,* whose face could easily grace the silver screens of Japan, defied the typical image of a Civil Engineer. Her hair—a riot of colours—and her kaleidoscopic-patterned outfit, reflecting her vibrant spirit, were all packaged in a frame tiny enough to tuck under my arm.

"One day? That would be quite the engineering marvel! It took us five days to complete the trek. The planned route demands endurance and careful pacing," she continued.

"Five days!? What I envision is doing one trek on one mountain in one day and coming back to sleep in my room down the hall," I said, the impossible challenge deflating my spirit. Memories of my desk-bound days clashed with their contagious atmosphere of adventure.

"Perhaps you like to do the 'O.' It make big loop. It start and end at *Torres.* You have to pack all you food and camp outside for ten days," teased *Amelia.*

"You are *Jubilada,* no?" asked *Lucas.*

"I'm what?" I asked.

"*Jubilada* is the Spanish word for retired woman," he said. "A word encompassing joy and freedom and jubilation. From a medical perspective, the word suggests concluding work and beginning a new, life-giving lifestyle. I believe you have the inner strength required for such a trek. It's a chance to embrace the majestic beauty of nature. Trust me, the therapeutic benefits are remarkable. Trekking together teaches us to be better persons; you must cooperate as a team to survive."

"I love the sound of that word. *Jubilada*! I'll always remember it. Thanks, *Lucas.*"

"Before coming here, my days revolved around a computer screen," I said, addressing all of them. "Sure, I'd canoe after work or hike in the mountains on weekends, but I didn't build up much strength. Now, as I've been travelling, long hours on buses have been making my tummy bulge instead of tightening. The concept of trekking for five days straight appears daunting. I doubt I possess the stamina required. Also, the thought of sleeping out in the wilderness unnerves me. And then what about tents, food, supplies, and other gear—none of which I currently own? How do I even begin to prepare for such an adventure?"

Looking into each youthful face—each one having completed the "W," I wondered how they could possess so much energy.

"You no need any tents for the 'W.' You stay in *Refugios,*" said *Amelia.*

"What is a *Refugio*?" *Sounds like the cities of refuge for criminals I'd read about in the Bible.*

"A *Refugio* is a lodge incorporating showers, and bunk beds, and a cafeteria. Similar to this facility," said *Lucas.*

Gazing through the misted window, where windswept trees danced wildly, I voiced my doubts, "I've been here for two days, and the rain hasn't stopped. Hiking in the rain doesn't sound like much fun."

"If you desire seeing all the colours of a rainbow, you must hike in the rain," said *Miko.*

"How long will it take me to prepare my out-of-shape body?" I said, turning back to the group, determination beginning to replace doubt.

Miko said, "Check out my ectomorphic body type, and I did it. Without any push-ups or dead-lifts."

Three eager faces looked expectantly at me. Observing their faces, I saw a reflection of my past self, the one who had taken in Leah, only to fail. But this time I would choose for myself, stepping into the wild for the joy of discovery. Deciding to trek would propel me into the unknown; away from my burdened past, toward a future filled with love, healing, and new-found freedom.

"Well?" asked *Amelia.*

"Do you really think I can complete the 'W' trek?" I stalled, pondering, the weight of my pending decision—heavy, yet exciting.

Lucas, catching my gaze, shared from his heart. "In these mountains, *Root,* you will expand your consciousness and improve your physicality. I know. I am a medical doctor from *Brazil.* I put my practice on hold for a year after a challenging surgery because I realized that to save lives, I needed to provide myself with life-giving time to travel, to explore both my internal fabric and South America's external landscape."

Lucas, whom I initially mistook for a young hostel employee in that tank top, shorts, and bare feet, astonished me when he revealed his profession. How hard this intuitive young man must have struggled to harness his wanderlust during those seven grueling years of medical school. His steady hands, now tracing trails on the map, spoke to me of the sacrifices he had made and the depth of his dedication to saving and living life.

They all nodded.

The allure of Fitz Roy, the dream that set me on this path, still calls to me, but a five-day trek through the Torres del Paine offers me an alternative to the sting of an unmet goal. Reflecting on those days when I'd once been shackled to my home office computer and imprisoned by imagined fears of an unsafe, scary, and unfriendly world, I knew I'd been wrong. My journey constantly revealed to me a world brimming with kindness, wonder, and fellowship.

"All right, I'll do it. I WILL climb the *Torres!* But only the 'W.' I'm ready for this journey," I finally said, a mix of panic and excitement bubbling inside me.

Three sets of high fives—resounding throughout the kitchen—along with three sets of enveloping hugs, felt like a warm tide washing over me, affirming my decision. Joy burst within my spirit.

When the others left, *Lucas* said, "*Root,* never forget that we are alive to live. This trek will help you to rediscover the value of life."

He bowed his head, placed his right hand under my right hand, then put his left hand on top of both of ours, and continued, "Beauty is within your reach for free. Blessings on your life, *Señora.*"

I am blessed! Especially to have met such a spiritual and gifted man.

Lucas and I parted; and as I lugged my laptop and porridge bowl into the kitchen, each step felt lighter, filled with a new-found purpose. Now certain that the sun would soon shine again, I hummed a happy tune. *How hard can it be?*

In the early light of Friday morning, *Marcela,* the owner of *Casa Lili,* and I stood facing each other across a makeshift reception counter, situated within a cozy former bedroom.

"Before you commence your *Torres del Paine* trek, you must book your

Refugios," *Marcela* began. "This will determine when you can leave. The treks start on a Monday and end on a Friday. A bus will take you from here to the *Torres Norte* trailhead, then you ride a ferry from *Paine Grande,* then bus back here. The 'W' trail has four *Refugios.* These are first-class accommodations with hostel-style rooms and restaurants."

"Can I book my tickets through you?" I asked. *Today being Thursday, I could be on the trails in three days!*

She laughed.

"No, no. Two separate agencies manage reservations. *Fantastico Sur* handles *Torres Norte* and *Cuernos,* and *Vertice* handles *Paine Grande* and *Grey.* The *Vertice* office is three blocks that way, so I suggest you start there. It will take some time."

"Sounds complicated to me. Why don't they just have all four bookings available through one agency?" I asked.

"You are in *Chile,*" she said.

Stepping outside after *Marcela*'s briefing, the tasks necessary for Monday departure hung heavily on me. My first of two goals for the day: buy a range of gear for *Patagonia*'s unpredictable weather. In a wool-scented shop bustling with trekkers, I bought a toque, mitts, a yellow raincoat, and black rain pants. Amidst the crowd, sharing smiles, and trying on "*Torres* approved" attire, I felt a kinship, as though I'd become part of an international tribe of outdoor enthusiasts.

When I passed a *Patagonia* store, I read the English sign near the door identifying the flagship store Yvon Chouinard and Doug Tompkins had established. But my hand, weighed down by my heavy heart, couldn't reach for the door. Seeing Yvon and Doug's names reminded me of my inability to travel to *Argentina* to climb Fitz Roy. *Yet, sacrificing that dream will teach me to find beauty and challenges wherever I travel. Trekking a mountain range similar to the majestic Fitz Roy offers me a solace I find appealing. I shall embrace this journey and prepare for this unforeseen adventure. I have enough gear. Keep walking.*

Carrying bags full of my new clothing, I turned my attention to my second goal: to book my first two nights at *Vertice,* the agency closest to *Casa Lili.* By the time I navigated my way along the streets near the coastline framed by the mountains, where the water lapped against the pilings of a pier, to *Vertice,* a locked door cluttered with signs greeted me. *Seriously?*

How can they be closed, it's only eleven o'clock? I studied the notices, hoping to find out when they would reopen. *Such a curious thing! Spanish uses the same letters English does, but they're arranged in patterns that don't make the least bit of sense to me.*

Beginning to grasp *Marcela*'s words, I wondered if I felt thwarted because of how *Chilenos* operated or if I felt divine retribution opposing me again—revealing my sins. *I should have gone to Vertice before I shopped.*

Back at *Casa Lili,* I asked *Marcela,* "What are *Vertice's* hours?"

"They are only open until noon on Fridays, but they will be open *mañana,* tomorrow is the best day to get things done in *Chile* anyways."

All night I slept fitfully, but once I heard my fellow trekkers stirring early Saturday morning, I leaped out of my bunk, ready to tackle the day's challenges.

My sole mission for that cloudy Saturday: reserve all four nights at my *Refugios.*

Vertice is open, what a pleasant surprise. The travel adventure company's open door seemed to spell success.

"We have beds at *Paine Grande* and *Grey* available Wednesday and Thursday. Unless you want to start at *Grey* and end at *Torres Norte.* Then we could book you for Monday and Tuesday," said the young clerk with jet-black hair swept up in a severe bun.

"No, I want to start at *Torres Norte,* so could I tentatively reserve Wednesday and Thursday nights, please?"

"No, I am unable to do that. First you must go to *Fantastico Sur,* make sure they have Monday and Tuesday free, and reserve your nights at *Torres Norte* and *Cuernos* there. Then come back here, show us your receipts for those nights, and I can then book Wednesday and Thursday for you."

"Really?" I asked, thinking she might be joking. Her face displayed not a glint of humour. "Well, um... all right then, so how far away is *Fantastico Sur* from here?"

"Just four blocks that way and three to the left. And *Señora,* we close at noon. And we open again Monday morning."

At ten thirty I arrived at *Fantastico Sur,* which misled me into believing I had received a good omen.

At *Fantastico Sur,* a wave of confusion washed over me because of language barriers, unavailable dates, and an uncooperative debit card.

An unusually tall, competent-looking man finally sorted out my concerns. "Now do you want bedding on your bed?" he asked.

"Um, well, yes, sure, that would be nice."

"Okay, bedding. Okay, yes. Now do you want to pay for your meals ahead of time?"

Do I look like a foraging animal that eats bark and roots? How many more questions?

"Yes," I said, "But wait, what are my other choices for food?" Given my peanut allergy, I normally took extreme care in selecting what to consume.

"You can pack in your own, or you can buy snacks when you are at the *Refugios*," he said.

Once we finally completed my bookings—clutching my priceless receipts—I returned to *Vertice* at 11:58, my lungs constricting and my calves aching.

My efficient clerk looked up briefly as I burst through the door, then resumed tidying her desk and told me, "Sorry, we are closed."

"What do you mean!? You are closed? I have my receipts from... *Fantastico Sur* for Monday night at *Torres Norte*... and *Tuesday* night at *Cuernos*," I could barely breathe the words past my lips.

"We will be open again Monday at nine," she most pleasantly said.

"But I leave on Monday..." I said as she walked me to the door and politely shut it in my face.

My heart sank. Returning to *Casa Lili*, I couldn't shake the mental images: seeking refuge beneath the starlit sky, my backpack doubling as a pillow, scrounging for sustenance under the river rocks. But the thought of braving puma territory alone overnight, unprotected, weighed most heavily on my mind. Oddly, wisdom from my Al-Anon days resurfaced to help me piece together this logistical jigsaw. During the years I had lived in an alcoholic marriage, I had met a friend in church who had told me about Al-Anon, the twelve-step program for spouses of alcoholics. She and I held secret phone meetings while the children slept and my ex-husband was away, as I didn't want to leave them with him or a sitter to attend public meetings. I had learned that I, too, was sick, and unable to change him, and that only with a higher power's help could I change myself. Just as those teachings had guided me through the storms of my past life, they now offered a wisdom I could apply to my current tumult. Once again, I repeated those wise words: "God grant me the serenity to accept the things I cannot change."

I know I might not get rooms for the nights at Paine Grande and Grey, too. So, I can't change it now; but I can change the way I'm reacting, so this would be a suitable time to let go and let God. And eat a big lunch.

"What's wrong, *Chica*? I thought you'd be excited when you came back; instead, your face looks blacker than a country teapot," said *Marcela* from her reception desk at *Casa Lili.*

After explaining to her that I had only succeeded in reserving my first two nights, I said, "I'm giving up. I don't want to risk having to sleep under the stars for two nights. I'll stay here for another week, sell my tickets to a fellow trekker, or attempt to get a refund from *Fantastico Sur*—if that is possible. Then I'd have time to book all four nights for the following week."

"This is not a problem," *Marcela* said, understanding my turmoil. "Many trekkers, and I also, have had such frustrations. The process is *muy complicado,* a test of your resolve, *Chica.* Go this Monday as you planned. When you arrive at *Cuernos,* ask them to phone ahead to *Paine Grande* and they will reserve a place for you. It is low season now because winter is coming. No problem."

"You're right, I can't let these logistical snags change my plans. That sounds like a satisfactory solution. I would rather leave this Monday now that I'm enthused to go. Okay, thanks, that's what I'll do."

Little did I know that the following week would only be "no problem" for *Marcela.*

The next day, in search of earrings for my daughters, I entered a store displaying crystals, jewelry, hand-blown glass, and bright paintings in the windows. The blended aroma of coffee and cinnamon buns added to its eclectic charm. Once inside, the bustling world outside faded away, replaced by a realm of artistic wonder. A freckle-faced young woman with frizzy curls peeking out from under a hand-knit toque greeted me.

"You are looking for earrings, ma'am; we have some funkier ones over here," she said. Her distinct European, not *Chilena,* accent confused me.

"Thanks, I'll have a look. Just curious, what is your heritage?" I asked.

"My home country is Poland. I am *Anya,* a pleasure to meet you."

"Hi, I'm Ruth. How does a young gal like you end up working in *Chile*? I always love to hear people's story."

"Ah yes, customers will ask me this. Before I left Poland and the ordinary life, I was a draftsperson. About six years ago, I worked at a horse ranch in Canada. This is where you are from, no? Now I prefer to ride motorcycles, they always go in the direction you want them to. A few years ago, while I was hitchhiking in *Chile,* a kind man named *Rodrigo* picked me up. This is our shop, and we live in the back."

My ears perked up, "You were a draftsperson? So am I." Our careers, along with our shared passion for horses and motorcycles, forged a bond between us, making us instant friends.

"Come to the back of my shop, I have something to show you," she said, her tone promising secrets yet to be unveiled.

Has she forgotten I'm a potential customer? A big sale could be slipping through her fingers. Intrigued, I followed her, each step revealing more of the shop's creative treasures. She stopped behind an easel set up on a table. Paint pots, paintbrushes, canvas, and driftwood covered every inch of the table's surface. She showed me canvases splashed with brilliant colours, beautiful flowers not found in Canada, and exotic birds also not found in Canada.

"Wow, I thought we draftspeople could only draw straight lines. You are so talented."

"Believe it or not, I just picked up a paintbrush since I've been in *Chile,*" *Anya* said.

I believed her. At this point in my travels, I easily understood how the bountiful beauty of *Chile* could draw the artist out of even a draftsperson; we whose primary skills lay in technical drawing rather than artistic explorations.

I noted with surprise how the entire afternoon had vanished in *Anya's* captivating world. After sipping jasmine tea and eating dried *Calafaté* berries with her, *Rodrigo* challenged me to a game of chess which we played on a creamy-tan wood board with four-centimetre-high roughly-carved wooden pieces; the Bishops were upright canoes, the Rooks were native men wearing headdresses, the Pawns were native women with long hair and headbands, the King and Queen were larger natives with headdresses, and the Knights were unicorns. Finally purchasing a pair of earrings made of blue jasper pendants with quartz gemstones, I made my way back to the hostel, savouring my unique shopping experience.

The noise level in the wee hostel kitchen area that evening grew in volume until I recognized that supper time approached, yet I wanted to complete my blog before I began preparing my meal, so I kept typing, trying to take up as little space as possible at the kitchen table. I'd nearly finished all my entries, thinking how anxious my fans would be to read my further adventures and marvel at my photos.

One voice, tinged with humour, rose above the cacophony of multiple languages.

Ramon, an imaginative athletic Spanish traveller I'd spoken with several times, pranced around the table with outspread "claws" above his head and his wide-open mouth showing his "fangs."

"I am a mutant of nature. My mother birthed a creature infected with the desire to travel. She just doesn't get me. I don't get her either," said *Ramon*.

When I looked up, I noticed that his antics had all the folks eating or preparing meals laughing—in stitches.

"I get you," I said. Sharing my story of solo travel at my advanced age had helped many a youthful trekker view their mothers in a fresh light. Among my fellow sojourners, I'd found my kindred spirits. The same goldy-green tones of the *Pampas* grasses and the blues-whites of the mountains that produced artists and attracted philosophers inspired me. Now I understood the desires associating me with a world of travellers. All my life I'd felt judged because I constantly desired a new job, a new place to live, or a new vacation destination. Among my work colleagues, I felt like the odd one out. While they were content to devote themselves to their professions year-round, I cherished the idea of a longer break, beyond the mere five-week summer holiday. As *Che Guevara* wrote in a book I once read, "We were always skimming the surface, never getting down to the roots." I totally understood *Ramon*'s lifestyle choice.

The way young people gravitated to me reminded me of how mosquitoes seek out bare flesh. No doubt rubbing shoulders with this "old" woman sparked their curiosity. And no wonder—I must have stood out in the same way a *guanaco* roaming the plains in Canada would stand out. Memories of when I'd first seen a herd of wild creatures that resembled an unusual blend of antelope agility and llama grace from a bus window surfaced. Curious, I'd asked my seatmate for an explanation.

"Those are *guanacos.* Notice their adorable black faces?" she had informed me, contrasting them with the smaller, white-faced *vicuñas,* which live at altitudes above 4000 feet. "They both belong to the camel family. One male *vicuña* has many females in his harem."

The woman behind us had spoken up, "That must be great for the male!"

The conversation took an unexpected turn when a man seated across the aisle had chimed in with, "Or it could be a nightmare!"

Laughter had erupted through the bus, creating a welcome moment of connection.

Ramon's exuberance lifted me from my reverie, when he bounded over to me and hugged me off my chair, "Will you adopt me?"

"*Si,*" I giggled, as he gave me the double-cheek kiss and trotted over to the gas stove.

Sluggishly, 320 pictures continued to upload to my blog. The sound of both *Ramon* and *Angel,* his Spanish travelling companion, chatting in Spanish and clanking dishes in the kitchen, provided soothing background music.

Ramon, who grinned from ear to ear, walked with minced steps toward me and said, "For you, *Mama Root.*"

Something smells so good. Snapping the laptop shut, I looked up at him. *My blog can wait.*

If he hadn't set a steaming plate of pasta smothered in a thin, lumpy tomato sauce onto the table, I would have thought he continued to joke around. He placed the plate in front of me with such a flourish that the sauce slopped onto the table where the dry wood—that appeared not to have been polished for years—soaked up every drop.

"You made this for me? Thank you so much!" I shook my head in wonder, settling back into my chair.

Angel followed him with three empty wine glasses in his hands, a dingy tea towel draped over his left arm, and a bottle of burgundy wine tucked under his right arm.

The three of us sat in familial company, clinking our glasses together, "To travel."

"*Lucas* told us about your 'W' trek, *Mama Root!*" *Ramon* said with a wink, "Going from a keyboard warrior to a wilderness warrior, *si*? You can do it!" He playfully nudged my shoulder, his eyes twinkling as he took an exaggeratedly large bite of pasta.

"Why, thank you for your confidence in me," I said. The sauce tasted delicious, yet the lumps were oddly crunchy.

"We are trekking the 'O,' leaving tomorrow," said *Ramon*. "The trail makes a big loop-de-loop starting and ending at *Torres Norte*. We pack all our food and camp under the stars for ten days. Are you sure you won't come with us?"

"I'm sure." We all helped ourselves to another serving of laughter.

I love being part of my new trekking tribe. These boys really make me feel like I'm accomplishing something special. They can't even begin to comprehend that I will treasure this moment as long as I live. Wonder had faded from my life—life had become too serious, too difficult. But in the depths of *Patagonia*, alongside folks like *Ramon* and *Angel*, I became aware anew of the joys and delights of life—a healthy life.

Conversations with *Ramon* and *Angel* still echoed in my ears as I stepped out alone to walk along the coastline in the cool evening air. Suddenly my stomach began to churn painfully, not from overeating, but with a familiar, dreadful unease. The back of my throat constricted, tingled; the inside of my mouth felt like sandpaper. A giant rubber band tightened around my neck and chest. Inhaling and exhaling took a Herculean effort. For the first time since I had eaten my "son's" tomato sauce, a sickening realization hit me. Initially, I refused to believe it. But as each laboured breath became a struggle and the tingle in my throat intensified, denial gave way to a paralyzing truth. Fear injected adrenaline into my bloodstream, not enough, however, to stop the reaction. As I stumbled away from the seawall, upsetting thoughts tumbled through my mind.

The crunchy sauce must have contained peanuts. No! How could I have been so careless? I'm face-to-face with my old arch-enemy—the peanut. My EpiPen is in my room about six blocks away by now. I should have brought it with me. Would a hospital here even treat me? Someone on a bus had told me Chilean mothers only feed their children peanuts after they're weaned, and Chile has a near-zero incidence of peanut allergies, so they wouldn't be skilled in treating an anaphylactic reaction. This is where I could die, alone in Chile. But I don't want to die, especially not now, before I even meet my grandchildren. What to do? Who can help me?

Gasping for air on the streets of *Puerto Natales*, overcome by nausea, and not wanting to make a smelly mess on a sidewalk, I bolted toward a section of lawn and with long, slow, wheezing inhales, I leaned forward and retched until my sides hurt. Unfortunately, dozens of cars barrelled down a main road right in front of me. Now I understood how humiliated homeless people must feel, forced to live all aspects of their lives out in the open. Perhaps a few passing motorists even mistook me for one of them. After I emptied my stomach contents onto that public piece of grass, my breathing eased, my stomach relaxed, and I felt grateful that the reaction had been mercifully mild; I knew the danger had passed. I meant to walk steadily, but my legs shook and my heart beat rapidly before I reached the consoling sturdiness of my bunk. Lying there, in a half-dreaming state, an old memory surfaced—a memory that had lain dormant until the night's scare unearthed it. It pulled me back through the years to a night in 1987, in a small trailer on the Bible College campus where a container of Thai food had nearly cost me my life. Relishing the idea of the free meal the cafeteria provided monthly for students, I opened the container. The excitement overshadowed my usual caution concerning my severe peanut allergy. After a few bites that familiar sense of my throat constricting preceded the wheezing as I struggled to breathe, and a wave of panic set in. Peanuts!

Fortunately, my neighbours were home, and they hurriedly drove me to the hospital. Lying in the white-sheeted bed, hooked up to monitors and receiving adrenaline, the gravity of my situation sank in. My brother had arrived within minutes, a look of inquiring concern on his face.

"I didn't check the free cafeteria food… for peanuts," I wheezed.

He sighed, exasperated. "Ruth, anaphylaxis is serious. You've got to be more careful. Your life isn't worth a free meal."

I nodded groggily, receiving his words. "I know, I promise to be more careful. Thank God I arrived here in time."

The memory faded into morning noisiness, leaving behind a renewed sense of gratitude for the life still pulsing through my veins. Sleeping longer than usually possible in the crowded rooms at *Casa Lili* restored me, I leaped out of my bunk on Sunday with a renewed sense of vitality. *I faced down my "kryptonite" and overcame. One by one, the fears that formerly plagued me are falling before me. Notes to self: always be wary of your personal kryptonite. And pay more attention to your friend Lesley's travelling tips for you—the 3 L's: lipstick, life jackets and life-giving EpiPen. My allergies, entangled with the fear of possible negative outcomes, can't rob me of the joy of travelling.*

To accomplish my first task of the day—to test the weight of my backpack—I filled every pouch and zippered compartment with all my necessities and hopes, then slung the loaded goliath over my shoulders. Attempting to step forward, I stumbled back four steps. Condensing my pack to the essentials, I tried again and managed to walk around the room.

Thank goodness I don't have to pack camping gear as well. Now I should be able to get out the door tomorrow morning. I should have exercised more before I left home. But I am committed—no turning back.

Late Sunday night, I crawled into my bunk and lay on my left side, and in a few seconds, rolled onto my right side. Jumping out of bed, I rearranged my pack out in the dark, cold hallway. Three times. The pelting *Patagonian* rain pounded a rhythm on the hostel's metal roof and the howling wind banged the metal eaves against the roof, echoing my restless thoughts and pounding heart. *Will sleep ever come? Am I truly prepared for what lies ahead?* Images of hiking in a deluge and a windstorm seeped into my fitful dreams.

Before Monday's sun rose, I gulped several cups of black tea, devoured some cheese and crackers, and tried to balance my trepidation with my excitement. Crossing the threshold of *Casa Lili,* in the dark, at 7:15 a.m., backpack slung over my shoulders, I took my first step into the unknown, one step deeper into the heart of *Patagonia*. Overnight, the wind had cleared the sky of clouds, revealing multitudes of stars that seemed to twinkle encouragingly, making me think of how the vastness of the universe dwarfed my fears. Reaching the bus depot at 8:00, I located the bus bound for *Torres del Paine* National Park and tripped up the stairs, heaved my pack into the upper luggage rack, and squished into my seat.

While the jumbo bus filled with at least 100 yawning *Torres del Paine* trekkers, I smiled at my reflection in the window. Sighing, I took a deep, cleansing breath, unaware that I would soon discover that *Marcela* had used those reassuring words "no problem" a little too freely.

CHAPTER 9

Wayfinding: Trekking in Torres del Paine

After a bone-rattling, two-hour, 120-kilometre bus ride, we arrived at the starting point for the *Torres del Paine* trek. What I had seen in the pre-dawn light of *Puerto Natales* as a dark, one-dimensional chalk line drawn across the distant horizon transformed outside my bus window into an up-close, three-dimensional panorama: vast olive-green meadows and woodland stretching to shattered, chiselled limestone peaks cutting into the heavens. Oh, the elation that surged through me at my first sight of the *Torres*! *From here my departure from civilization begins. I have the stamina to do this, I have the stamina to do this, I have the stamina to do this.* Only a few clouds remained from last night's rain, floating above the summits in a bounteous blue sky. The immense wildness of *Torres del Paine* National Park spread before us. Nothing *Lucas, Miko,* or *Amelia* had told me about the beauty prepared me for the thrill that galvanized me when my eyes swept across those fields and hills! The lofty crags and sheltered valleys beckoned me onward.

The bus driver screeched to a halt in the parking lot of the Park. The scent of distant pines and the ozone-infused smell of damp earth blew in through the open bus door. *Bring it on, I am Canadian; at least I know how to dress in layers.* The thermometer near the console read only +4 °C. The cold metallic railing stung my bare fingers as I stepped outside. Snow-covered peaks clawing for the highest place in the range transferred their icy energy into the wind tearing against my cheeks. Park attendants herded us into the Park Office where they collected their admission fee of 18000 *pesos* from every trekker. *All the businesses arising from this whole trekking scene are sure skilled at efficiently extracting money from us tourists. I've certainly noticed that each natural attraction in Chile has an attached fee.*

At 10:20 a.m., all 100 of us were seated in the Park Office, excited to watch our orientation video.

"Please, please do not hike alone here. Pumas are the only predatory species in this area and mothers with young can be especially dangerous. Always walk with a trekking buddy," the warden reiterated after the graphic presentation ended.

His cautionary words about pumas lingered in the air, reminding us of the unpredictability of wildlife and nature. He then directed us outside to wait for the *Torres Norte Refugio* shuttle bus. Most of my fellow wanderers exited the office in pairs or groups. As I proceeded to the parking lot, I scanned the trekkers standing alone, trying to identify a solitary soul whom I could outrun in the event of a puma attack. Back home among the hiking community, our little joke was that you didn't need to run faster than the bear, you just needed to run faster than your hiking partner. Therefore, I approached a flustered looking woman whose leather hikers shone, her un-frayed laces tied in perfect bows; no scuff or dust marred the beauty of those boots.

"Hey, hi. I notice that we have matching Canadian flags," I said, pointing to a decal sewn onto her lopsided pack with thick red-and-white threads.

"*Mais oui, mon ami.* I just left Montréal one week ago. I work at a desk all day, I'm an accountant. I decided that I needed a challenge, you understand what I mean, sometimes life gets so predictable. So, I googled 'best hikes in the world' and... *voila;* here I am."

"I think you are very brave," I said.

"I think I'm going to die."

After studying her fitness level, I knew she'd make a useful candidate to ramble with while in puma country—I knew her unbendable leather boots would give her painful blisters after her first few steps, ensuring that I could outrun her.

"Would you like to hike with me? I'm going to spend my first night at *Torres Norte Refugio.*"

"*Mais non.* I would love to, you look strong, but I plan to start from *Refugio Grey* and end at *Torres Norte. Au revoir, mon ami.*"

"*Au revoir,* and good luck to you," I said, watching her walk stiffly toward her shuttle bus, wondering if I could safely venture into these untamed landscapes alone. *I've come this far on my own, I can handle this too.* Resolved to embark on the trail solo, I hoisted my pack onto my back, and focused on how the solitude would allow me to savour each moment, to immerse myself in the keen beauty of *Patagonia,* pumas notwithstanding.

After a fifteen-minute ride on a shuttle bus, I spotted the *Torres Norte Refugio.* Partly hidden behind trees in full green leaf, the building looked large enough to accommodate hundreds of trekkers, and sturdy enough to keep out pumas. A blue roof, horizontal wooden slat exterior, and floor to ceiling windows rose above a disordered lawn that I surmised a herd of goats had mowed.

Beyond the glass door, a coffee-scented calm replaced the roar of the wind. As I stood by the parquet-style oak desk, I watched the clerk's fingers slide back and forth down the register, in search of my name. Every time she scrolled over a name, my heart sank lower. *Had I made a blunder in my booking? Or worse, ended up at the wrong Refugio?* Each time I repeated my name for her, my voice wavered.

While I waited, I set my blue-and-purple knapsack down on the patterned stone floor, careful to display the side with my Canadian flag to all passers-by. My backpacking community all assumed from my "accent" that I must be American; now all would know that this trekker proudly hailed from Canada. As time ticked by, snippets of conversation from fellow trekkers spoke of the day's remaining light, enough to allow for the eight-hour round trip to the *Torres* peak. Their words added to my inner tension.

Finally, I heard the clerk sigh in relief, and she said, "Oh. *Root*! Now I find you." She put a check mark by my name, then pointed down the hall to my dorm room.

Propping myself against my backpack, I placed Hatchi on my pillow, then sprawled across the lower bunk in the *Torres Norte Refugio.* Gratitude washed over me. *We have a place to sleep tonight, Hatchi!* The sight of the *Torres,* visible through the large open window, grounded me—like ancient titans forged of granite, they soared into the heavens. These spires, resembling three long dinosaur toes, pierced the azure sky, their grandeur dwarfing the valleys below where brown grasses swayed, and coniferous forests cloaked the bases of snow-covered rocks.

The once-empty dorm room buzzed with life as trekkers swarmed in to claim their bunks, their excited, multilingual chatter filling the air. Realizing this offered me another chance to locate a hiking buddy, I searched for a fellow wanderer. While I had recently battled my internal enemy, the peanut; now I faced the external threat of the puma. This contrast of threats—one fought within my own body, and the other lurking in the *Patagonian* wilderness—resonated with me. *I know I need to carry an EpiPen for my peanut allergy, and I'd like to find a partner to prevent me from becoming the one solo trekker who fulfills the warden's dire prophecy of a mercifully swift death-by-puma.* Pumas and peanuts had intensified my awareness of danger, yet both had brought me closer to understanding both my strength and the fragility of life, and instilled in me a deeper spiritual resilience.

My search for a trekking partner led me to pass on both a lively young woman, whose brisk tempo might challenge my own, and a seasoned gentleman, whose leisurely gait might slow my pace. *I think I am going solo. But—my past adventures have taught me the value of solitude—by travelling alone, I control my timing and my speed.* Leaving Hatchi guarding my backpack on my bunk, I laid claim to my personal space. Slinging my leather purse over my shoulder—filled with enough snacks and water to sustain me for the next eight hours—I set out alone, yet undaunted, and journeyed onto the path that beckoned me toward my first hike of the *Torres del Paine*!

Minutes later the throngs of eager hikers had thinned, leaving me to my thoughts. My sun-loving self would have preferred to keep walking out in the open pastures where long-maned horses grazed near bright red-and-white buildings, and to remain oriented to the sunny *Torres*; but within half an hour, the trail led into the verdant cathedral of deciduous and coniferous trees that prevented the daylight from filtering through to the ground. The low-hanging bough of a pine tree called down the wind with her thin moaning voice, and asked the wind to breathe movement into her branch until soft needles brushed my shoulder, as if to welcome me into the pine-family woodland. The well-trodden path beckoned, where, for centuries the wild things had travelled in search of water—the pumas and foxes, bold, sure-footed, silent; the deer, wide-eyed, curious, hesitant.

Suddenly, an agitated voice captured my attention after my fifteen minutes of pleasurable nature solitude. A woman, about my age, approached with a younger companion.

"What do you think you're doing hiking solo?" she asked.

These were the last words I understood as she transitioned into rapid-fire

Spanish—only the words "daughter," "doctor," and "hospital" were familiar. *Does she mean that her daughter needs to go to the hospital? The young woman looks fine, although perhaps they aren't mother and daughter. Maybe she's a doctor and wants to help me. Oh, how a common language could simplify communication.* After I heard the word *solo* again several times, I figured they—complete strangers—were conscious of my safety. The woman seemed driven by a protective instinct—perhaps she had seen other solo hikers underestimate the wilderness. I looked down into her eyes, unsure of how to assure her that I felt safe hiking alone. *Or do I really feel safe? I could feign ignorance and continue on my way, but that would hardly be courteous. I could attempt to answer her in Spanish, but I could inadvertently insult her.*

The silence hung between us as we stood face-to-face, until, on the trail behind me, the sound of rocks crunching and twigs snapping alerted me to the arrival of another fleet-footed youth intent on overtaking me.

Instead of passing us, however, the skinny rail of a man with less wispy blonde hair on his head than on his chin stopped, looking quizzically at us both. He, too, walked alone, and the woman quickly directed her advice to him. He appeared to understand her concern. *He's obviously not Chileno, but maybe he can help me.*

"I'm hiking with him," I indicated to her with sign language.

The newcomer understood both my words and my situation. He winked and agreed to play along. Despite the unexpected encounter with her, I felt a growing confidence in my ability to navigate the challenges of this foreign land.

They conversed in Spanish for some time, while I stood quietly, scuffing the pine-needle-carpeted underbrush with the toe of my hiker. Finally, the woman acquiesced, then she and her daughter left us in peace.

"Once we're out of her sight you can speed on down the trail," I said to the man, gesturing ahead to a bend in the footpath.

"Aye, no need. I'd love some company," he said. "G'day, I'm Peter from New Zealand. And you are?"

In walking with Peter—who slowed his pace to match mine—I found a surprising camaraderie. Our conversations, ranging from philosophy to the raw beauty around us, added a layer of richness to the trek that I hadn't anticipated.

"Sweet as! You are wearing the *Torres* on your tee," he said with a grin, as we distanced ourselves from the self-appointed enforcers of trail etiquette.

"Yes, I bought this T-shirt back when I stayed in *Villarrica*. Kind of a goal-setting thing," I said. The bright blue shirt displayed a vivid photograph of the unmistakable white *Torres* and the green *pampas* grasses.

"Right, soon we'll be here," he said as he pointed to an area near my neck.

We came out of the trees via a rickety wooden boardwalk with railings made of stripped logs, crossed a frothing creek, stopped to gaze up at a sky dotted with light-hearted popcorn clouds, then continued our conversation.

"Studied a bit of philosophy back home. Travelling out in the wild gives you heaps to ponder on, eh? I'm into this virtual gig, making educational animations. As long as I have Wi-Fi, I'm sorted. Advertisers on my website sign my paycheques. It's a beaut job, lets me roam wherever the wind takes me."

"For sure, that's a dream job. You're the second digital nomad I've met on this trip," I said.

"Yeah, nah. This life's a cracker, isn't it? Been tramping around South America for eight years now. It's choice, mate. And bonus; now I'm bilingual."

As much as I am enjoying all this changing scenery, I doubt if I could make a lifestyle of travel.

"You're amazing! Oh, look at that black bird with the huge wingspan thermalling along that cliff. I think it's a giant bald eagle," I said. The awkwardly proportioned black-and-white bird suggested function above form, but the way the creature soared gave it a grace not even the bald eagles back home possessed.

"Ah, welcome to *Chile,* mate. That's not a bald eagle, it's an Andean Condor. Legend goes, with their sharp eyes, if you spot one, means you have a bit of that vision too, eh? Trusting what you see in your mind's eye, that's knowing you're on the right path."

"Thank you, I receive that."

The condor circled with wings outstretched to catch the rising warm air, thermalling higher and higher, until the tiny dot vanished, leaving me breathless at the pageantry of its flight. *This journey has given me the condor's perspective—my journey through a foreign country is enlightening me, refocusing me. Travelling is letting the mysteries, the awes, and the beauties break into the shell my small life had constructed around me. I yearn to fly with a bird's vision over these pointed snow-sprinkled peaks to confirm that I am on the right path.*

That condor is free—free to fly where he wills, free from any restraints, free from stop signs, traffic lights, and others' expectations. He overcomes the law of gravity. The price of my freedom is accepting my inability to change Leah and acknowledging my mistakes. My evolving transformation grants me the clarity to accept Leah as she is, to live and let live. Just like that condor carving out its space in the sky, my journey is carving out a space for me to figure out what true freedom means. Thank you, condor!

For the last 800 metres, the steep ascent on the single-file trail slowed everyone's pace—soon we were almost stepping on the heels of the person in front of us, and I could hear the conversations of the people behind us. No longer level, the trail wound straight up through rocks ranging from gravelly scree to car-sized boulders. When my lungs screamed at me to stop and to catch my breath, I thanked this mule train—youth in orange framed sunglasses, youth in green bandanas, youth with embroidered backpacks, youth yelling with glee—for encouraging me to ascend to the crest. I vowed to maintain the rhythm of the undulating line. *I will keep going. I will keep going. I will keep going.*

Now I understood why the Spanish described the saw-toothed ridges as *Torres* (Towers). The closer Peter and I came to the summit, the more the *Torres* grew, and the faster my heart beat; although the ground had levelled out.

"Wow!" I said, breathing heavily.

"Good on ya, mate. You made it! These peaks are mint, aye? Nothing back home quite like it. Makes you appreciate the wide, wild world," said Peter, breathlessly. His smile—mirroring mine—looked pumped enough to fly us to the tip of the *Torres.*

We gaped at the *Torres* of stone proclaiming the passing of much geological time. They rose straight up from an azure-blue high-mountain lake that only came into view once we reached the pinnacle. Three hundred and sixty degrees of silent rock, big sky, and rough exposed nature guarded the *Torres* secret. Dozens of beaming faces on the summit shone with the joy of achievement. Peter and I ran around giving high-fives to our trail mates. Raising his camera, Peter preserved a timeless moment of me against the

Torres, my arms outstretched as if to gather all that tranquil radiance into my heart.

The renewed exuberance of a stream of trekkers scrambling up onto a colossal boulder inspired me to accompany them—the sight of the lake from that perch took my breath away.

Instead of joining me on the boulder, Peter said, "I'll be right back, mate. Gotta check out the lake, eh?"

A meditative awe settled over me as I waited and gazed at the incredible beauty before me. *How can I feel so comfortable with someone I only met hours earlier? I can't believe that Peter never left me after our first encounter. But will he really come back?*

As Peter wandered off, doubt clouded my mind as I recalled promises broken in my past—each "I'll be right back" a string of empty words from my ex-husband.

"I'll see you after work," my ex-husband had said when he left in the morning.

At supper time, when all the other fathers in our cul-de-sac were pulling into their driveways, Annie and I would watch at the front window for him. Finally, we would eat alone, and I would put his untouched supper in the fridge. Any number of days later he would show up again. Until the time he had vanished when I was pregnant with our second child and returned months after I'd given birth to our son.

"I love you and the kids," he'd profess on his reappearance.

Although I knew he wanted to be the man I had married, once he'd broken my trust, I no longer believed his words.

And now I am doubting Peter's words. I can't see him anywhere and people are leaving to go back down now. We only have about three hours of daylight left. He must have started down without me.

Aware that I already missed the companionship of this digital nomad, I climbed off the erratic and walked toward the groups of trekkers bound for *Torres Norte.*

The descent down the rugged mountainside required picking my way through a slippery labyrinth of rocks and boulders using every ounce of balance and precision I could muster. The jagged terrain tested my agility and resolve, but the savage majesty of the surrounding peaks served as a rewarding backdrop. After I'd descended for ten minutes, I heard a breathless, "Ruth, wait for me. *Amiga,* why leave? I said I'd be right back, eh? I looked all over for you up at the summit." Peter's feet kicked up nose-clogging puffs of dust as he ran down the trail toward me.

"Oh, Peter, I'm so sorry. You are truly a man of your word. I don't know what I was thinking. Forgive me," I said, relieved to see him.

"The code of the road says that hikers who travel together stay together." His hand on my shoulder felt warmly reassuring, he looked at me with compassion in his eyes, and I trusted him.

We fell into step with each other once again, discussing topics as diverse as Christianity and how our upbringings inform our belief systems. We shared in the excitement of seeing an elegant red fox near *Campamento Chileno,* where *caballeros* were saddling horses for their dude rides.

"I don't think I've ever seen such exquisite rock formations as the *Torres del Paine,*" I said.

"Hard out! And me, I've seen heaps of mountains. And we can congratulate ourselves; today we tramped twenty-two kilometres with an altitude gain of 1366 metres," he said, looking at his GPS.

Upon arriving at Peter's camping spot near the *Refugio,* a few scattered clouds caught the sun's waning rays as it descended below the hills. Each passing moment transformed them from white into breathtakingly gentle pinks that melted into fiery reds, casting a contemplative glow on us, as we stood facing each other.

"Been choice hiking with you, Ruth. I've never had anyone order me to hike with them before!" he laughed. "But hey, I'm glad you did. I enjoyed your company immensely."

"Can you stay for a late supper with me in the *Refugio*?" I asked, yearning for more time with him.

"I wish, but our paths split now, I'm *Ushuaia*-bound. Got more adventures waiting. Catch you later!"

The transient display of the setting sun to the west of us spoke to me of the fleeting nature of our seven-hour connection—forged on the trail and by our shared understanding of life. When he hugged me, he compressed me against the hard muscles toned from years of cycling and hiking. Watching him disappear into a leafy bush, then emerge pushing his already-packed bicycle, and wave to me—a part of me longed to hop on the back of his bike, to journey together beneath the ethereal beauty now painted in the heavens. A big part of me—I unravelled like a three-strand rope.

Awakening to the sound of rousing backpackers on Tuesday at 7:30 a.m., the anticipation of the trek from *Torres Norte* to *Los Cuernos* fluttered within me. Peeking outside through the curtains, I thought, *I've been birthed into a realm of serrated granite giants bent and folded into the most spectacular shapes. I've truly embarked on a monumental journey, haven't I?*

How I managed to walk in a straight line will always remain an unknown; because my eyes were glued to the peaks; marvelling that their rugged rough-hewn features had somehow resisted the chiselling gusts that had for centuries tried to smooth their features. A colourful stream of kindred spirits teemed along the trail—some moving in my direction and others journeying the opposite way—each with their own pace and their own reason for trekking. Brief exchanges with fellow pilgrims created fleeting but profound connections—sometimes a simple *hola* (hello), and sometimes a *suerte* (good luck). All assessed my advanced age and solo status. My presence prompted smiles and the universal thumbs-up.

Feeling drawn by *Lago Nordenskjold,* lying blue and beautiful to the south, I veered slightly off the trail to stop a moment and absorb the view.

"Look, *Amiga,* Unidentified Flying Objects," a playful traveller said, pointing to the sky beyond the lake.

Bright, solid-white oblong clouds hanging motionless far above the serene waters rippling with shimmering heat waves, indicated that the wind roaring past our ears did have the power to sculpt the clouds, the power to reveal the true nature of our core.

"Oh, yes, those clouds do look like spaceships! They must be delivering aliens who are also interested in this fascinatingly wild topography."

"What are they called—do you know?" he asked.

"Lenticular. Or leni. They form in extremely windy conditions. I think this area qualifies. I know about them from when I used to glide. A leni-day was a no-fly day for me."

Another moment of connection, then solitude. Alone in the enlightening wilderness. Walking alone more than walking with fellow travellers made me value each conversation.

The song of a babbling waterfall soon beckoned, inviting me to enjoy a moment of respite. *Perfect timing. My feet are so hot and swollen. This will feel great!*

Sitting on a rock, I unlaced my runners, tugged at my sweat-soaked socks until I peeled them from each foot, laid them on a stone to dry, rolled up my jeans, and plunged my feet into the icy embrace of the river churning down the side of the mountain. I splashed in the frothing water, then lay back on the cool rock, luxuriating in the hot sun, smiling at the lenticular clouds, feeling a surge of childlike energy. The simple act of lying with my feet submerged beneath the crystal-clear water, opened an aquatic portal to my past. As a child, I loved to walk in the muck and make paths for the rivulets of melted snow with the toes of my yellow rubber boots—a network of channels, cleared of leaves and gravel and mud—and watch the fast release of the water, and dream of the distant lands awaiting me, my thoughts carried along by the current. Wherever I have lived, I've always sought out a river. *This moving water still fascinates me, and the sound calms my spirit. As beautiful as the lake appears, it fails to fascinate me—it rests, it is motionless.*

After bobbing my feet in the icy mists of the flowing water for mere seconds, they already began to tingle, and I felt ready to continue my trek—ready to feast my eyes on the countryside from new and glorious angles.

Around the next bend in the trail, a familiar yet forlorn figure sat on a rock, her head in her hands. The pale face slowly lifting to greet me looked strained and exhausted.

"Julia? What's happening?" I asked, placing my hand on her shoulder. The young blonde German and I had eaten several meals together at *Casa Lili*.

"Ugh, Ruth, hi. I'm not going to survive this. I've been puking all day. It's too hot during the day and too cold at night. This backpack weighs a ton. And that infernal wind. The wind!"

"Mind if I share your rock?" I asked, lowering my pack to the ground, and sitting beside her. "I remember you telling me how proud you were when you got off the plane from Germany. And remember how you dreamed of trekking the 'W' for years, and how you worked and saved up the money for the flight?"

"Uh, ja, but that was before I started walking." She glanced at me then dropped her head into her hands.

"You need to get off this rock and start walking again. You can do it; I know you can. Look, I'm weaving reality into my dream, too, and I'm almost wise enough to be your grandmother. I'm doing it. So can you," I said, with my arm around her stiff shoulders.

No response.

"Focus on all the beauty around us," I said, scanning the rugged peaks.

Julia's gaze followed mine, lingered on the skyline, and she inhaled deeply.

"Ja. Thanks, Ruth. But hello, now I'm totally up for keeping on!" she nodded, her lips spreading to a wane smile.

"Alright," I said, "You'll be at the *Torres Norte Refugio* in a few hours. Then you can celebrate your dream come true!"

We helped each other to gear up, exchanging a warm embrace before bidding farewell. My gaze focused on her pack, bobbing up and down heavily with each step, until she vanished from view, beyond the gushing falls. *She's a survivor.* My heart glowed.

Continuing along this bountiful trail, I felt so energized I believed I could grow as tall as the mountains.

Near the heat of the day, I felt God speak to my heart. "You gave Julia a gift, now here is my gift for you—the gift of your first love of horses—rekindled."

Gradually, a rhythmic, sharp click-clacking of iron-shod hooves on the rocky path behind me overtook the sound of wind-borne birdsong. Riding on the lead horse, the gaucho—who wore a luxuriant black jacket and fringed chaps—tipped his black traditional *Chileno* beret, perched jauntily at the back of his head, and smiled at me. A smile that touched a primal place within me. He smiled at me! His saddle lay hidden under a thick sheepskin saddle blanket. Underneath his saddle, another tasselled sheepskin blanket flopped in the wind—a vivid mosaic of yellows, reds, and greens seeming to capture the essence of vitality. Leather on leather groaned under the weight of the massive burdens precariously straddling six horses' spines. I wondered if they were laden with gear for trekkers attempting the rugged 10-day "O" trek or perhaps provisions bound for one of the *Refugios.* Sturdy white ropes linked the pack string together. Strong chestnut steeds with flowing black manes, their muscles expanding and contracting under their sweaty coats, marched alongside caramel and creamy-ivory pintos. Trailing at the end of the string, came an albino with spooky, otherworldly pink eyes.

They snorted as the dust tickled their nostrils, and the wind carried the sweet, musky scent of horse sweat into mine—the fragrance of freedom. This fleeting encounter made my heart burst with drops of liquid laughter that splashed vermilion and gold across the wide, wide sky. Only after I could no longer locate the string of pack horses in the distance, did I step back onto the trail. Here, amidst the beauty and majesty of God's creations, I felt as though I had communed with the divine. Thank you! What a gift!

When my mind floated back to earth, I noticed that I stood at a fork in the trail. Ahead I saw trees, grasses, shrubs, mountains—everything but the reassuring sight of fellow trekkers. The formerly well-marked trail seemed to fail me now. A few paces along one path, I spotted a miniscule sign that said, "Shortcut." *Could this be the way to Los Cuernos?* I felt uneasy at the prospect of becoming lost. Imagined dangers lurked—pumas on the prowl, the creeping cold of sleeping alone in the wild. The chorus of "what ifs" played through my mind until—lacking any guides—I decided that a shortcut should eventually connect me to the main trail, and I could conserve some energy.

THIS is a shortcut? Or did the sign actually mean, "If you take this route, you'll be sorry" or "This is the shortcut to heaven?"

The sign also failed to mention the trail rose at an eighty-degree incline. I climbed upward—each stride overcoming gravity—my feet seeking firm purchase, my progress one step forward to two steps back, each pause allowing me to catch my breath before reaching out for a solid boulder or bush to steady myself. All the while, I leaned ahead to keep my pack from tumbling me backward. Murphy's Law may have ensured that no one had been around to help interpret that sign, but no law prevented an audience from forming now.

When I next raised my sweating brow, I saw above me a man my age perched on a large rock, watching me quizzically. A short word about sitting on rocks. Rocks are unforgivingly hard, and they don't come with back supports; they do increase the probability that one can return to a standing position with one's loaded backpack.

"Going down is easier, mate," he laughed. His wavy black hair and entrancing smile momentarily rooted me to the spot.

"Is this... or is this not... the shortcut to *Cuernos*? I asked, gripping a handful of branches.

"I believe it is. Do all Canadians take the 'straight up the cliff' shortcuts?" he asked, still amused.

"Very funny. You're good at identifying accents! But I need to ask where you are from."

I'd learned to say that instead of my former, "Are you Australian?" Because they would answer, "No. We are English." If someone called me an American, I corrected them just as quickly.

"I'm Nate, from New Zealand," he said, rising. "See those miniature people down the hill; my wife and son. Hope you find your trail."

Knowing that his family awaited him below dimmed any prospect of further encounters with him.

When I finally gained my footing on high, a well-earned sense of achievement washed over me—my spirit nearly burst, as if suspended halfway between openness and vastness. The cobalt lake, towering mountains, and leafy green trees wrapped around me, evoking memories of swathing my newborns in thick, soft winter blankets. In this landscape, I felt like a tiny being: an infinitesimal speck in the centre of majestic grandeur.

I balanced a while longer in my moment of triumph, then, with the well-marked main trail to *Los Cuernos Refugio* beckoning me forward, I walked on and pondered. That day, an amusing illusion took hold of my weary mind; the final kilometre of any long trek surely must expand beyond 1000 metres, defying all scientific measurements. *I'll never make it. My legs can't walk another step.* Hunger gnawed at me, and I fantasized that those pack horses carried mobile *empanada* stands, now set up and waiting to serve me a savoury snack around the next bend in the trail. Then I thought of my words to Julia. *This is the final stretch; I can do it.* At 4:30 p.m., the *Refugio* welcomed me as the sun began its descent behind the mountains, marking the end of an awe-filled day. In contrast to *Torres Norte's* refined, spacious, and upscale amenities, *Los Cuernos* appeared rustic and crowded. Mere steps from the buildings, a waterfall—which provided the hostel with their electricity and fresh water—thundered, so unlike the calm *Lago Nordenskjold.* Buoyed by the elation of completing the second leg of my trek, I approached the receptionist. He swiftly located my reservation and directed me to my assigned room. "First, may I please ask you to reserve my night at *Paine Grande*? I tried, but I couldn't reserve it in *Puerto Natales*," I said.

"We belong to *Fantastico Sur*, but *Paine* belongs to *Vertice*, so I no can book your night at *Paine*. But no problem. Make sure you book a bed as soon as you get to *Paine Grande* tomorrow. This is our offseason, so no problem."

Where have I heard that before?

Excellent. His confident words, ensuring me of a warm safe place to sleep, comforted me.

The *Refugio* buzzed with life, different languages, and laughter—making me feel welcome in this communal space. Entering a room crammed with twenty bunks, I noticed that a group of four men and three women from one touring caravan had just arrived, along with their tour guide, claiming the last of the lower bunks. Determinedly, I hefted my pack up onto an upper bunk, foreseeing complications with my nocturnal bathroom trip. Extending my hand, I introduced myself to six of my bunkmates, who shared that they were also doing the "W" trek. Instead of only a brief smile and nod, the seventh person took the time to chat.

"Hi, I'm Don from Ecuador. My doctor told me I'm too fat. This trekking tour is my dieting program," he joked, shaking my hand with one hand, and jiggling his ample waistline with the other, "Yeah, five days from now I'll be a svelte eighty kilograms. In Ecuador, we say *'paso a paso, libra por libra'*—'step by step, pound by pound'. That's my motto for this trek!"

Don's jet-black eyes sparkled like a newly opened can of Cola—they absolutely effervesced with light and life. A fountain of wavy ebony hair graced the tip-top of his head, and his grin stretched his round face into dimples.

"I'm Ruth from Canada. I don't know whether to congratulate you or say I'm sorry," I said, and he chuckled, those eyes twinkling.

"Say congratulations. Our group is launching off into a great adventure. Which tour group are you with, Canada?" he asked, christening me with his own trail name.

"None, I am travelling alone, but I've sure noticed most people our age do travel in a guided tour group. That idea hadn't occurred to me. I thought only seniors travelled in groups."

He laughed and said, "I won't be a senior for another five years."

"I'll never be a senior," I said.

That night I managed to fall asleep despite all the noise and commotion of the busy hostel. How is it that a seemingly insignificant incident can have consequences that leave you shaking your head in wonder? Little did I realize that in two nights' time, tonight's bathroom run would lead to securing me a bed and satisfying my hunger.

In the darkness that shrouded the room, I woke. *Oh, no. My bladder can waken me even when dozens of snorers can't.*

Carefully employing stealth mode, I crawled out of my bunk and tiptoed across the pitch-black space, pausing in the silences between snores. The creaking of the door hinges pierced the nocturnal stillness. Walking down the long, cold empty hallway I groped for the door to the ladies' room. Success! As I inched the bathroom door open for the return journey, loud breathing caused me to jerk a step backward to prevent colliding with the dark form of a hulk of a man on the other side of the door. A strong arm grabbed my left arm and whispered, "Shush."

My right hand flew to my heart. *Should I wrench my arm from his grip and run back into the ladies' room? Should I practise my Tai Chi kicks on him? Should I scream? My brain seems to be awake, but this darkness is so thick I can't even tell if my eyes are open. Am I dreaming?*

Above all my split-second scenarios, I thought I heard him whisper my newly dubbed trail name.

"Canada, this is Don," he said, recognizing me in the dim light. "One of your bunk mates. I met you this afternoon."

"Oh, Don, you almost gave me heart failure."

He whispered, "Wait for me, then we can go back into the room together. Only one creak this time."

Which we did; two times in one night.

Drifting off to sleep again, I am the condor—soaring, seeing the world anew, embodying its expansive perspective. *I can only imagine what tomorrow will bring.*

Stirring from my slumber on Wednesday morning, I heard the steady patter of raindrops tapping against the windowpane, portending an unwelcome shift in the weather—weather that would demand that I resurrect my long johns. After two glorious days of sunshine and warmth, I woke to an altered landscape. Peering out the drapeless window beside my bunk, what I saw stunned me—a dissonant mixture of cloud shapes and colours, hidden among dark, vaporous, lurking sky-shadows that obscured the treetops.

Why is everyone rousing already? It's so dark.

The world outside looked grey—the matte-grey of a gun barrel, with shades of winter. *I don't want to go trekking in that!* I pictured myself slowly sinking into the cold depths of the outdoors—like that day on the Stave River, paddling my leaky canoe—and it didn't seem appealing or safe. I rolled over. The dank smell of sweaty socks and sweating bodies saturated the *Refugio's* small, confined space. *Could I spend an entire day hanging around with restless travellers, though? Oh! I must hike, or I'll be a day behind and miss my shuttle back to Puerto Natales!* Whipping off my bedsheets, I swung my feet onto the frigid floor and shuffled stiffly to the window. Rubbing the condensation from a square on the windowpane, I gazed out again, this time imagining a world full of new wonders beyond the hostel, only waiting to be discovered.

Miko's words drifted across time from *Puerto Natales* into my mind, "If you want to see a rainbow, you have to walk in the rain." *So, I will walk in the rain.*

In the small cafeteria, runny, greasy scrambled eggs, and toast darker than I preferred slid around on my plate while I looked for a place with an empty chair. I spotted Don from Ecuador and his group at a long table. My steps slowed. *Would they mind if I joined them? They seem so close-knit, like family. I'll be the intruder—the outsider. Maybe I'll find another seat.* Just then, they began to pack up. Stacks of dishes clattered as they prepared to leave. Don caught my eye, and we both burst out laughing, both thinking of our synchronized bladder adventures. *My baño-buddy (bathroom-buddy)!* Watching Don snicker, I remembered my sombre months of caregiving, and felt a kinship with this fellow traveller's uninhibited joy.

"We must stop meeting like this," he said, finally controlling his mirth.

"Indeed!" I said, laughing freely.

I'm so grateful I am travelling solo, I don't need to rise on command, and follow the leader, or in Don's case, follow the last person in the queue.

From my seat at an empty table, Don's movements held my focus as he struggled to sling his bloated backpack over his shoulders, then take two bouncy skips and a hop to catch up to the woman at the end of the line, as his group filed toward the door. My fork kept shovelling runny eggs into my mouth. Despite all the trekkers criss-crossing back and forth in my field of vision, Don and I maintained eye contact. *My connection with Don makes me feel like I'm eating warm porridge smothered in thick white cream covered in a golden maple syrup drizzle.*

I couldn't have known then what a key role Don would yet play in my life. Then, I only knew that I admired an overweight man who lightheartedly accepted a challenge that forced him to be more mobile than he'd been for years. *This guy has taken charge of his destiny. He's making wise decisions that years from now will make his ninety-year-old self say, "thank you." The realization dawned on me: I met this man only because I chose to travel, to embark on adventures, and to embrace solitude. Don had noticed me when the others in his group couldn't see me beyond their fellow trekkers.*

Joy had already lit up my face even before Don turned in the doorway, looking back at me, grinning. Don winked at me—no doubt once again recalling our shared nocturnal secret. Flashing my biggest smile, I waved goodbye as the door slammed behind him; then I swallowed the last of my "porridge," and returned to my room to compress my remaining gear into my backpack.

Hoisting it onto my back still required a sumo wrestling pose, and no wonder; for it contained four seasons' worth of clothing. Repacking for the day, I stashed my hot weather items creased and flattened near the bottom—but wore two fleeces and two jackets layered on top of my *Torres* T-shirt to keep out the clammy chill, deciding against taking the umbrella offered by the hostel so I could feel the rain on my face; it couldn't possibly dampen my spirits.

"If I were you, I'd do this," a female voice beside me said.

Her tracksuit pants matched her rain jacket, her rain hat covered the back of her neck, her pack looked thin and bulge-free, and her tone said, "Listen, the experienced trekker will tell the rookie something important." So, I listened.

She removed the items from her pack, placing them on her bunk, and folding them neatly into a large green plastic bag; then she tucked everything back into her pack, without even overstretching the seams.

"This way, even if you walk through a downpour, your stuff stays dry," she said, tossing me a bag courtesy of herself, and floated into the hallway.

"Thanks, I appreciate that." *But do I really want to take all my gear out and start over? On the other hand, do I really want to have a wet pack full of soggy heavy clothes?*

Minutes later, I'd layered the contents of my backpack inside the green rain barrier then ventured into the drizzle, grateful that she had shared her wise organizational method. Eager to greet the world beyond, I charged ahead, scarcely aware of the weight of my pack pressing against my shoulders and back. Due to the rain, the number of trekkers on the trail had dwindled, making the walk even quieter than the previous day. Over the boggy trail lay a gloomy, faint light through which the gun-barrel-grey clouds tumbled; I knew no dismay; faced with nature's display of her misery, I felt sad to be deprived of the views I'd seen yesterday. The air—rich with the scent of damp earth—evoked a primal aroma that connected me to the wild landscape around me.

Less than an hour later, the sun suddenly found a path through the clouds and spotlighted a thing so tiny—something I would otherwise have walked past, or even stepped on. At my feet, a radiant yellow flower atop an exquisitely formed plant cradled a glistening orb in its upturned leaves, the bloom showcasing the raindrop more beautifully than the finest crystal vase could. Just as the buttercup growing out of the salmon bones had given me hope for a better future beyond Leah, seeing this delicate flower-vase gave me hope that I'd be sleeping on a bed that night.

Continuing on, I squelched along the sodden path toward an archway ushering me into that land of the unknown. Sunshine fuelled three bright, complete single rainbows overlaid against trees, rivers, waterfalls, and mountains, splashing colour across the saturated trail. *Miko's rainbow!* The blue of yesterday's sky transformed into two radiant blue curves between the red, orange, yellow, green, indigo, and violets of a double rainbow. The bow arched upward from the whitecaps on *Lago Nordenskjold. Chilean rainbows are far superior to Albertan rainbows!*

Contemplating each petal of the delicate flower-vase, and each glowing arc of the rainbows spanning the heavens, I marvelled at the boundless creativity of the Divine Artist. But only when I came upon the rough cairn, where time and eternity converged, did I feel the deepest communion with my Creator. A sizable boulder with a cairn of assorted rocks in varying shapes and hues balanced on top, hinted that many others had also cherished this spot. Reverently, I added my flat sandstone rock to the apex of the stack, a gesture of connection, honouring the sacred journey of faith that had led me here—a journey in which I continually encountered God amidst nature's splendour. Pausing to absorb the cairn's significance, I exclaimed, "Surely the Lord is in this place!"

One third of the way between the *Los Cuernos* and *Paine Grande Refugios, Campamento Italiano* unexpectedly came into view. Dozens of trekkers lounged and bustled about, their tents pitched under the canopy of ancient trees. Lacking brick-and-mortar walls to protect against pumas, the makeshift C-can office embodied rustic simplicity, missing essentials like running water and a cafeteria.

The first bench that greeted my eyes since morning made the perfect place to set my pack alongside two fatigue-green canvas rucksacks covered with America flags. Light-footedly, I eagerly explored the campsite.

A youth with a Spanish accent asked me a question that gave me pause.

"Are you going to hike the 'W'?

"I am hiking the 'W,' aren't I?" I asked.

"It's only a 'W' if you trek up *Frances Valley* and return here; otherwise, it's just a 'U.' Then from here, you continue to *Paine Grande*." He pointed toward the north with an arm covered in a profusion of black curls. "You can leave your pack against the office wall, no one will steal it."

"How much time does the round-trip take?" I asked.

"Two hours," he said, his words hanging in the air as light snow began to fall, turning the mountains into a faint, phantasmal line that haunted the horizon and echoed my inner turmoil.

Two extra hours of walking—with stiff legs and a lower back that reminds me of its existence with a constant ache—might not be wise. I still have half a day of trekking ahead of me, with the spectre of night inching closer. This would not be the first or last time that I demanded my body perform more than I had the physical resources to sustain.

"What's the reward?" I found myself asking, the spark of adventure kindling inside.

"The most beautiful glacier, *Glacier Frances, Amiga*. Take the trail to the viewpoint called *Mirador Britannica*. It's worth every step," he said.

Once, the invisible chains of others' expectations for my life had constrained me, but isn't my journey about continuing to break them? Now, why wouldn't I follow the rhythm of my heart? I could tell my friends and family that I had conquered the "W," as Lucas at Casa Lili had described it, not just the "U." I've travelled all the way to South America—why not see everything I can?

"Alright, I'll take the challenge! Where is the trailhead?"

He pointed again, this time toward masses of thick juniper bushes dwarfed by even thicker, green broad-leafed trees, then bade me farewell.

After waving goodbye, I protected my ears with my wool toque and tugged my yellow raincoat and black rain pants from my pack stretching them on over all my other clothes, which made bending my elbows and knees difficult.

I stacked my backpack among rows of older canvas and newer nylon packs leaning against the metal office wall and set off behind three travellers who were confidently striding toward the juniper bushes. *They must be taking the two-hour round trip to Mirador Britannica, as well, so I'll follow them—they must know the way.* They veered left, where the dense underbrush—looking impenetrable moments before—yielded to a hidden trail. I veered left.

Fragments of my fellow travellers' muffled chatter floated back, as we slogged along the surprisingly level terrain.

Suddenly I realized something. *Level terrain? Wait! To reach a viewpoint, one must ascend.* A sinking feeling gripped me. Had I, in my eagerness to belong, relinquished my sense of direction?

Their bulky, overladen packs also puzzled me. *Why would they need packs for a quick two-hour round trip? Training for an Ironman event, perhaps?* I tried to quell the rising tide of doubt. My hikers glimmered with moisture, but my feet remained dry—a small victory for my forethought of lining them with plastic bags.

I envisioned the group ahead laughing at my folly. Yet, more than their imagined mockery, the echo of my questions stung. *Why am I blindly following these people? Why didn't I think for myself? Why did it take so long to notice I'm going the wrong way? Now I won't have time to see the glacier or make it to the next Refugio before dark.*

According to my persistent punctuality paradigm, seventeen precious minutes had slipped away, lost in the labyrinth of my misplaced trust. The group I'd been tailing dissolved into the thicket, just as another trekker materialized in front of me.

"*Buenos Dias*, is this the way to *Mirador Britannica*?" I asked.

"No, *Señora*, you go wrong way. Is back. That way," she pointed toward the way I'd come.

"*Gracias*," I thanked her, as our paths crossed, and I turned around in mid-stride.

As I retraced my steps, a familiar sting of realization pricked my conscience, transporting me back five years to another time I'd blindly followed someone, to my detriment.

Just before the Labour Day weekend, Chad had breezed into my office.

"Hi, Ruth. Got plans for the long weekend?" he asked, sitting in my extra swivel chair.

"No, nothing yet," I replied, curious.

"Do you want to come on a three-day ride to Revelstoke with my cousin Jeff and me?

Initially, his proposal sent a flurry of worries through my mind. *The mountains, with their steep winding roads, intimidate a novice rider like me. What if I crash? What if I get lost, or, worse, cause an accident? What will our co-workers think?*

The picture he had painted, though, of a scoot through mountain passes, along rivers, and taking a ferry across a lake, had made me decide to go. Three days of motorcycling was exhilarating, until the return trip. The sweltering sun shone on my black leather jacket, chaps, and boots as we idled behind a long lineup of cars waiting to purchase Park Passes at the Alberta Park gate.

Suddenly Chad had swerved around the motionless vehicles and sped toward the highway. I'll never know whether it was the psychological group-mentality factor, the thrill of getting away with breaking the law, or just being oppressively hot, hungry, and tired—but—abandoning my better judgment—I chose to kick into gear and follow Chad. Later—after a brief but pleasant ride through the mountains—humiliatingly painful consequences were meted out. When I saw the flashing red-and-blue lights in my rear-view mirror, I pulled into the shoulder, kicked down *Pegasus*'s kickstand, swung my leg over the scorching black seat, peeled off my sticky chaps, helmet, and jacket, and flung the heavy heap into the ditch.

"I don't have a Park Pass," I had admitted to the warden, my voice a mixture of defeat and realization. A later court appearance, and a fine, and a community service term had all stemmed from that one moment of unthinkingly following Chad.

Shaking off the memory, I refocused on the path before me. *Not this time. This time, I choose my route—learning from my past, not repeating it. Yes,*

I have learned to be a way-finder. I can correct wrong turns. I can be gentle with myself. In my new world, I desire only the less-travelled path or the more-travelled path; not the right path or the wrong path. I can learn to do my trip intentionally, wholeheartedly, and with joy.

And without asking for further help, I rustled through the distant edge of the juniper thicket and—lo and behold—discovered the sign marking the trailhead for *Mirador Britannica*. The frigid air dulled the pungent, organic scent of the mud. When the chilled earth along the trail felt the warmth and connection of my footfalls, she spoke into my spirit: "Wait, linger here, spend time with me." Yet, driven to compensate for lost time, while simultaneously desiring to pause, I chose to ignore her summons, instead scrambling up the steep gradient. As I climbed, an uneasy sense of solitude tightened my stomach with each step—thirty minutes passed—no fellow travellers, no more signs, no assurances. *Could I have missed another directional sign?*

Then, amidst the muck of the less-trodden path I noticed a well-defined boot tread. His wiggly, wavy pattern became as dear to me as the basketball *Wilson* had become to Tom Hanks in *Castaway*—a connection in the wildness, an assurance. The imprint—whom I dubbed "Wiggle Tread"—meant a living, breathing human had walked here, its larger size affirming its owner's masculinity. "Wiggle Tread" and I scrambled up the trail together for half an hour, my foot fitting within the curves of his track—both of us engaged in conversation, both of us revelling in the splendour of our tranquil surroundings. As I approached a rocky threshold, "Wiggle Tread" vanished. His absence heightened my dread of getting lost or of arriving at *Grande* after dark—until I shifted my focus skyward.

Directly above me, I beheld the grandeur of *Glaciar del Frances*! *Thanks, "Wiggle Tread!"* My pace slowed; my breath caught. The radiating glacier, dense with snow and ice, lay cradled in the mountain from apex to valley, displaying its ageless majesty, standing out against the dismal grey sky as brightly as my lemon-yellow motorcycle helmet. Large, fluffy snowflakes floated hesitantly earthward, as if contemplating the idea of returning to their heavenly treasury.

Twenty minutes later I joined the company of six fellow trekkers at the *Mirador Britannica* viewpoint. We all leaped with glee—faces upturned in the falling flurries. Wet snowflakes clung to our gear, painting the world in shades of winter white. A young woman offered to capture pictures of our new, temporary tribe—our tribe, the keepers of a fleeting, shared joy. Her camera froze our moment of triumph in time—thumbs-up, victory signs, exuberant mid-jump poses with toes pointing skyward, our laughter echoing in the snowy expanse. None tarried beyond these precious moments, all of us sensing that the path to our next *Refugio* still stretched long and inclement before us.

From the pinnacle of the glacial bowl, I descended back to *Campamcnto Italiano*. Once I'd hoisted my pack onto my back, I stepped forward alone, leaving behind the earnest camaraderie of the camp. The sombre contrast between the vibrant life at the lookout and the eerie desolation on this solitary section of trail jarred me. Inhaling deeply, I braced myself for this next leg of the journey, unaware of the impact it would have on me.

This section of the forest—bearing the scars of nature's purifier: fire—lay silent before me. A cold gust of wind rattled through the heat-blasted branches of thousands of trees with charred bark and smooth silver trunks. The faint scent of ash and burned resin stirred in the air, suggesting that the blaze had not been long past. The leafless, lifeless trees reached their crooked and barren arms upward imploring the towering peaks that had been spared the effects of fire to console them—peaks that were always there to accompany me from beyond this land of despair.

My fingers slid along a gnarled, twisted, snapped-off branch that jutted out from the polished, silvery-sleek trunk, conjuring a comforting thought that lifted my spirits: "Don't see us snags as dead. Instead, you must view us as nurturers of the new life—the next generation—that will feed on our decomposed trunks."

In the heart of this charred territory, I stumbled upon something unexpected—an anomaly in the long-extinguished embers on the forest floor that caught my eye and halted me in my tracks.

CHAPTER 10

Trails End

STEPPING CAREFULLY OVER THE DEADFALL STREWN RANDOMLY ACROSS the trail, I paused, my heart heavy, as a patch of colour caught my eye. I stooped down, my curiosity piqued. There, half-buried under the seared foliage of the scorched earth, and encircling the bases of the snag, a lone clump of delicate, red, bell-shaped flowers bloomed on a thorny green stem. Strength flourishing silently in solitude.

Kneeling before the Phoenix blossoms, I placed a finger on either side of the stalk, slid my hand up, feeling the softness of the velvety-shimmery petals, and turned her face toward mine. *How can you grow in this place so stripped of life? Are you aware of your beauty? Do you desire appreciation and recognition? You're thriving in this post-apocalyptic environment where no one is likely to see you, yet here you are—beauty from ashes. Maybe your exquisiteness doesn't need an audience, just the courage to exist.*

The flower's sunshiny fragrance released a memory of Vicki. We sat side-by-side on our picnic blanket, the sun shone in a clear blue sky. My youngest daughter Lenora was dressing her Cabbage Patch doll. A younger girl danced her Barbie doll along the moist green grass beyond the blanket. Their play and laughter made us chuckle and clink our chilled lemonade glasses together. A perfect day for cousins to play together, and sisters to chat. Then a not-so-perfect memory that had happened fourteen years after our picnic intruded.

I saw myself exiting an elevator and walking down a corridor past open rooms—rooms with cement block walls painted an anemic yellow, and narrow metal beds that should have been scrapped in a demolition sale. Doctors and patients wandered around me, indifferent to my presence, while I waited in a messy waiting area, where the TV blared, and nurses breezed past me without making eye contact. *This is chaos, utter and total chaos. I've come to visit my sister, not a prisoner! Surely, she doesn't belong here.*

After what felt like an eternity, the psychiatrist finally called me into his office. He gave me a disinterested glance and placed a folder on the table.

"The case is not cooperating with us," he told me, as though she were a Robertson screwdriver that didn't fit into a Phillips screw.

He flipped through sheaves of papers in a thin folder, clapped it closed, then asked his assistant to locate the correct notes.

"She is not a 'case'! She is my sister! And she has a name. Vicki!" I said, clenching my fists under the table.

Unmoved, the psychiatrist said to his assistant, who had returned with the correct file folder, "Make a note. The case's family is caring."

The assistant wrote those words on a blank sheet of paper.

"What is Vicki's diagnosis?" I had asked him for the second time.

"I can't tell you. But if a hypothetical case presented with these symptoms, I would diagnose schizophrenia."

Dear God. No! Something I'd long suspected but had long denied.

"To prevent further psychotic breaks, I would prescribe medication. The case will remain here until we are assured that she is following protocol. As for the daughter, the medical team would hypothetically diagnose her with Shared Psychotic Disorder. They will release her from the hospital where she is situated, in due time. The daughter is prohibited from returning home with the mother. You may now have a ten-minute visit with the case."

My heart broke when I entered Vicki's room. She'd been sitting on her bed, reading her Bible, a towel draped over her head, her posture stooped, and for a second I saw our grandmother in her.

"I don't want to talk to you, okay? I told the nurses I didn't want anyone to know I was here. How did you get in? You came all the way here to see me?" she mumbled.

"I don't see why I can't talk to you since I'm here. After all, I haven't seen you for eight years!"

"You say that as if you think I am crazy."

"I'm here to support you, Vicki."

"I admit I have been lying to you, okay, but there are more lies out there that you are listening to. Don't listen to what they tell you, it's all a sham.

Okay? The doctor is not helping me, and I am not going to cooperate with any family meeting."

"Well, maybe the doctor can help us deal with how this is affecting us."

"But who will help me then?"

Her involuntary plea had torn at my heartstrings—I swallowed hard, blinking back the hot prickle of tears stinging my eyes. She couldn't comprehend my offer of support. The sad truth settled in; my love alone couldn't bring back the sister I remembered. I had to leave her there.

The wind blew in gusts through the forest. The memory released my tears—I let them fall freely onto the red-velvet flower. *Vicki, if you allow me to see you again, I will love you for who you are, and not try to fix you. I miss you Vicki, my sister, my friend.* Right in the middle of the burned forest—with only the sometimes malevolent, sometimes caressing wind that morphed into a living identity to witness me—I mourned the loss of my sister. The sister schizophrenia had taken from me.

As my grief ebbed, another memory surfaced. I settled deeper onto the floor of the forlorn forest, its quiet sadness reminding me of that summer's day in 2013 when I had settled onto the hospital bed beside Leah where, after eight long years, I once again looked into her eyes. Immediately I'd thought of how she had long since outgrown her Barbie doll, and long since left her childhood innocence behind.

"Oh, Auntie Ruth," she said, rising from her bed to give me the tightest, longest hug.

Through our tears—mumbling, head and eyes down—she jerkily pieced together the events of those missing years.

"I am so sorry for what I put you through, I thought you hated us. My hair is too frizzy. I look ugly in pants. I hate my eyes. I'm eighteen years old and I haven't had any fun. I want to buy twenty bras! I just don't know what I want. At first it was exciting to think that we had to get away from people, then I started to think either I was crazy, or Mom was. That was when I wanted to end it all, but first I called 911. They brought me here. They took her to some psych hospital in Vancouver."

"I'm sorry too, Leah. I tried to get your mom to come live with me when they released her from the hospital, but she wouldn't come. I was angry with her for harming you, until I learned that she couldn't be a normal mother because she suffers from a disease. I'm so sorry that you also suffer from a disease because of how she raised you."

"Yeah, they told me. Shared Psychotic Disorder. At least I'm still alive. I had to go out and buy food for us. I stopped exercising and stopped going to school in Grade 6 because she said it was bad."

Her mumbling faded from my memory, and I focused on the velvety red bloom that reflected my rebirth, a life rising from the ashes of days filled with caregiving, anger, and tears—shared with Leah. *I do miss you Leah, my niece. I can only hope you will find your way in the world.* Encircled by forest—where life is both lost and regenerated—I saw the choices Vicki, Leah, and I had—to remain tethered to past sorrows or to step into futures filled with new growth. Choosing growth seemed like the better way. I imagined a wonderful future for each of us—free from old wounds, unbound from our pasts, and filled with forgiveness. Shaking off the memories—and the sooty, musty undergrowth from my rain pants—I rose and set my eyes on the trail ahead, my heart lighter. *Be thankful for everything. Listen to nature.*

Slogging through various permutations of hydrogen and oxygen falling from the heavens in an intriguing display of nature's chemistry, I reflected on the day's lessons, allowing them to guide me beyond the pallor and foul smell of the burned forest toward the welcome haven of *Paine Grande Refugio.* I sang aloud, "He gave me beauty for ashes, the oil of joy for mourning, the garment of praise for the spirit of heaviness, that they might be called oaks of righteousness, the planting of Adonai, that He may be glorified." Late afternoon had settled in—hopefully only a two-hour journey to *Paine Grande* remained—yet the overcast sky made the path look deceptively dim.

Eight hours after I'd left *Los Cuernos,* I spotted the rambling cedar buildings of *Grande,* framed by the black-capped, *Paine*-blue, precisely folded rock masses. By the time I stepped through the double doors at the *Paine Grande Refugio,* my body felt like a paradox of sensations—my legs trembled, and my muscles rebelled with every movement. But on the inside, my heart raced—adrenaline-fuelled, exhilarated—I had turned a "U" into a "W!" Even as I pondered my momentous achievement, I chuckled—thanks to the snowfall, I could've easily walked in the shape of a "W," or fashioned a giant trekster's snow angel. The warmth of the supper-scented air whispered comfort to my weary self. Here within this spacious, high-ceilinged lobby, the non-reservation drama would near its climax.

The confident words of the clerk at *Los Cuernos* last night, and *Marcela*'s assertion, "It is low season now because winter is coming. No problem," still rang in my ears. Two groups of trekkers queued ahead of me at the reception desk.

Please, please, please, God, let them have a bed for me.

To quell my apprehension while waiting, I studied the wall posters illustrating the geology of the mountains. Among the displays were explanations about sedimentary rocks called turbidites, fossils, belemnites, magma, submarine avalanches, intrusive rocks, and granites that formed the spectacular cliffs. One poster stated, "If you ever see a middle-aged man on his own in *Patagonia,* he is probably a geologist." *I wish I could meet a geologist who could explain this to me.*

Just then the door opened and, along with a blast of frigid air, a clump of ecstatic adventurers tumbled inside. Not one looked like a geologist. Upon closer inspection, though, I recognized them as the tour group from my room at *Cuernos.*

"Don!"

"Canada!"

We both broke into Cheshire Cat grins and embraced, both remembering our middle-of-the-night, synchronized skulks to and from the bathroom.

"Wasn't that the most absolutely exhilarating and challenging trek? Can you believe we walked twenty-four kilometres? I must have shed ten kilograms already," he said, contracting his abs.

The male receptionist beckoned me before I could reply; but my nod, my jubilant face told Don all he needed to know.

My voice, carrying the weight of my day's journey, barely managed to convey my plea.

"I tried to make a reservation in *Puerto Natales,* but they closed before I could reserve a bed for this night. Do you have a room available?" I asked.

"*Señora,* all our rooms are already booked for tonight."

You're kidding! I couldn't miss the lack of empathy, the way he pushed his papers around on his counter, how he looked past me to the growing lineup of trekkers behind me.

"What about a tent?" I pressed.

"Let me check for you. One moment please," he said, shuffling more papers back and forth, his face maintaining professional detachment. "I am sorry. All our tents are already reserved, *Señora.*"

"Could I sleep in the lobby? Just for the one night?"

"I am sorry, we prohibit this," he said firmly.

What am I supposed to do? I can't walk for eight hours to the next Refugio before dark. I'm exhausted, my legs have bounced their last bounce. Will I have to sleep under the stars? I shuddered.

"Well, can I at least buy myself dinner?" Perhaps a full stomach would lessen my panic. Once again, he shuffled his papers. The queue behind me had grown to about two dozen tired-looking and, probably, hungry trekkers in the few moments I'd been stalling the inevitable. *I have nowhere to sleep tonight.*

"*Señora,* I regret that all the dinners are sold out. But please come back later; if someone doesn't show up, you can reserve their bed and their meal. But please be aware, it will be first-come, first-serve."

"And what if everyone shows up, what then?" I asked. *Breathe slower.*

"*Señora,* please to let me attend to these other clients first. As I said, you can return to see me later."

This can't be happening.

Sighing loudly, I shifted the dead weight of my pack around on my slumped shoulders. Shuffling my feet, I sank into a couch snugged against the lobby wall, dropping my gear beside me. My mind whirred with scenarios as I searched for a solution to my predicament. Out of the corner of my eye, I saw Don pushing his way through the maze of tired but wired trekkers toward me. His approach brought a flicker of hope.

"*Mande,* Canada, you look like you wore a hole in the bottom of your hikers or something. What happened?"

Instead of laughing with him, I could only manage a pasted-on smile. Don slung his arm around my shoulder, settling in beside me with his listening ear.

"Let me clarify, the hike was incredible; but they don't have a room for me here; and the clerk needs a lesson in innovative problem-solving skills. I have nowhere to sleep! I'll have to keep walking to Grey tonight. It's only eleven kilometres, so how hard could that be?" I said.

"Check back often with Mr. Personality; someone is bound to be a no-show. But if you can't get a bed, you can have my extra sleeping bag and curl up on the floor in our dorm. I'm so fat I'd be warm enough even without any bedding. Remember, *Paso a paso, libra por libra,*" he said.

He gave his stomach a playful jiggle for effect. I giggled, amused by the thought that excess weight had insulation value! Suddenly, the flowers on the lobby coffee tables smelled sweeter, the level of noise from talking travellers seemed less annoying, and hope shone through the windows.

"Are you serious?! You would do that for me? You are so kind!" I blinked, incredulous.

"Of course, Canada, of course, that's how we Latinos are. We show love to people. And you would show love to me if you ate my dinner. My dieting program prohibits eating. I want to eat *mucho,* but..."

"Oh, thank you, thanks so much, Don. How can I ever thank you? Thank you," I said as I crushed his pillowy girth with a bear hug.

"Whoa, I'm just giving you my dinner, not the left lobe of my lung," he laughed and jiggled.

Don turned to the six others in his group and asked, "Are you okay if we adopt this homeless Canadian for the night?"

Their nods brought a genuine smile to my face, though a knot of worry lodged in my stomach.

"Thanks, everyone, this means a lot to me," I said.

We carried our paper plates piled high with aromatic *Chilean* beef, steaming baked potatoes, *ceviche,* and salad upstairs to a cozy lounge. We sat on three couches surrounding a wood-grain coffee table with our hot, sagging plates on our laps; and with our plastic goblets of thick purple *Chilean* wine, we raised a toast to travel. Don introduced me first to Maggie and Gabe.

"Wow, are you two marathon runners?" I asked, envying their biceps and calves.

"Right, mate," Gabe said, with a New Zealand accent. "Last year we ran forty kilometres in the Antarctic. This year, we're taking it easy, just doing this trek."

Just?

Don looked at me as he rolled his eyes. He sipped his wine again while introducing me to Steve and Emma, an English couple visiting their daughter while she studied for a year at *Santiago* University.

"Hi, pleased to meet you," I said, using my potato—instead of my tongue—to soak up all the sauce from the meat and swallowing the remaining tangy *ceviche.*

"Your supper was delicious. Thanks, Don," I said, the uncertainty of my sleeping arrangements still casting a shadow over the jubilant atmosphere around me.

"Better you eat it than me. Go check at reception now. The floor could feel mighty hard by 3 a.m. I'm just sayin'," Don said, thunking his wine glass onto the coffee table.

I acknowledged that my own bed promised the ideal solution to getting a good night's rest before the challenge of day three's trek, and ran down the stairs to the lobby.

"Nothing yet." The receptionist's monotone voice fell heavily on me.

My expressive face couldn't hide my concern when I returned to the group.

"No luck so far," I said, sinking back into the couch. The laughter and clinking of wine glasses felt distant to me.

Don gestured toward the pair at the end of the table, a father-and-son duo hailing from Glasgow; their quiet expressions suggesting a strenuous yet rewarding day on the trail.

"Hey, Canada," said the father, "You travelling alone, hey? You know you're in puma country, hey?

"I'm pretty sure the wind blows them all away, hey, Glasgow," I tried to joke.

At 8:00 p.m. Don yawned, and said, "It's been dark for ages. Who in their right mind might straggle in now? Go check again, Canada."

A few moments later, I danced back up the steps two at a time.

"I have good news and bad news. They have a bed for me! But they don't provide bedding," I reported.

The group responded immediately and encouragingly—seven sets of hands smacked high-fives all around our table.

"As wonderful as your offer was, I chose a soft mattress over a hard floor. Seriously, though, how can I ever thank you, Don?"

"Just keep smiling, Canada," he said, rubbing my back. "Come down to our dorm and we'll solve the 'no bedding' problem for you."

Their generosity overwhelmed me and vaporized the evening's tension. Seven sets of hands pulled sweaters, socks, extra sleeping bags, and pillows from packs and piled them onto my outstretched arms. When I watched those hands—hands that had travelled from New Zealand, England, Ecuador, and Scotland—I shook my head in awe. *We've only just met, yet, because we're on the same trail, we are all kindred spirits; sharing moments, sharing lives, sharing bedding.* Strolling down the dimly lit corridor to my room, I marvelled at the serendipitous midnight encounter with Don near *Los Cuernos's* washroom doors. *I am not trekking alone, after all.*

Cocooned under my odd collection of borrowed bedding, I lay on my warm, comfy mattress, enjoying my full stomach. Reflecting on dinner, I realized how just months ago, the idea of mingling with strangers had seemed scary. Yet now, here I am! I'm feeling at ease with strangers and connected to this tribe of travellers. Each kilometre I've traversed has not only moved me from Canada to *Chile* but has moved me inwardly. I'm forging a bond with the person I truly am—the person I couldn't be in Maple Ridge.

Hatchi peered at me from my pillow.

"You know, Hatchi, booking online from Canada could have simplified things."

"Ach aye, no, Lassie. 'Letting go and letting God' works better." At least that's what I thought I heard him say.

Instantly the day's anxieties dissolved, my aching muscles relaxed, and my snores soon harmonized with all the others in the room.

We didn't meet in the washrooms that night, yet the next morning Don greeted me with a wink when I appeared in their dorm's doorway to return all his group's bedding.

"I'm still too fat to eat breakfast. I seem to have gained weight overnight. So, take this voucher and go eat my breakfast for me. I still have a long way to go to get to 160. *Paso a paso, libra por libra,* you know. We're leaving *el pronto.* And don't forget to call me when you come to Ecuador, the most beautiful place on earth. And keep smiling," he said.

Don handed me the unassumingly valuable voucher, together with his email address scribbled on a paper towel. His hug enveloped me, evoking the sensation of sinking into an overstuffed easy chair, and his two-cheek kiss carried the aroma of an angel. Then his group closed the dorm door behind them, and they all exited the lobby, leaving me alone in the commotion of the early morning.

"Goodbye, my friends. Let's keep in touch," I said, waving to them through the double glass doors.

Solo in the cafeteria, I enjoyed a Papa-bear-sized bowl of porridge smothered with fresh mango slices, and a steaming *maté*. For the first few spoonfuls, my thoughts dwelt on my new trailmate, Don, and his appreciation of my smile. *Did my smile draw him to me, or did the love he has for every human draw me to him? I felt like we were two separate melodies that were played together, for too-short a time. I will miss that guy.*

Movement beyond the window caught my eye, and I watched as the treetops wildly thrashed as though to a celestial hip-hop beat in a cosmic aerobic class. At a nearby table, four athletic-looking youth had also noticed the wind and carried on a discussion that unnerved me.

"Yeah, the trek to *Glacier Grey* is famous for its freaky winds. Our guide told me it blew over a tour bus last month," said a woman's voice.

A slice of mango lodged mid-swallow, gagging me. *Surely, she's exaggerating.*

Next a man spoke. "Wild. And I met a bloke on the trail who told me a wind gust knocked them off balance. All three of his group fell backward onto their packs. And that happened just yesterday."

I swallowed too quickly, the *maté* burning my throat. My heart sped as I absorbed their stories. *Could it be true? Should I rush after Don's group, seeking safety in numbers? We'd face and overcome the wind as a team.* The wind rattled the windowpanes, stirring my thoughts enough to make me reconsider the wisdom of facing nature's power unprepared and alone.

After finishing my meal, I shouldered my pack and headed for the glass door. When I looked outside from the calm of the cafeteria, I saw a world in motion. The loose straps on the early-rising trekkers' backpacks writhed and twisted as if trying to break free from their loads. Lenticular clouds raced across the turbulent air, casting ever-changing shadows on the landscape. I paused there, my hand on the handle, my mind whirling indecisively.

I could see Don trundling along, his red-and-yellow pack visible in the distance; I knew I'd never catch up with his group. But the thought that I had maximum ballast in place—Don's breakfast and a heavy backpack—reassured me, giving me the courage to open the door and venture into the day solo. How bad could the roaring tempest be?

The pampas grasses swirled and rippled as though an intergalactic hair dryer on high speed were challenging their resilience. To my ear, that celestial hip-hop music I'd first imagined began to sound like a constant rumbling, highlighting the absence of birds. Growing up with the Chinooks of Alberta, I'd learned to manage the wind: I'd fashion makeshift wings from my jacket, skating swiftly across frozen rivers propelled solely by wind power. But the tearing gales of *Patagonia* surpassed even my expertise! Each staggering step reminded me of nature's untamed force. Such a wind, in such a wild place, must have torn unencumbered through these mountains since time began. Yet, in this moment, the wind encountered me. *Now I believe the overheard conversations of the trekkers, and I know what Julie meant about the fierceness of the wind.* If I planned to reach *Glacier Grey* in such a gale, I would need a miracle.

I'd take walking through quicksand over walking in this wind any day. My attempts at forward movement made my eyes water and my nose drip, blurring the trail ahead. Instead of berating myself with an "I should have," I thought, *next time I will bring my motorcycle goggles.*

The *Patagonian* winds carried the sound of Bob's voice from *Mexico* into my ears.

"Learn to harness the power of forces going against you. If you do it right, you will progress faster headlong into that force, instead of flowing to where the force wants to take you," he had said.

Recalling Bob's words, I tried to relax my rigid stance, tried to let the wind guide rather than control me. Before I'd walked half an hour, I stumbled from the path, holding my breath, and cupping my hands over my ears, and trundled toward a rocky outcrop surrounded by a grove of trees to rest—to escape the din rattling in my brain. *I'll park myself on this rock and wait until the wind settles down; only then will I continue.*

Suddenly, a figure emerged from the blur—the *Chileno* leader of a nearby tour group. The guide's weathered face, the considerable number of tourists trailing him, and his perfect English-language skills gave me every confidence that he'd be passing along valuable wisdom. He approached steadily, seemingly at ease with the tempest around us. I leaned closer to him.

"What? I can't hear you," I yelled.

"I said, I see you are having difficulty navigating the wind," he shouted back at me. "And since the wind here never desists, I believe it is far superior to learn to trek in it. Fortunately for you, I do offer a service in which I instruct people how to walk in the *Patagonian* winds. It is normally a three-day course but as you look intelligent, I am prepared to teach you in a five-minute demo."

His grin relaxed me, and as he extended his hand, I reached out, my deliverer's strong grip stabilizing me until I regained my balance.

"Pleeeeeasse show me," I laughed so hard, but the tears streaming down my cheeks were unrelated to the intense wind whipping around us.

"Put your legs apart like you are riding a very fat horse, like so. Now lean forward at a 45-degree angle, like so. Do not lean too far forward or the weight of your backpack will precipitate a nose-plant. Now walk."

He lumbered ahead, looking like a foraging caveman—indeed if his arms had been longer, his knuckles would have dragged on the ground.

My first attempt at mimicking his form resulted in me leaning too far forward so that when the wind paused to reload, I took a series of swift dance-like steps to keep from falling.

"Impressive save. An effective beginning for an amateur," the guide said, trying hard to control his laughter.

"Thanks so much. Now I have a hope of arriving at *Glacier Grey* in one piece," I said, thinking how—with his invaluable lessons—he had unknowingly gifted me a slice of his world.

The guide and his group foraged ahead of me, leaving me to turn my thoughts inward. *Since Mexico I have relaxed my white-knuckled grip on the tiller of my life, I have gone on alone. I have done things that have scared me. But never have I faced such a wind.* Inside my determined brain, as I matched the rhythm of the guide's gait—rocking and swaying against the wind—I realized I needed to learn this skill; the same skill Judge Bob in *Mexico* used at the tiller of *Ethos* to show me that we have power over the wind, whether at sea or on this wind-shorn trail.

I staggered on. My left shoulder ached, so I shifted my pack's weight, adjusting the flapping straps. Deliberately, I focused on the ground beneath my feet, psyching myself into believing that a level path—instead of the dauntingly steep ascent—lay ahead. For hours I walked, I inhaled the pine-sap-scented air, feeling more alive than a newborn foal. I thanked God for a new day. The wind, once a buffeting adversary, seemed to ease as my wind-walk improved, transforming into a friendly companion.

Shifting my pack's weight again, I pondered my love-hate relationship with this loyal travelling companion of mine. Every step I took convinced me that at times some strange force would bring it to life. Clairvoyant powers enabled it to know when I neared a *Refugio*, and it became heavier and more unwieldy. It craved being held and carried around, like a baby, the epitome of neediness, relentless neediness. How often had it cried out to be fed with souvenirs whenever I passed an *artesan* booth? On the positive side, I'd already met four trekkers whose backpacks suffered from broken straps, so I loved how my gear maintained its good form; it certainly took a beating.

Crossing paths with large numbers of hikers made me want to laugh and twirl in a polka with each, then dance on alone again to enjoy my solitary place in the vast empty spaces of God's incredible creation. Sunshine backlit the peaks shrouded in dark, mysterious clouds, outlining jagged contours. The clouds moved across the sky as deliberately as the crowds of trekkers moving across the trails.

Even from a distance, I recognized *Pocahontas* walking toward me. She bore out her trail name with her waist-length, ebony hair tied back securely in a braid, and tiny yet ample form. Her coal-black eyes sparkled with light and life.

"Cavewoman!" she yelped as we kissed and hugged several times, in classic, exuberant *Chilena* fashion.

Thinking back to when we'd first met at *Casa Lili,* I recalled the shadowy depths where she gave me my nickname. She and I had spent an afternoon exploring the dark, dank bowels of the *Mylodon Cave* in *Puerto Natales,* looking for the hidden remains of the extinct animals. *Pocahontas's* playful antics beside the towering statue of a *Mylodon* and her spirited poses on *La Silla del Diablo* had added a touch of whimsy to our escapade. After our shared exploration, marked by selfies with our tongues sticking out, and *Pocahontas's* infectious energy, we had walked arm in arm back to the taxi, where she announced, "Your new name—'Cavewoman.'"

"*Pocahontas*!" I said, recalling our adventures in the cave and sitting on the "Devil's Chair." "So good to see you again."

Her presence momentarily lifted the physical demands of the journey from my shoulders.

"You meet my brother? He also live in *Santiago*. *Manuel,* this is Cavewoman," she said, introducing us.

Manuel, with his tall, sinewy frame, stood with his eyes lowered. His quiet presence, in stark contrast to his sister's energy, reminded me of an opened can of Cola gone flat. Silence.

I hushed my voice and asked, "I wonder, does he speak English?"

"My brother is strange case," she said affectionately, smiling at him.

Manuel gazed at the mountains while *Pocahontas* and I cherished our moments of laughter and chatter. A whisper of worry wove its way through my thoughts—the unsettled question of tonight's shelter—as the sun arced lower in the sky, portending that the missing *Refugio* reservation drama would reach its climax at *Grey*. But by balancing the joy of the present moment against the uncertainty of what lay ahead, I allowed myself to enjoy her friendship and her buoyant energy many minutes longer.

"We need to keep going, don't we?" I finally said. "Until we meet again, *Pocahontas*... and *Manuel*."

We kissed and hugged again, promising to stay in touch, and went our separate ways. Though fleeting, our out-of-the-blue meeting buoyed my spirits immensely. Feeling rejuvenated, I faced squarely into the wind once more; confident of my victory over the invisible, once-malevolent force.

Noticing the seemingly insignificant things gave me as much joy as did the grand expanses of spiked mountains surrounding me. A boulder split by the force of freezing water blocked the trail ahead of me. Two smaller rocks, wedged tightly within the boulder's crevice, appeared unable to break free. My fingers curled over them, feeling their rough edges and the weight of their imprisonment, attempting to release them—but they remained trapped, held fast in the boulder's grasp. The plight of the smaller rocks reminded me of the sporadic good times in my marriage that had once held me in place. This image transported me to a spring day in 1982—to my living room full of lovely Christian mothers wearing floral-patterned dresses. A wonderful memory marred by my ex-husband's abrupt entrance, interrupting the bible study being led by our pastor.

"What's going on here? Why aren't you paying attention to our children? I want all you people out of my house. Now!" he said, his voice sharp, silencing our conversations. He pointed a rigid finger at the front door.

But in the next few minutes, the pastor's loving words, gentle yet powerful, turned my ex's intended disruption into peace. That day marked a pivotal moment, as Bill joined me in prayer and, later, in baptism. He promised to make a new life for the four of us; but alcohol had a vice grip on him, and those brief vapours of hope would evaporate the day the phone rang at five in the morning. Jolted awake, I reached for the receiver and, in that moment, realized Bill hadn't come home. An unfamiliar female voice on the other end asked for something unexpected—something immoral—and shattered the fragile peace Bill and I were trying to build.

"I want you to give Bill a divorce. He loves me and I want to marry him," she stated in a cigarette-smoke-husky voice.

I envisioned her having recently left a dimly light bar, calling from a phone booth on some dark street, with Bill standing behind her. Until then, my suspicions were only notions, inklings. Overcome with shock and sorrow, I ended the call, the receiver slipping from my grasp as I crashed onto the floor. While the children slept on, I lay on the floor for hours unable to move or think, able only to cry my very being out. The fragile crate that held my life with him splintered into a million pieces in those moments; and all my hurt seeped down into my soul, spreading pain along with every movement I made. The betrayal swallowed up the remnants of my trust and love; and I vowed to divorce him; yet, a mere two months later, I had taken him back. He had held me in place with another promise.

Walking around the boulder, I reflected on those rocks, trapped in their granite prison, as I had once been. Using a resolute kick, I freed them, mirroring my own liberation. Smiling, I rejoiced in a spirit reborn, rejoiced in my journey from the confines of a broken marriage to the joys of self-discovery.

A trail sign with a red dot next to the words *Usted Esta Aqui* showed my location at 1,589 metres above sea level (ASL). Congratulating myself, I sat down on a rock to eat a stale lunch and rehearsed a speech filled with pathos, designed to secure me a bed at the *Refugio*. Another hour later, the "You are here" sign indicated I'd descended to an elevation of 570 metres ASL, with another steep incline lying ahead. I ignored it. For the next couple of hours, I kept a rapid gait intended to outpace the sun dipping toward the western horizon. Then, from my elevated position on the mountain ridge—roughly 2000 metres ASL—I gazed down on a compact, white-roofed building set amidst a dense mass of towering green trees. Beyond them, golden sunbeams, splaying across the lake created from the meltwater of *Glacier Grey*, made this tranquil scene enchanting. Exhausted, and hoping against hope that a soft bed and a warm meal awaited me, I scampered—as best I could with feet of lead—down the trail with uplifted arms, unaware of my backpack swinging discomfortingly from side to side. Yes! *Refugio Grey* at last!

Pausing to catch my breath, I leaned against the rough bark of a tree. My gaze drifted upward, following the lines of the towering, erect conifers shielding me from the wind. They seemed to peer down, silently questioning me, "Why do you need to wander? Why move from a perfectly good place to an unknown place?" Unlike me, they were rooted deeply in their chosen home. "How do you do it?" I asked them. "How can you possibly live out your lives in one location?" Sighing, I moved forward, sensing their protective aura guiding my steps.

In the clearing, the main building of the *Refugio* stood firm, a variety of tents and outhouses sprawling around it. My eyes scanned about two dozen trekkers ambling around—making the promise of a safe space to sleep seem like a mirage. After eight hours of crusading against the wind, I'd arrived—only to face another challenge.

Once again, I lumbered directly to reception. The aroma of hot food teased my senses, intensifying the gnawing emptiness in my stomach.

"*Hola,* I tried to reserve a bed," I began. I finished my lengthy explanation then added my "I'm tired and grubby" card to my rehearsed speech. "Do you possibly have a bed available?" I gazed expectantly into the receptionist's dark eyes.

"*Señora,* I am sorry, but every one is booked," he said.

I felt akin to *Ethos's* sails when they had faltered, their angle all wrong for the wind that Judge Bob had tried to teach me to harness. My anticipatory vision of a safe and soft bed in a warm *Refugio* popped. Sleeping under the stars seemed the least reassuring of prospects in puma country, but a tent would at least complicate a feline's meal preparation.

"Do you have any tents available?" I asked.

"*Si Señora,* and they are cheaper than rooms, but you have no indoor plumbing. *Jorge* can set up a tent for you and show you where the outhouses are. Will you need to rent a sleeping bag and air mattress? Did you wish to reserve a tent, then?" he asked.

"Yes, yes, and yes! And *gracias.*" Suddenly, my backpack felt as light as a cotton ball.

Jorge navigated the terrain expertly, greeting other staff and trekkers with a smile that spoke of a deep love for this rugged land. *Jorge* and I chose a spot at the far edge of the open field near the *Refugio*. The altitude had stolen the warmth from the long rays of sunshine that highlighted a dozen neon-yellow tents. The private space their fabric walls offered—there amidst dense green forests and towering mountains, standing like sentinels—looked as welcoming as the Queen's palace.

"You need anything else, *Señora?" Jorge* asked, with a tone that conveyed his expertise and his desire to assist me.

"I have everything I need, *gracias,*" I said, watching him jog through the tents to help another trekker.

Kneeling, I opened the flaps and pushed my gear inside. A wave of disappointment washed over me as the smell of musty sweat hit my nostrils. As I slowly dragged my weary body into the exposed vulnerability of my flimsy tent, looking for the least bumpy place to lay my air mattress, I thought of how I'd longed for the comfort and security of the *Refugio* during my trek. Still fully clothed, I burrowed into the sleeping bag and tucked my legs up to my chest, with only my head peeking out above the draw-stringed top, like a gopher scanning the sky for hawks. My new reality had jarred me, but embracing the total wilderness-explorer experience felt liberating. *I'm polishing up my persona as an expert trekker; plus, this rugged camping experience will add a captivating dimension to my upcoming blog post.*

Lying on my right side, enjoying the roaring silence, my mind wandered back to the nighttime noises of the past few months, when I'd drift off to sleep listening to slamming doors, creaky floors, smells of supper, coughing, laughter, chatting trekkers, and snores. But then darkness fell, summoning with it nerve-wracking sounds out of their lurking places. Unknown bird screeches, scrapings and scratchings, twig-snapping sounds, the thought of unknown animals all made even the intermittent silences feel ominous. Several interminable minutes later, clumsily untangling myself from the sleeping bag, I made a decision. *I'm going into the Refugio, to be safe with my fellow travellers. Someone might not have arrived for the night, and I could get a room. Do I really know how to be alone successfully? Am I even wired to function as an individual?* But as I groped for the tent flap, I changed my mind. *I have the spirit of a pioneer, and I will brave the wilderness rather than seek the comfort of the familiar.* Tucking myself back into my bag, I fell into the sleep that only fresh mountain air can induce.

Disoriented—from being awakened suddenly—my heart pounded. *What was that? What woke me? Is the wind playing tricks on me, or is a puma lurking around my tent?* I sat upright, unable to see my hand a centimetre from my face. I strained my ears to catch any sound, any clue. Outside, the night held its breath, and so did I, waiting for the sound to repeat itself.

Breathing deeply to steady my rapidly beating heart, I lay still, listening intently. Only dense silence followed. A glance at my phone showed two a.m. My bladder must have wakened me, that's all. Sheepishly, I unzipped the tent, and, with every sense alert, slowly stepped out into the black mystery of night—earnestly hoping to remember the location of the outhouse. The eerily calm, crisp air smelled raw and organic like damp, ozone-infused soil after a thunderstorm. Then I tilted my chin upward. Millions upon millions of stars—those invisible-by-day, silent, orderly-orbiters of the sun—flickered across the immense sky. Wrapping my arms around my waist to stave off the biting chill of the night, I stood still, scanning in an arc from one horizon to the other, gradually turning in a circle until I had absorbed the majesty of every star, every constellation. Gazing at the boundless heavens, a wise thought dawned on me: seeing the world from this vast, star-studded perspective made all the circumstances in my life seem insignificant against the backdrop of eternity. Suddenly a once-memorized Bible verse popped into my mind.

"Lift up your eyes on high, and see! Who created these? The One who brings out their host by number, the One who calls them all by name. Because of His great strength and vast power, not one is missing."

How can I feel alone when surely God the Creator is with me? My solo trip to Chile is my darkness that let me see that God created me to shine like a star. I may have only booked Refugios for two nights, but, wow, that choice allowed me to meet Don and witness the breathtaking expanse of stars!

Pondering the night's wonder like a precious treasure in my heart, I fell back to sleep upon my return to my tent. Four hours later, at 6 a.m. on Thursday morning, I set my large bowl of sweet, steamy porridge on a wooden table inside *Glacier Grey*'s hostel. Across from me, a young man—whose white-blue eyes made me think they'd been carved from *Glaciar del Frances*—glanced up briefly from his own meal.

"Do you mind if I eat breakfast with you?" I asked.

"Hello, not at all. Please, have a seat. I am Marko, from Helsinki, Finland. But since the government deported me, I consider myself a citizen of the world. By the by, if you are also hiking to *Glacier Grey* today, this is what we can anticipate," he said, indicating the topographical map on his GPS.

"Yes, I'm anxious to see the glacier. That's my plan for the morning. Then I'm trekking back to *Paine Grande* to catch the ferry, and bus-it back to *Puerto Natales* tonight. But wait. You have to cross a suspension bridge, you say? Just what is this bridge suspended over, and how high is it?" I asked, pointing to his screen.

"Below it is a river, at the bottom of a ravine, about 200 metres deep."

"What materials were used to construct it? And how long is it?" I asked.

"The bridge has standard wooden slats and cable railings. I guess it is about 300 metres in length. The sign indicates a maximum of four people at a time. It is fortunate you are slender. Are you afraid of heights, given all the mountains you have just climbed?"

"No. Well. I'm more afraid of depths. Despite my ability to fly in a glider and walk along the edge of a cliff, seeing the ground so far away directly under your feet evokes an unsettling feeling of vertigo. So does trying to balance with all that wobbly bounciness. And let's talk about the insubstantial railings," I said.

Marko leaned closer, his voice a taunting whisper, "And when you look down into that chasm, it's like staring into the abyss itself."

Nervously, I twirled my spoon around in my bowl, spreading porridge up the sides. In my mind's eye I saw, almost in a panic, the bridge breaking and me free-falling into the depths.

"So, you can only access *Glacier Grey* if you cross the bridge?" I asked.

"Certainly not. One can easily climb down the ravine, cross the river, and climb back up. It would take approximately two hours each way. However, since you need to catch the evening ferry from *Paine Grande,* perhaps you should cross the bridge. Then it only takes half an hour to hike to the glacier. It will be worth it, I assure you," he laughed.

He picked up his breakfast tray, while I tucked my porridge bowl and spoon onto his plate sticky with egg yolk, and followed him outside.

"Why don't you join me?" he asked, retrieving his pack from under the veranda.

"Sure," I said, gathering my resolve along with my gear, trying to focus on the goal, not the obstacle.

For the next half an hour, Marko entertained me with non-stop scripts of American movies from the 1980s, causing me to change the trail name I'd given him from Stretch—for his excessive height—to Hollywood. As we wound our way along the footpath—the atmosphere saturated with the earthy aroma of the rich, bushy green forest, patches of blue sky peeking through the thick canopy above—he impersonated characters so convincingly that I laughed until my sides ached; and, my dread of crossing the suspension bridge dissipated into the humid air.

A disconcerting, intermittent sound, grew louder with every step. Instead of the melodic chirping of birds, I sensed—but couldn't yet see—that something eerily unnatural lay ahead. *What is that noise?* The path, now narrowing and winding, brought us face-to-face with the sagging suspension bridge and I saw the source of the noise. Every time a trekker's weight stretched the metal cable against the bolts buried deep in the rock, I heard the unnerving squeal of metal-on-metal—the bridge seemed to protest the intrusion. My stomach knotted. My options dwindled. *Marko is right—crossing the bridge is the only way to get to Glacier Grey.*

"You first," he said, his blue eyes twinkling with mischief, as he urged me to take the lead.

Once the bridge emptied of trekkers, I drew in a deep breath and stepped onto the bridge, my first step away from the dirt path. In that one step, the ground dropped 200 metres to the icy depths of the foaming, swiftly racing river—rushing urgently toward the lake. The trees on the other side swallowed up the far end of the bridge, and scraggly trees clung to the near-vertical ravine walls. A jumble of trees had fallen headfirst into the river, likely landing there after a gust of wind had loosened them from the time-eroded rocks that had once supported them.

Don't look down. Shifting my gaze to my hands, I noticed they gripped the cold, flimsy cable railing so tightly my knuckles turned white. When I glanced beyond my feet through the wooden slats to the ravine below, my vision defocused in a dizzying blur. *Don't look down.*

Stiff-legged and rigid-armed, I resisted the bridge's gentle sway, inching forward cautiously, each step in tune with the thud of my racing heart. Suddenly, while attempting to channel my apprehension into a determination to cross, the bridge pitched sideways, up, and down all at once. My sweating hands made gripping the railing difficult. Behind me, the stomp of someone's boots hitting the boards made me turn my head.

"Stop! You're scaring me," I yelled back at Marko.

"Not to worry, my fair damsel—I—Indiana Jones, am here to rescue you," he said as he continued to leap around on the bridge.

"This is not funny," I said, looking forward, trying to ignore the creaking wooden slats.

Finally, I convinced Indiana Jones to walk like Marko, letting me cross the bridge successfully. After an hour-long five minutes, I reached the first of five stairs carved into the rock at the opposite cliff, my wooziness gone; I started plotting the most effective means to lose Marko. Now, with Marko's peculiar antics fresh in my memory, I decided that the Finnish government probably had valid reasons for deporting him. Fortunately, he spotted a cute young, unsuspecting female and bade me farewell. *How will I ever cross that bridge on the way back?*

For the next 120 glorious minutes, I hiked through the warm forest, revelling in my new-found solitude. As the terrain transitioned, frigid air—smelling raw and wild—drifted toward me along the ground, prompting me to retrieve my toque and jacket from my pack. Peering between two standing-dead trees and the odd, wind-warped evergreens, my gaze stalled on the distant horizon. There, a curved mountain range boldly asserted its craggy outline against the charcoal clouds that appeared to have oozed out of their cloud-form containers. Wedged between two granite slabs, the glacial sheet extended back from the grass-covered slopes beneath my feet all the way to the mountain range. My feet danced on the trail; my heavy pack anchored me and kept me from flying. Climbing onto a lichen-covered boulder, I gained my personal viewpoint to marvel at the moon-crater-like tip of the glacier floating on the lake it had created. Tears of joy welled up as I observed the jagged, wrinkly surface of the serrated, blue-white ice.

The paradox struck me—how frozen water could simultaneously melt and calm my heart. A glacier is a living tool God uses to sculpt the mountains. Dormant yet alive, the ice holds the power to carve fantastical forms from solid granite. Ice—gifted with the power to change the seemingly unchangeable. A power I knew that I shared albeit only over myself.

As I sat contemplating the symbiosis of mountains and ice, I reflected on the profound symbolism of this frozen giant, and wondered how the mountains and ice of *Glacier Grey* shaped the *Chilean* people. And in that moment, I realized how they were shaping me—transforming the trajectory of my life, steering me toward the unexplored depths of my being. And to think—all this had been ignited seventeen long months ago by the pages of the little book, *Extreme Landscape.*

A smile lightened my face; I breathed in and shifted taller on my boulder, all the while absorbing the revelations gifted by the glacier—cherishing them. Basking in the warmth of my new-found clarity, I allowed the awe to permeate my entire being. When the chatter of other trekkers reached my ears, I took one last look—reluctant to tear my eyes from the glacier—as I yielded my vantage point to them and descended the trail toward the suspension bridge. The river cascaded down the ravine far below my feet, sparkling and spirited. It seemed friendly this time, its energy reflecting the exhilaration of my completed trek. My body moved and swayed with the rhythm of the wobbling bridge, in a stark contrast to the resistance I'd felt on my initial crossing. The cable railing felt smooth and cold under the light touch of one finger tapping each side with each step. The skies cleared and the sun's brilliance bathed my awakened heart during my uneventful trip back to *Refugio Paine Grande*—the twelve kilometres behind me marking the completion of my five-day trek. An overwhelming sense of achievement, fatigue, and euphoria accompanied every step. I'd more than survived the challenge—I'd cherished and loved every exhilarating moment. But little could I know that upon returning to *Casa Lili,* my hostel in *Puerto Natales,* a dense shadow would settle over my elation.

Wandering around the *Refugio's* lobby, I glimpsed an outlet beside a flamenco-red leather couch in the communal space. Seating myself on the hard tile floor, I eagerly awaited the revival of my long-dead phone battery, the smooth white charging cable a lifeline to my outside world.

Back here at *Grande,* us weary trekkers needed to decide whether to take a further two-hour trek to the bus stop to catch the bus to *Puerto Natales* or pay for a short twenty-minute Catamaran ferry trip across *Lago Pegoe* to the bus. The 15,000-peso ferry fare posed a fiscal dilemma. Hunger gnawed at my stomach, urging me to choose thrift over comfort. The ferry fee seemed an extravagance I couldn't afford; if I walked that far, I knew I'd be even hungrier. But if I took the ferry, I wouldn't be able to afford to eat. *What to do?* My desire for an enormous supper eventually won—I would walk. While I sat watching my phone's battery percentage increase, I sensed eyes observing me.

Her blonde hair fell across her arm as she craned her neck to look down over the arm of the couch into my face.

"We just can't disconnect from civilization, can we? Hi, I'm Dagmar, from Denmark."

"True. I'm Ruth," I laughed.

Dagmar patted her stubby fingers against the leather. "Come, sit up here, and let's have a chat. Just imagine if we had crossed paths at the start of our trek. But hey, I have some unsolicited advice for you. After soaking in the *Torres* high, you need a new goal. A fresh quest awaits you. Fitz Roy, in *Argentina,* beckons, my friend," she said, continuing to tap the couch with an adventurous energy seeping through her calm exterior.

Ouch. I winced. I shared how my dream to climb Fitz Roy had taken shape providentially and about my disappointment in failing to reach *Argentina,* then quickly shifted the subject.

Excitement lit up her eyes, revealing a kindred spirit who also loved to explore. After meeting her, I felt less wary of people from Scandinavian countries—whereas I envisioned Marko at the Fringe Festival, I envisioned Dagmar playing Grandma at our community theatre. Our conversations unveiled the layers of her journey so far—a six-month ramble in Tibet, an ongoing exploration in South America, and, now, her plan to walk to the nearby *Lago Pegoe* lookout before taking the ferry.

"I'd be delighted if you joined me. The lake is just a fifteen-minute walk from here," she said, her invitation offering a glimpse into the world of a nomadic soul.

"I will, thanks. I'd love to hear more of your adventures. Plus, I'll still have time to hike to the bus before dark."

Upon reaching the summit, we settled onto the most inviting rocks, sharing in the simple pleasure of yogurt and crackers smeared generously with cream cheese. The wind, a sculptor of snowscapes in my world, had laid bare the desolate, obsidian peaks of the mountains. A yearning enveloped me, tempting me to linger, to commune with the forest fairies, my mind conjuring images of them painting those blackened tips with their glistening, ebony pigments. The flat, azure surface of the lake below served as a mirror reflecting the verdant hills and the playful, scattered cumulus clouds.

Dagmar bent to pull her water bottle from her pack.

"Oh! I just remembered; I have an extra ticket for the ferry. Yes, a guy in my trek group bought a round-trip ticket but chose to walk. He handed it to me, and I think you're the lucky recipient. Yes, this is for you," she told me.

In stunned gratitude, I watched as she retrieved the ferry ticket from her pocket and extended it to me.

"Seriously? You'd give this to me? Thank you, a thousand times, thank you," I exclaimed.

Overwhelmed by her unexpected generosity, I leaped off my rock, enveloped her in a spontaneous bear hug, and silently breathed a prayer of heartfelt thanks for the extraordinary gift from a perfect stranger.

An hour later, Dagmar and I dumped our backpacks onto a jumble of packs and suitcases at the stern of the small Catamaran ferry. We settled near the bow, where the gurgling and whooshing of the engine in the water hampered our attempts at conversation. In the queue for the washroom at the hostel, I'd met a friendly *Chileno* with whom I'd sustained a tolerable chat. To my surprise, he, his wife, and their teenage son sat down across from Dagmar and me. They adopted us, treating us as family during the ferry ride! Witnessing adolescents journeying with their parents seemed so odd to me—rarely had I seen that in Canada. Later, when we bade farewell, they kissed us, and their kindness shone through when the wife instructed her son to fetch the *mochilas* (backpacks) for the *Señoras.* This heartfelt gesture spoke to me of their communal spirit and hospitality, a value deeply cherished in *Chilean* society.

As the ferry churned farther across the lake, I gazed out over the water, grappling with the reality that the visual feast I had savoured for the past five days would soon reside only in my memory. The shoreline receded, and the peaks gradually faded into the distance. My heart whispered a plea as I watched the vanishing scenery. "Captain, please turn back. I don't want to leave." The urgency of this thought rang through my being, encapsulating the emotional struggle of parting with the transformative wilderness that had relentlessly pushed me to the raw edge of my perceived abilities, my known existence—then demanded more.

Yet, from this trial emerged a revelation—the new identity I'd sought.

Every *Refugio* required guests to sign registers, likely because they feared losing an exuberant but unprepared trekker. In *Refugio Grey's* register, I had scanned the list under the heading "Occupation" and been impressed with the person who had written, "Traveller." The word resonated deeply with me, even more than *Jubilada*. Beside my name, I too had penned "Traveller," in a declaration as bold as the landscapes I'd traversed. "Traveller" felt like a calling, a valid occupation, and a role unbound by familiar titles. After all, travel is an agency for transformation—a way to revitalize one's spirit, restore wonder to one's life, and express oneself.

The experience is changing me, inspiring me to be wiser, braver, more creative. My voice is finding me. Joy is surprising me. My voice releases from within as I immerse myself in this country's unique history and culture. Each encounter, each revelation, has guided me toward leaving the hurt behind and finding peace, helping me to see and remember the good that emerged from my marriage and my time with Leah.

I resolve to face whatever lies beyond with an open heart. From here, I'll go forward with intention, seeking joy in each step. I've had to let go of my dream to travel to Argentina, its borders feeling as impassable as the doubts I once carried. But now, I'm tickled that I've been able to move on and I feel a new hope emerging. The Lodge—the place where my transformation will continue—lies ahead, yet the journey within has already begun. The Lodge will be a place where the adventure deepens, where I can embrace every part of myself that these travels have uncovered.

Approaching the end of my ferry trip, with the wind-resistant peaks gradually fading, the deeper meaning of my solo sojourn to Chile becomes clear to me. I'm ready!

END OF VOLUME 1

As you reach the final pages of this memoir's "Volume 1: The Beginning," you are invited to accompany Ruth in her journey, where every thoughtful step brings to light surprises of strength, courage, and joy; where Ruth's path is marked with out-of-the-blue connections to fellow travellers, and moments of everlasting fulfillment. Read *Travelling Into the Patagonian Wind—A Solo Journey to Joy, Volume 2: The Destination,* A memoir.

Printed in the United States
by Baker & Taylor Publisher Services